THE ROMANTIC
IMAGINATION

THE ROMANTIC IMAGINATION

C. M. BOWRA

OXFORD UNIVERSITY PRESS

LONDON   OXFORD   NEW YORK

OXFORD UNIVERSITY PRESS

Oxford London New York
Glasgow Toronto Melbourne Wellington
Cape Town Salisbury Ibadan Nairobi Lusaka Addis Ababa
Bombay Calcutta Madras Karachi Lahore Dacca
Kuala Lumpur Hong Kong Tokyo

TO

THE MASTER AND TUTORS

OF

ELIOT HOUSE

οἴκοθεν οἴκαδε

PREFACE

This book contains the lectures which I gave at Cambridge, Massachusetts, during the happy months of 1948–1949, when I was Charles Eliot Norton Professor of Poetry at Harvard University. I have thought it right to publish them as they were delivered and not to transform them. The book will probably suffer from the circumstances of its origin and show certain traits which are undesirable in the printed page but inevitable to lecturing, especially when the audience does not always consist of the same people and each lecture has to be complete in itself. I must also apologize for speaking on a subject in which I am in no sense an expert or even a scholar. But the subject seemed to me to have been unjustly treated in recent years, and the welcome given to my handling of it has comforted me in my choice. Since the material presented is essentially "popular," I have given hardly any references other than what is necessary for identifying important texts.

C.M.B.

Cambridge, Massachusetts
March 10th, 1949

CONTENTS

CONTENTS

THE ROMANTIC
IMAGINATION

I

THE ROMANTIC IMAGINATION

I F WE wish to distinguish a single characteristic which differentiates the English Romantics from the poets of the eighteenth century, it is to be found in the importance which they attached to the imagination and in the special view which they held of it. On this, despite significant differences on points of detail, Blake, Coleridge, Wordsworth, Shelley, and Keats agree, and for each it sustains a deeply considered theory of poetry. In the eighteenth century imagination was not a cardinal point in poetical theory. For Pope and Johnson, as for Dryden before them, it has little importance, and when they mention it, it has a limited significance. They approve of fancy, provided that it is controlled by what they call "judgement," and they admire the apt use of images, by which they mean little more than visual impressions and metaphors. But for them what matters most in poetry is its truth to the emotions, or, as they prefer to say, sentiment. They wish to speak in general terms for the common experience of men, not to indulge personal whims in creating new worlds. For them the poet is more an interpreter than a creator, more concerned with showing the attractions of what we already know than with expeditions into the unfamiliar and the unseen. They are less interested in the mysteries of life than in its familiar appearance, and they think that their task is to display this with as much charm and truth as they can command. But for the Romantics imagination is fundamental, because they think that without it poetry is impossible.

This belief in the imagination was part of the contemporary belief in the individual self. The poets were conscious of a wonderful capacity to create imaginary worlds, and they could not believe that this was idle or false. On the contrary, they thought that to curb it was to deny something vitally necessary to their whole being. They thought that it was just this which made them poets, and that in their exercise of it they could do far better than other poets who sacrificed it to caution and common sense. They saw that the power of poetry is strongest when the creative impulse works untrammelled, and they knew that in their own case this happened when they shaped fleeting visions into concrete forms and pursued wild thoughts until they captured and mastered them. Just as in politics men turned their minds from the existing order to vast prospects of a reformed humanity, so in the arts they abandoned the conventional plan of existence for private adventures which had an inspiring glory. As in the Renaissance poets suddenly found the huge possibilities of the human self and expressed them in a bold and far-flung art, which is certainly much more than an imitation of life, so the Romantics, brought to a fuller consciousness of their own powers, felt a similar need to exert these powers in fashioning new worlds of the mind.

The Romantic emphasis on the imagination was strengthened by considerations which are both religious and metaphysical. For a century English philosophy had been dominated by the theories of Locke. He assumed that in perception the mind is wholly passive, a mere recorder of impressions from without, "a lazy looker-on on an external world." His system was well suited to an age of scientific speculation which found its representative voice in Newton. The mechanistic explanation which both philosophers and scientists gave of the world meant that scanty respect was paid to the human self and especially to its more instinctive, though not less powerful, convictions. Thus both Locke and Newton found a place for God in their universes, the former on the ground that "the works of nature in every part of them sufficiently evidence a deity," [1] and the latter on the principle that the great machine of the world implies a mechanic. But this was not at all what the Romantics demanded from religion. For them it was a question less of reason than of feeling, less of argument than of experience, and they complained that these mechanistic explanations were a denial of their innermost convictions. So too with poetry. Locke had views on poetry, as he had on most human activities, but no very high regard for it. For him it is a matter of "wit," and the task of wit is to combine ideas and "thereby to make up pleasant pictures and agreeable visions in the fancy." [2] Wit, in his view, is quite irresponsible and not troubled with truth or reality. The Romantics rejected with contumely a theory which robbed their work of its essential connection with life.

Locke is the target both of Blake and of Coleridge, to whom he represents a deadly heresy on the nature of existence. They are concerned with more than discrediting his special views on God and poetry: they are hostile to his whole system which supports those views, and, even worse, robs the human self of importance. They reject his conception of the universe and replace it by their own systems, which deserve the name of "idealist" because mind is their central point and governing factor. But because they are poets, they insist that the most vital activity of the mind is the imagination. Since for them it is the very source of spiritual energy, they cannot but believe that it is divine, and that, when they exercise it, they in some way partake of the activity of God. Blake says proudly and prophetically:

This world of Imagination is the world of Eternity; it is the divine bosom into which we shall all go after the death of the Vegetated body. This World of Imagination is Infinite and Eternal, whereas the world of Generation, or Vegetation, is Finite and Temporal. There Exist in that Eternal World the Permanent Realities of Every Thing which we see reflected in this Vegetable Glass of Nature. All Things are comprehended in their Eternal Forms in the divine body of the Saviour, the True Vine of Eternity, The Human Imagination.[3]

For Blake the imagination is nothing less than God as He operates in the human soul. It follows that any act of creation performed by the imagination is divine and that in the imagination man's spiritual nature is fully and finally realized. Coleridge does not speak with so apocalyptic a certainty, but his conclusion is not very different from Blake's:

The primary IMAGINATION I hold to be the living Power and prime Agent of all human Perception, and as a repetition in the finite mind of the eternal act of creation in the infinite I AM.[4]

It is true that he regards poetry as a product of the secondary imagination, but since this differs only in degree from the primary, it remains clear that for Coleridge the imagination is of first importance because it partakes of the creative activity of God.

This is a tremendous claim, and it is not confined to Blake and Coleridge. It was to some degree held by Wordsworth and Shelley and Keats. Each was confident not only that the imagination was his most precious possession but that it was somehow concerned with a supernatural order. Never before had quite such a claim been made, and from it Romantic poetry derives much that is most magical in it. The danger of so bold an assumption is that the poet may be so absorbed in his own private universe and in the exploration of its remoter corners that he may be unable to convey his essential experience to other men and fail to convert them to his special creed. The Romantics certainly created worlds of their own, but they succeeded in persuading others that these were not absurd or merely fanciful. Indeed, in this respect they were closer to earth and the common man than some of their German contemporaries. They have not the respect for unsatisfied longing as an end in itself or the belief in hallucination and magic which play so large a part in the mind of Brentano, nor have they that nihilistic delight in being detached from life, of which Novalis writes to Caroline Schlegel:

I know that imagination is most attracted by what is most immoral, most animal; but I also know how like a dream all imagination is, how it loves night, meaninglessness, and solitude.[5]

This was not what the English Romantics thought. They believed that the imagination stands in some essential relation to truth and reality, and they were at pains to make their poetry pay attention to them.

In doing this they encountered an old difficulty. If a man gives free play to his imagination, what assurance is there that what he says is in any sense true? Can it tell us anything that we do not know, or is it so removed from ordinary life as to be an escape from it? The question had been answered in one sense by Locke when he dealt so cavalierly with poetic wit, and a similar answer was given by Blake's revolutionary friend, Tom Paine, in his *Age of Reason*:

I had some turn, and I believe some talent for poetry; but this I rather repressed than encouraged as leading too much into the field of imagination.

This is a point of view, and it is not new. It is based on the assumption that the creations of the imagination are mere fantasies and, as such, divorced from life. The problem had troubled the Elizabethans, and Shakespeare shows his acquaintance with it when he makes Theseus say:

The poet's eye, in a fine frenzy rolling,
Doth glance from heaven to earth, from earth to heaven;
And, as imagination bodies forth
The forms of things unknown, the poet's pen
Turns them to shapes, and gives to airy nothing
A local habitation and a name.[6]

This would have won the approval of an Italian philosopher like Pico della Mirandola, who thought that the imagination is almost a diseased faculty, and would certainly have welcomed Theseus' association of the poet with the lunatic and the lover. Even those who did not venture so far as this thought that the creations of the imagination have little to do with actual life and provide no more than an agreeable escape from it. This was Bacon's view in *The Advancement of Learning*:

> The imagination, being not tied to the laws of matter, may at pleasure join that which nature hath severed and sever that which nature hath joined, and so make unlawful matches and divorces of things.

Bacon regards this as a harmless and not unpleasant activity, but not more. Though the Elizabethans excelled almost all other ages in the creation of imaginary worlds, their gravest thinkers made no great claim for them and were on the whole content that they should do no more than give a respite from the cares of ordinary life.

Such a position is plainly unsatisfactory for poets who believe that the imagination is a divine faculty concerned with the central issues of being. Indeed, it must be difficult for almost any poet to think that what he creates is imaginary in the derogatory sense which Bacon and his like give to the word. Poets usually believe that their creations are somehow concerned with reality, and this belief sustains them in their work. Their approach is indeed not that of the analytical mind, but it is none the less penetrating. They assume that poetry deals in some sense with truth, though this truth may be different from that of science or philosophy. That Shakespeare understood the question is clear from what Hippolyta says in answer to Theseus' discourse on the imagination:

> But all the story of the night told over,
> And all their minds transfigur'd so together,
> More witnesseth than fancy's images,
> And grows to something of great constancy,
> But, howsoever, strange and admirable.[7]

Hippolyta has sense enough to see that a poet's inventions are not an "airy nothing" but stand in some relation to reality. In this she presents a view which is in opposition to that of the Platonist Pico but which has some affinity with that of Guarino, who says that the statements of poetry are true not literally but symbolically.[8] For Hippolyta the creations of the imagination are related to living experience and reflect some kind of reality.

The Romantics face this issue squarely and boldly. So far from thinking that the imagination deals with the non-existent, they insist that it reveals an important kind of truth. They believe that when it is at work it sees things to which the ordinary intelligence is blind and that it is intimately connected with a special insight or perception or intuition. Indeed, imagination and insight are in fact inseparable and form for all practical purposes a single faculty. Insight both awakes the imagination to work and is in turn sharpened by it when it is at work. This is the assumption on which the Romantics wrote poetry. It means that, when their creative gifts are engaged, they are inspired by their sense of the mystery of things to probe it with a peculiar insight and to shape their discoveries into imaginative forms. Nor is this process difficult to understand. Most of us, when we use our imaginations, are in the first place stirred by some alluring puzzle which calls for a solution, and in the second place enabled by our own creations in the mind to see much that was before dark or unintelligible. As our fancies take coherent shape, we see more clearly what has puzzled and perplexed us. This is what the Romantics do. They combine imagination and truth because their creations are inspired and controlled by a peculiar insight. Coleridge makes the point conclusively when he praises Wordsworth:

It was the union of deep feeling with profound thought; the fine balance of truth in observing, with the imaginative faculty in modifying the objects observed; and above all the original gift of spreading the tone, the *atmosphere*, and with it the depth and height of the ideal world around forms, incidents, and situations, of which, for the common view, custom had bedimmed all the lustre, had dried up the sparkle and the dew drops.[9]

So long as the imagination works in this way, it cannot fairly be accused of being an escape from life or of being no more than an agreeable relaxation.

The perception which works so closely with the imagination is not of the kind in which Locke believed, and the Romantics took pains to dispel any misunderstanding on the point. Since what mattered to them was an insight into the nature of things, they rejected Locke's limitation of perception to physical objects, because it robbed the mind of its most essential function, which is at the same time to perceive and to create. On this Blake speaks with prophetic scorn:

Mental Things are alone Real; what is call'd Corporeal, Nobody Knows of its Dwelling Place: it is in Fallacy, and its Existence an Imposture. Where is the Existence Out of Mind or Thought? Where is it but in the Mind of a Fool? [10]

Coleridge came to a similar conclusion for not very different reasons:

If the mind be not *passive,* if it be indeed made in God's image, and that, too, in the sublimest sense, the *Image of the Creator,* there is ground for the suspicion that any system built on the passiveness of the mind must be false as a system. [11]

When they rejected the sensationalist view of an external world, Blake and Coleridge prepared the way to restoring the supremacy of the spirit which had been denied by Locke but was at this time being propounded by German metaphysicians. Blake knew nothing of them, and his conclusions arose from his own visionary outlook, which could not believe that matter is in any sense as real as spirit. Coleridge had read Kant and Schelling and found in them much to support his views, but those views were derived less from them than from his own instinctive conviction that the world of spirit is the only reality. Because he was first a poet and only secondly a metaphysician, his conception of a universe of spirit came from his intense sense of an inner life and from his belief that the imagination, working with intuition, is more likely than the analytical reason to make discoveries on matters which really concern us.

In rejecting Locke's and Newton's explanations of the visible world, the Romantics obeyed an inner call to explore more fully the world of spirit. In different ways each of them believed in an order of things which is not that which we see and know, and this was the goal of their passionate search. They wished to penetrate to an abiding reality, to explore its mysteries, and by this to understand more clearly what life means and what it is worth. They were convinced that, though visible things are the instruments by which we find this reality, they are not everything and have indeed little significance unless they are related to some embracing and sustaining power. Nor is it hard to see what this means. Most of us feel that a physical universe is not enough and demand some scheme which will explain why our beliefs and convictions are valid and why in an apparently mechanistic order we have scales of values for which no mechanism can account. Locke and Newton explain what the sensible world is, but not what it is worth. Indeed, in explaining mental judgements by physical processes they destroy their validity, since the only assurance for the truth of our judgements is the existence of an objective truth which cannot be determined by a causal, subjective process. Such systems embody a spirit of negation, because in trying to explain our belief in the good or the holy or the beautiful they succeed only in explaining it away. That is why Blake dismissed atomic physicists and their like as men who try in vain to destroy the divine light which alone gives meaning to life, and proclaimed that in its presence their theories cease to count:

The Atoms of Democritus
And Newton's Particles of light
Are sands upon the Red sea shore,
Where Israel's tents do shine so bright.[12]

The Romantics were concerned with the things of the spirit and hoped that through imagination and inspired insight they could both understand them and present them in compelling poetry.

It was this search for an unseen world that awoke the inspiration of the Romantics and made poets of them. The power of their work comes partly from the driving force of their desire to grasp these ultimate truths, partly from their exaltation when they thought that they had found them. Unlike their German contemporaries, who were content with the thrills of *Sehnsucht,* or longing, and did not care much what the *Jenseits,* or "beyond," might be, so long as it was sufficiently mysterious, the English Romantics pursued their lines of imaginative enquiry until they found answers which satisfied them. Their aim was to convey the mystery of things through individual manifestations and thereby to show what it means. They appeal not to the logical mind but to the complete self, to the whole range of intellectual faculties, senses, and emotions. Only individual presentations of imaginative experience can do this. In them we see examples of what cannot be expressed directly in words and can be conveyed only by hint and suggestion. The powers which Wordsworth saw in nature or Shelley in love are so enormous that we begin to understand them only when they are manifested in single, concrete examples. Then, through the single cases, we apprehend something of what the poet has seen in vision. The essence of the Romantic imagination is that it fashions shapes which display these unseen forces at work, and there is no other way to display them, since they resist analysis and description and cannot be presented except in particular instances.

The apprehension of these spiritual issues is quite different from the scientific understanding of natural laws or the philosophical grasp of general truths. Such laws and truths are properly stated in abstract words, but spiritual powers must be introduced through particular examples, because only then do we see them in their true individuality. Indeed, only when the divine light of the imagination is on them do we begin to understand their significance and their appeal. That is why Blake is so stern on the view that art deals with general truths. He has none of Samuel Johnson's respect for the "grandeur of generality," and would disagree violently with him when he says, "nothing can please many and please long, but just representation of general nature." Blake thought quite otherwise:

> To Generalize is to be an Idiot. To Particularize is the Alone Distinction of Merit. General Knowledges are those Knowledges that Idiots possess.[13]

> What is General Nature? is there Such a Thing? what is General Knowledge? is there such a Thing? Strictly Speaking All Knowledge is Particular.[14]

Blake believed this because he lived in the imagination. He knew that nothing had full significance for him unless it appeared in a particular form. And with this the Romantics in general agreed. Their art aimed at presenting as forcibly as possible the moments of vision which give to even the vastest issues the coherence and simplicity of single events. Even in "Kubla Khan," which keeps so many qualities of the dream in which it was born, there is a highly individual presentation of a remote and mysterious experience, which is in fact the central experience of all creation in its Dionysiac delight and its enraptured ordering of many elements into an entrancing pattern. Coleridge may not have been fully conscious of what he was doing when he wrote it, but the experience which he portrays is of the creative mood in its purest moments, when boundless possibilities seem to open before it. No wonder he felt that, if he could only realize all the potentialities of such a moment, he would be like one who has supped with the gods:

> And all should cry, Beware! Beware!
> His flashing eyes, his floating hair!
> Weave a circle round him thrice,
> And close your eyes with holy dread,

For he on honey-dew hath fed,
And drunk the milk of Paradise.

It was in such experience, remote and strange and beyond the
senses, that the Romantics sought for poetry, and they saw that
the only way to convey it to others was in particular instances and
examples.

The invisible powers which sustain the universe work
through and in the visible world. Only by what we see and hear
and touch can we be brought into relation with them. Every poet
has to work with the world of the senses, but for the Romantics
it was the instrument which set their visionary powers in action.
It affected them at times in such a way that they seemed to be
carried beyond it into a transcendental order of things, but this
would never have happened if they had not looked on the world
around them with attentive and loving eyes. One of the advantages which they gained by their deliverance from abstractions
and general truths was a freedom to use their senses and to look
on nature without conventional prepossessions. More than this,
they were all gifted with a high degree of physical sensibility and
sometimes so enthralled by what they saw that it entirely dominated their being. This is obviously true of Wordsworth and of
Keats, who brought back to poetry a keenness of eye and of ear
which it had hardly known since Shakespeare. But it is no less
true of Blake and Coleridge and Shelley. The careful, observing
eye which made Blake a cunning craftsman in line and colour
was at work in his poetry. It is true that he was seldom content
with mere description of what he saw, but, when he used description for an ulterior purpose to convey some vast mystery, his
words are exact and vivid and make his symbols shine brightly
before the eye. Though Coleridge found some of his finest inspiration in dreams and trances, he gave to their details a singular
brilliance of outline and character. Though Shelley lived among
soaring ideas and impalpable abstractions, he was fully at home
in the visible world, if only because it was a mirror of eternity and

worthy of attention for that reason. There are perhaps poets who live entirely in dreams and hardly notice the familiar scene, but the Romantics are not of their number. Indeed, their strength comes largely from the way in which they throw a new and magic light on the common face of nature and lure us to look for some explanation for the irresistible attraction which it exerts. In nature all the Romantic poets found their initial inspiration. It was not everything to them, but they would have been nothing without it; for through it they found those exalting moments when they passed from sight to vision and pierced, as they thought, to the secrets of the universe.

Though all the Romantic poets believed in an ulterior reality and based their poetry on it, they found it in different ways and made different uses of it. They varied in the degree of importance which they attached to the visible world and in their interpretation of it. At one extreme is Blake, who held that the imagination is a divine power and that everything real comes from it. It operates with a given material, which is nature, but Blake believed that a time would come when nature will disappear and the spirit be free to create without it. While it is there, man takes his symbols from it and uses them to interpret the unseen. Blake's true home was in vision, in what he saw when he gave full liberty to his creative imagination and transformed sense-data through it. For him the imagination uncovers the reality masked by visible things. The familiar world gives hints which must be taken and pursued and developed:

> To see a World in a Grain of Sand
> And a Heaven in a Wild Flower,
> Hold Infinity in the palm of your hand
> And Eternity in an hour.[15]

Through visible things Blake reached that transcendent state which he called "eternity" and felt free to create new and living worlds. He was not a mystic striving darkly and laboriously towards God, but a visionary who could say of himself:

> I am in God's presence night and day,
> And he never turns his face away.[16]

Of all the Romantics, Blake is the most rigorous in his conception of the imagination. He could confidently say, "One Power alone makes a Poet: Imagination, The Divine Vision," [17] because for him the imagination creates reality, and this reality is the divine activity of the self in its unimpeded energy. His attention is turned towards an ideal, spiritual world, which with all other selves who obey the imagination he helps to build.

Though Blake had a keen eye for the visible world, his special concern was with the invisible. For him every living thing was a symbol of everlasting powers, and it was these which he wished to grasp and to understand. Since he was a painter with a remarkably pictorial habit of mind, he described the invisible in the language of the visible, and no doubt he really saw it with his inner vision. But what he saw was not, so to speak, an alternative to the given world, but a spiritual order to which the language of physical sight can be applied only in metaphor. What concerned him most deeply and drew out his strongest powers was the sense of a spiritual reality at work in all living things. For him even the commonest event might be fraught with lessons and meanings. How much he found can be seen from his "Auguries of Innocence," where in epigrammatic, oracular couplets he displays his sense of the intimate relations which exist in reality and bind the worlds of sight and of spirit in a single whole. His words look simple enough, but every word needs attention, as when he proclaims:

> A Robin Red breast in a Cage
> Puts all Heaven in a Rage.

Blake's robin redbreast is itself a spiritual thing, not merely a visible bird, but the powers which such a bird embodies and symbolizes, the free spirit which delights in song and in all that song implies. Such a spirit must not be repressed, and any repression of it is a sin against the divine life of the universe. Blake was a visionary who believed that ordinary things are unsubstantial in themselves and yet rich as symbols of greater realities. He was so at home in the spirit that he was not troubled by the apparent solidity of matter. He saw something else: a world of eternal values and living spirits.

Keats had a more passionate love than Blake for the visible world and has too often been treated as a man who lived for sensuous impressions, but he resembled Blake in his conviction that ultimate reality is to be found only in the imagination. What it meant to him can be seen from some lines in "Sleep and Poetry" in which he asks why the imagination has lost its old power and scope:

> Is there so small a range
> In the present strength of manhood, that the high
> Imagination cannot freely fly
> As she was wont of old? prepare her steeds,
> Paw up against the light, and do strange deeds
> Upon the clouds? Has she not shown us all?
> From the clear space of ether, to the small
> Breath of new buds unfolding? From the meaning
> Of Jove's large eye-brow, to the tender greening
> Of April meadows?

Keats was still a very young man when he wrote this, and perhaps his words are not so precise as we might like. But it is clear that he saw the imagination as a power which both creates and reveals, or rather reveals through creating. Keats accepted the works of the imagination not merely as existing in their own right, but as having a relation to ultimate reality through the light which they shed on it. This idea he pursued with hard thought until he saw exactly what it meant, and made it his own because it answered a need in his creative being.

Through the imagination Keats sought an absolute reality to

which a door was opened by his appreciation of beauty through the senses. When the objects of sense laid their spell upon him, he was so stirred and exalted that he felt himself transported to another world and believed that he could almost grasp the universe as a whole. Sight and touch and smell awoke his imagination to a sphere of being in which he saw vast issues and was at home with them. Through beauty he felt that he came into the presence of the ultimately real. The more intensely a beautiful object affected him, the more convinced he was that he had passed beyond it to something else. In *Endymion* he says that happiness raises our minds to a "fellowship with essence" and leaves us "alchemized and free of space":

> Feel we these things? that moment we have stept
> Into a sort of oneness, and our state
> Is like a fleeting spirit's. But there are
> Richer entanglements, enthralments far
> More self-destroying, leading by degrees
> To the chief intensity.[18]

The beauty of visible things carried Keats into ecstasy, and this was the goal of his desires, since it explained the extraordinary hold which objects of sense had on him and justified his wish to pass beyond them to something permanent and universal. Keats' notion of this reality was narrower than Blake's, and he speaks specifically as a poet, whereas Blake included in the imagination all activities which create or increase life. Moreover, while Blake's imagination is active, Keats suggests that his is largely passive and that his need is to feel the "chief intensity." But he is close to Blake in the claims which he makes for the imagination as something absorbing and exalting which opens the way to an unseen spiritual order.

Coleridge, too, gave much thought to the imagination and devoted to it some distinguished chapters of his *Biographia Literaria*. With him it is not always easy to disentangle theories which he formed in later life from the assumptions upon which he acted almost instinctively before his creative faculties began to fail. At times he seems to be still too aware of the sensationalist philosophy of his youth. From it he inherits a conception of a world of facts, an "inanimate cold world," in which "objects, *as* objects, are essentially fixed and dead." But as a poet he transcended this idea, or turned it to an unexpected conclusion. Just because the external world is like this, the poet's task is to transform it by the imagination. Just as "accidents of light and shade" may transmute "a known and familiar landscape," [19] so this dead world may be brought to life by the imagination. Coleridge justified this by a bold paradox:

Dare I add that genius must act of the feeling that body is but a striving to become mind — that is mind in its essence. [20]

What really counted with him was his own deep trust in the imagination as something which gives a shape to life. What this meant to him in practice can be seen from the lines in "Dejection" in which he explains that nature lives only in us and that it is we who create all that matters in her:

Ah! from the soul itself must issue forth
A light, a glory, a fair luminous cloud
Enveloping the Earth —
And from the soul itself must there be sent
A sweet and potent voice, of its own birth,
Of all sweet sounds the life and element!

Coleridge does not go so far as Blake in the claims which he makes for the imagination. He is still a little hampered by the presence of an external world and feels that in some way he must conform to it. But when his creative genius is at work, it brushes these hesitations aside and fashions reality from a shapeless, undifferentiated "given." In the end he believes that meaning is found for existence through the exercise of a creative activity which is akin to that of God.

Coleridge advanced no very definite view of the ultimate reality which poetry explores. If we may judge by "Kubla Khan," he seems to have felt, at least in some moods, that the mere act of creation is itself transcendental and that we need ask for nothing more. But perhaps the evidence of "Kubla Khan" should not be pressed too far. Indeed, if we turn to "The Ancient Mariner" and "Christabel," it seems clear that Coleridge thought that the task of poetry is to convey the mystery of life. The ambiguous nature of both poems, with their suggestion of an intermediate state between dreaming and waking, between living people and unearthly spirits, gives an idea of the kind of subject which stirred Coleridge's genius to its boldest flights. Whatever he might think as a philosopher, as a poet he was fascinated by the notion of unearthly powers at work in the world, and it was their influence which he sought to catch. Of course, he did not intend to be taken literally, but we cannot help feeling that his imaginative conception of reality was of something behind human actions which is more vivid than the familiar world because of its sharper contrasts of good and evil and the more purposeful way in which it moves. This conception was developed only in poetry, and even then only in two or three poems. Coleridge seems to have been forced to it by a troubled and yet exciting apprehension that life is ruled by powers which cannot be fully understood. The result is a poetry more mysterious than that of any other Romantic, and yet, because it is based on primary human emotions, singularly poignant and intimate.

Wordsworth certainly agreed with Coleridge in much that he said about the imagination, especially in the distinction between it and fancy. For him the imagination was the most important gift that a poet can have, and his arrangement of his own poems shows what he meant by it. The section which he calls "Poems of the Imagination" contains poems in which he united creative power and a special, visionary insight. He agreed with Coleridge that this activity resembles that of God. It is the divine capacity of the child who fashions his own little worlds:

For feeling has to him imparted power
That through the growing faculties of sense
Doth like an agent of the one great Mind
Create, creator and receiver both,
Working but in alliance with the works
Which it beholds.[21]

The poet keeps this faculty even in maturity, and through it he
is what he is. But Wordsworth was fully aware that mere creation is not enough, that it must be accompanied by a special
insight. So he explains that the imagination

Is but another name for absolute power
And clearest insight, amplitude of mind,
And Reason in her most exalted mood.[22]

Wordsworth did not go so far as the other Romantics in relegat-
ing reason to an inferior position. He preferred to give a new
dignity to the word and to insist that inspired insight is itself rational.

Wordsworth differs from Coleridge in his conception of the
external world. He accepts its independent existence and insists
that the imagination must in some sense conform to it. Once
again he sees the issue illustrated by childhood:

A plastic power
Abode with me; a forming hand, at times
Rebellious, acting in a devious mood;
A local spirit of his own, at war
With general tendency, but, for the most,
Subservient strictly to external things
With which it communed.[23]

For Wordsworth the imagination must be subservient to the external world, because that world is not dead but living and has
its own soul, which is, at least in the life that we know, distinct

from the soul of man. Man's task is to enter into communion with this soul, and indeed he can hardly avoid doing so, since from birth onward his life is continuously shaped by nature, which penetrates his being and influences his thoughts. Wordsworth believed that he helped to bring this soul of nature closer to man, that he could show

> by words
> Which speak of nothing more than what we are[24]

how exquisitely the external world is fitted to the individual mind, and the individual mind to the external world. This, it must be admitted, was not to Blake's taste, and he commented: "You shall not bring me down to believe such fitting and fitted." [25] But for Wordsworth this was right. Nature was the source of his inspiration, and he could not deny to it an existence at least as powerful as man's. But since nature lifted him out of himself, he sought for a higher state in which its soul and the soul of man should be united in a single harmony. Sometimes he felt that this happened and that through vision he attained an understanding of the oneness of things.

Though Shelley's mind moved in a way unlike that of his fellow Romantics, he was no less attached to the imagination and gave to it no less a place in his theory of poetry. He understood the creative nature of his work and shows what he thought of it when in *Prometheus Unbound* a Spirit sings of the poet:

> He will watch from dawn to gloom
> The lake-reflected sun illume
> The yellow bees in the ivy-bloom,
> Nor heed nor see, what things they be;
> But from these create he can
> Forms more real than living man,
> Nurslings of immortality!

Shelley saw that though the poet may hardly notice the visible world, he none the less uses it as material to create independent beings which have a superior degree of reality. Nor did he stop at this. He saw that reason must somehow be related to the imagination, and he decided, in contradistinction to Wordsworth, that its special task is simply to analyse the given and to act as an instrument for the imagination, which uses its conclusions to create a synthetic and harmonious whole. He calls poetry "the expression of the Imagination," because in it diverse things are brought together in harmony instead of being separated through analysis. In this he resembles such thinkers as Bacon and Locke, but his conclusion is quite different from theirs, since he insists that the imagination is man's highest faculty and through it he realizes his noblest powers.

In his *Defence of Poetry* Shelley controverted the old disparaging view of the imagination by claiming that the poet has a special kind of knowledge:

He not only beholds intensely the present as it is, and discovers those laws according to which present things ought to be ordered, but he beholds the future in the present, and his thoughts are the germs of the flower and the fruit of latest time . . . A poet participates in the eternal, the infinite, and the one.[26]

For Shelley the poet is also a seer, gifted with a peculiar insight into the nature of reality. And this reality is a timeless, unchanging, complete order, of which the familiar world is but a broken reflection. Shelley took Plato's theory of knowledge and applied it to beauty. For him the Ideal Forms are a basis not so much of knowing as of that exalted insight which is ours in the presence of beautiful things. The poet's task is to uncover this absolute real in its visible examples and to interpret them through it. It is spiritual in the sense that it includes all the higher faculties of man and gives meaning to his transient sensations. Shelley tried to grasp the whole of things in its essential unity, to show what is real and what is merely phenomenal, and by doing this to display how the phenomenal depends on the real. For him the ultimate reality is the eternal mind, and this holds the universe together:

> This Whole
> Of suns, and worlds, and men, and beasts, and flowers,
> With all the silent or tempestuous workings
> By which they have been, are, or cease to be,
> Is but a vision; — all that it inherits
> Are motes of a sick eye, bubbles and dreams;
> Thought is its cradle, and its grave, nor less
> The future and the past are idle shadows
> Of thought's eternal flight — they have no being:
> Nought is but that which feels itself to be.[27]

In thought and feeling, in consciousness and spirit, Shelley found reality and gave his answer to Prospero's nihilism. He believed that the task of the imagination is to create shapes by which this reality can be revealed.

The great Romantics, then, agreed that their task was to find through the imagination some transcendental order which explains the world of appearances and accounts not merely for the existence of visible things but for the effect which they have on us, for the sudden, unpredictable beating of the heart in the presence of beauty, for the conviction that what then moves us cannot be a cheat or an illusion, but must derive its authority from the power which moves the universe. For them this reality could not but be spiritual, and they provide an independent illustration of Hegel's doctrine that nothing is real but spirit. In so far as they made sweeping statements about the oneness of things, they were metaphysicians, but, unlike professional metaphysicians, they trusted not in logic but in insight, not in the analytical reason but in the delighted, inspired soul which in its full nature transcends both the mind and the emotions. They were, too, in their own way, religious, in their sense of the holiness of reality and the awe which they felt in its presence. But, so far as their central beliefs were concerned, they were not orthodox. Blake's religion denied the existence of God apart from men; Shelley liked to proclaim that he was an atheist; Keats was uncertain how far to accept the doctrines of Christianity. Though later both Coleridge and Wordsworth conformed almost with enthusiasm, in their most creative days their poetry was founded on a different faith. The Romantic movement was a prodigious attempt to discover the world of spirit through the unaided efforts of the solitary soul. It was a special manifestation of that belief in the worth of the individual which philosophers and politicians had recently preached to the world.

This bold expedition into the unknown, conducted with a scrupulous sincerity and a passionate faith, was very far from being an emotional self-indulgence. Each of these poets was convinced that he could discover something very important and that he possessed in poetry a key denied to other men. To this task they were prepared to devote themselves, and in different ways they paid heavily for it, in happiness, in self-confidence, in the very strength of their creative powers. They were not content to dream their own dreams and to fashion comforting illusions. They insisted that their creations must be real, not in the narrow sense that anything of which we can think has some sort of existence, but in the wide sense that they are examples and embodiments of eternal things which cannot be presented otherwise than in individual instances. Because the Romantics were poets, they set forth their visions with the wealth that poetry alone can give, in the concrete, individual form which makes the universal vivid and significant to the finite mind. They refused to accept the ideas of other men on trust or to sacrifice imagination to argument. As Blake says of Los,

I must Create a System or be enslav'd by another Man's.
I will not Reason and Compare: my business is to Create.[28]

The Romantics knew that their business was to create, and through creation to enlighten the whole sentient and conscious self of man, to wake his imagination to the reality which lies behind or in familiar things, to rouse him from the deadening routine of custom to a consciousness of immeasurable distances and unfathomable depths, to make him see that mere reason is not enough and that what he needs is inspired intuition. They take a wider view both of man and of poetry than was taken by their staid and rational predecessors of the eighteenth century, because they believed that it is the whole spiritual nature of man that counts, and to this they made their challenge and their appeal.

II

SONGS OF INNOCENCE
AND EXPERIENCE

IN 1789, the year of the French Revolution, William Blake issued his *Songs of Innocence* as the first volume to be produced in his new manner of illuminated printing. In 1794 he reissued it in the same manner, but with the addition of *Songs of Experience* to form a single book. This book is noteworthy among Blake's works because it is the only volume of poems which he himself published. The *Poetical Sketches* of 1783 was published by the Reverend Henry Mathew, no doubt with Blake's approval or acquiescence but not with his own loving care. Blake's other publications were either prophetic books or prose works, not poetry in the strict sense. The fact that Blake published the *Songs* as he did shows what importance he attached to them. There can be no doubt that he intended them to be as good as he could make them both in contents and in appearance. The Rossetti manuscript shows not only what pains he took in revising his texts but what self-denial he exerted in omitting from the book poems which are among the best that he wrote but which for some reason he did not think suitable for publication in it. A book formed with such care deserves special attention. Blake was thirty-seven when he issued it in its complete form, and it represents his mature, considered choice of his own poems. It is perhaps not surprising that in recent years scholars have tended to neglect the *Songs* for the prophetic books; for the *Songs* look limpid and translucent, while the prophetic books are rich in unravelled mysteries and alluring secrets. But the *Songs* deserve special attention if only because they constitute one of the most remarkable collections of lyrical poems written in English.

Blake made in practice a distinction between poetry and prophecy. In the first place, he recognized and maintained a difference of form. In the *Songs* he uses the traditional metres of English songs and hymns without even repeating the experiment, made in *Poetical Sketches*, of lyrical blank verse; in the prophecies, modelling himself on the Bible and Ossian, he uses what is in fact free verse, and his reasons for this are given in the foreword to *Jerusalem*:

> When this Verse was first dictated to me, I consider'd a Monotonous Cadence, like that used by Milton and Shakespeare and all writers of English Blank Verse, derived from the modern bondage of Rhyming, to be a necessary and indispensible part of Verse. But I soon found that in the mouth of a true Orator such monotony was not only awkward, but as much a bondage as rhyme itself.[1]

In the prophecies Blake speaks as an orator and needs an orator's freedom: in the *Songs* he sings and needs the regular measures of song. In the second place, Blake's purpose differs in the *Songs* and in the prophecies. In the prophecies he had a great message for his generation, an urgent call to awake from its slothful sleep, a summons to activity and to that fuller life which comes from exerting the imagination. At the beginning of *Milton* he displays his purpose:

> Rouze up, O Young Men of the New Age! set your foreheads against the ignorant Hirelings! For we have Hirelings in the Camp, the Court and the University, who would, if they could, for ever depress Mental and prolong Corporeal War.[2]

This is not the spirit in which Blake begins the *Songs of Innocence* with a poem significantly called "Introduction":

> Piping down the valleys wild,
> Piping songs of pleasant glee,
> On a cloud I saw a child,
> And he laughing said to me:

"Pipe a song about a Lamb!"
So I piped with merry chear.
"Piper, pipe that song again;"
So I piped: he wept to hear.

These are the words of a poet who sings because he must, not of a prophet whose first wish is to summon his generation to a new life.

The differences of form and intention between the *Songs* and the prophetic books are paralleled by comparable differences in the presentation of material. When he completed the *Songs,* Blake had already written some of his prophetic books and begun that remarkable system of myths and symbols which gives them so special a character. In the *Songs* there is almost no trace of Blake's mythical figures. Though he wrote *Tiriel* and *The Book of Thel* at the same time as the *Songs of Innocence,* their characters do not appear in the *Songs.* And this is all the more remarkable since the experience in these prophetic books is ultimately not very dissimilar from that in the *Songs* and belongs to the same important years of Blake's life. In the *Songs* Blake pursued a more traditional and more lyrical art, because some deep need in him called for this kind of expression. It is therefore dangerous to try to explain the *Songs* too exactly by the prophetic books. There are undeniable connections between the two, but the *Songs* go their own way in their own spirit. In them Blake speaks of himself from a purely personal point of view. It is true that he uses his own remarkable symbols, but not quite in the same way as in the prophetic books, and certainly not with the same desire for a new mythology to supplement or correct that of the Bible.

It is possible to read the *Songs* and to be so enchanted by them that we do not stop to ask what in fact they mean. Such a procedure has the formidable approval of A. E. Housman, who says of them that "the meaning is a poor foolish disappointing thing in comparison with the verses themselves." [3] This is of course true. The mere meaning, extracted from the poems and paraphrased in lifeless prose, is indeed a poor thing in comparison with what Blake wrote. The poems succeed through the magnificence of their poetry, and no analysis can take its place. At the same time, it is almost impossible to read and enjoy poetry without knowing what it means, for the good reason that the meaning is an essential part of the whole and makes an essential contribution to the delight which the poems give. To acquiesce in ignorance of the meaning is more than can reasonably be asked of us. Human curiosity and the desire to gain as much as possible from a work of art reject this limited approach and force us to ask what the subjects of the poems are. Nor does this destroy our pleasure in them. When we know what Blake means, we appreciate more fully his capacity for transforming complex states of mind into pure song and for giving to his most unusual thoughts an appeal which is somehow both intimate and rapturously exciting.

That Blake intended his readers to understand what he said and to pay an intelligent attention to it is clear from his title-page, which describes the songs as "showing the two contrary states of the human soul." Blake groups his verses under two main headings, and there is plainly a great difference of character between the two parts. In so arranging his work, Blake followed his own maxim that "without Contraries is no progression." [4] The contrast meant much to him, and we neglect it at the risk of misunderstanding his intention. So emphatic a division is not to be found in the prophetic books and shows that, when he chose, Blake could impose a fine architectural order on his work. Perhaps he was able to do this because the material and manner of the songs fall more easily into a definite shape than does the various stuff of the prophetic books. In the *Songs* Blake limits himself to a special section of material which is relatively clear in its outlines and limits. He has distilled his thoughts into the shape of song, and his appeal is more direct and more immediate than it can be in the more complicated technique of prophecy.

The two sections of Blake's book, the songs of innocence and the songs of experience, are contrasted elements in a single design. The first part sets out an imaginative vision of the state of innocence: the second shows how life challenges and corrupts and destroys it. What Blake intended by this scheme can be seen from the motto which he wrote for the book but did not include in it:

> The Good are attracted by Men's perceptions,
> And think not for themselves;
> Till Experience teaches them to catch
> And to cage the Fairies and Elves.
>
> And then the Knave begins to snarl
> And the Hypocrite to howl;
> And all his good Friends shew their private ends,
> And the Eagle is known from the Owl.

This little poem shows how the *Songs* are related to some of the most persistent elements in Blake's thought. Since for him the primary reality and the only thing that matters is the active life of the creative imagination, he has nothing but contempt for empiricist philosophers who build their systems on sense-perceptions instead of on vision. Blake believes that the naturally good are deceived by such theories and so corrupted by them that they cease to think for themselves, and restrict those creative forces which he calls "fairies and elves." When this happens, knavery, hypocrisy, and self-seeking enter into the soul, and the state of innocence is lost; but for those who have eyes to see, the free, soaring spirit of the eagle is visible in all its difference from the sleepy, night-ridden owl. This is the main theme of the *Songs*. In the first part Blake shows what innocence means, in the second how it is corrupted and destroyed.

Blake's state of innocence, set forth in symbols of pastoral life akin to those of the Twenty-third Psalm, seems at first sight to have something in common with what Vaughan, Traherne, and Wordsworth say in their different ways about the vision of childhood which is lost in later life, and it is tempting to think that this is what concerns Blake. But he is concerned with the loss not so much of actual childhood as of something wider and less definite. For him childhood is both itself and a symbol of a state of soul which may exist in maturity. His subject is the child-like vision of existence. For him all human beings are in some sense and at some times the children of a divine father, but experience destroys their innocence and makes them follow spectres and illusions. Blake does not write at a distance of time from memories of what childhood once was, but from an insistent, present anguish at the ugly contrasts between the childlike and the experienced conceptions of reality.

With a book which deals with so poignant a subject, it is tempting to look in Blake's own life for some event or circumstances which forced this issue so powerfully on him. That he was deeply troubled by it is clear not merely from the agonized poems of *Songs of Experience* but from the prophetic books, *Tiriel* and *The Book of Thel*, which seem to have been written in 1788 and 1789. In Thel Blake presents a symbolical figure who lives in an Arcadian state of innocence but finds herself appalled and helpless before the first appearances of reality; in *Tiriel* he makes his chief figure die when he realizes that he has erred in substituting the deadening rule of law for the free life of the imagination. Both books are, in a sense, concerned with the tragedy of innocence. Just as Thel is unable to endure reality when she sees it and flies back into eternity, so Har and Heva, who represent an innocence which has outlived its real strength, are unable to help Tiriel in his great need. The problems suggested in these two books are not the same as in the *Songs*, but there seems to be a common basis of experience, something which, even when he was writing the *Songs of Innocence,* deeply troubled Blake and forced him to think about this issue in more than one way.

When he composed the *Songs of Experience,* Blake seems to have passed through a spiritual crisis. He, who was in many ways the healthiest of men, wrote in 1793: "I say I shan't live for five years, and if I live one it will be a wonder." Something had shaken his trust in himself and in life. What this was we can only guess, and such clues as are available point to a combination of different causes. The trouble was already there in 1788 when he wrote *Tiriel,* but it seems to have grown and to have preyed more insistently on his mind in the following years. It did not in the least interfere with his creative powers. Indeed, at this time he did an astonishing amount of work both as a poet and as an artist, and most of it is as good as anything that he ever did afterwards. But Blake's genius was not discouraged by trouble and anxiety, and that he had these in full measure is beyond reasonable dispute. In the first place, his rapturous hopes in the French Revolution, expressed in his prophetic book called after it and written in 1791, were soon replaced by the recognition that events were taking a course not to his liking. The English Government was hostile to the Revolution, and Blake's own friends, like Thomas Paine, whom he saved from arrest by a timely warning in 1792, were in danger. What such a disillusionment meant to a visionary like Blake can be seen from his *Visions of the Daughters of Albion,* with its passionate denunciations of oppression and slavery. He was brought down with a terrible shock from his visions of reformed humanity to a realization of what political events really were.

In the second place, Blake's domestic life seems at this time to have passed through a strange phase. His excellent wife did not sympathize with his idealistic views of free love and resolutely opposed them. To Blake at first this was an unforeseen denial of the spirit, and it shook him deeply. It seems even for a time to have broken his trust in himself. He found his solution soon enough, and the rest of his life was spent in unclouded happiness with his wife. But what he felt at the moment can be seen from his strange poem "William Bond," and especially from three verses in it:

> He went to Church in a May morning
> Attended by Fairies, one, two and three;
> But the Angels of Providence drove them away,
> And he return'd home in misery.
>
> He went not out to the Field nor Fold,
> He went not out to the Village nor Town,
> But he came home in a black, black cloud,
> And took to his Bed, and there lay down.
>
> And an Angel of Providence at his Feet,
> And an Angel of Providence at his Head,
> And in the midst a Black, Black Cloud,
> And in the midst the Sick Man on his Bed.

Since by "fairies" Blake means the impulses of the creative imagination, it is clear that in this crisis his inner life has received a terrible blow from "Angels of Providence." In his language they are the forces of legality and moralism in which he saw the most sinister enemies of the free life of the imagination. He, who had put all his trust in this free life, found himself frustrated and depressed by the forces which he most condemned. Partly in politics, partly in domestic life, partly no doubt in other matters, Blake seems to have discovered that his central and most cherished beliefs were not shared by others but were the object of hatred and persecution. At some date in these years the common world was revealed to him, and he found it more frightening than he had ever suspected. From this discovery the *Songs* were born.

Blake's crisis takes place in a spiritual order of things and involves spiritual values, and for this reason he has to speak of it in symbols. What he describes are not actual events as ordinary men see and understand them, but spiritual events which have to be stated symbolically in order that they may be intelligible. In the *Songs of Innocence* Blake's symbols are largely drawn from the Bible, and since he makes use of such familiar figures as the Good Shepherd and the Lamb of God, there is not much difficulty in seeing what he means; but in the *Songs of Experience* he often uses symbols of his own making, and his meaning is more elusive. Indeed, some poems in this section are fully understandable only by reference to symbols which Blake uses in his prophetic books; and since the meaning of most symbols tends to be inconstant, there is always a danger that we may make his meaning more emphatic or more exact than it is, especially since, as Blake grew older, he developed his symbols and by placing them in precise contexts gave them a greater definiteness. But in both kinds of song it is clear that Blake anticipates those poets of a hundred years later who forged their own symbols in order to convey what would otherwise be almost inexpressible, since no adequate words exist for the unnamed powers of a supernatural world. Blake's own view of his method can be seen from a letter to Thomas Butts:

   Allegory addressed to the Intellectual powers, while it is altogether hidden from the Corporeal Understanding, is My Definition of the Most Sublime Poetry.[5]

Since by "Corporeal Understanding" Blake means the perception of sense-data, and by "Intellectual powers" the imaginative spirit which is the only reality, it is clear that in his view poetry is concerned with something else than the phenomenal world, and that the only means to speak of it is what he calls "allegory." It is true that elsewhere he sometimes speaks disparagingly of allegory, but that is because he distinguishes between true and false allegory.[6] For him allegory in the good sense is not the kind of "one-one correspondence" which we find in *Pilgrim's Progress,* but a system of symbols which presents events in a spiritual world.

   In the *Songs of Innocence* the symbols convey a special kind of existence or state of soul. In this state human beings have the same kind of security and assurance as belongs to lambs under a wise shepherd or to children with loving parents. Nor is it untrue to say that both the shepherd and the father of Blake's poems is God. It is He who is Himself a lamb and becomes a little child, who watches over sleeping children and gives his love to chimney-sweepers and little black boys. In the fatherhood of God, Blake's characters have equal rights and privileges. But by it he means not quite what orthodox Christians do. Blake, despite his deeply religious nature, did not believe that God exists apart from man, but says expressly:

Man is All Imagination. God is Man and exists in us and we in him . . . Imagination or the Human Eternal Body in Every Man . . . Imagination is the Divine Body in Every Man.[7]

For Blake, God and the imagination are one; that is, God is the creative and spiritual power in man, and apart from man the idea of God has no meaning. When Blake speaks of the divine, it is with reference to this power and not to any external or independent godhead. So when his songs tell of God's love and care, we must think of them as qualities which men themselves display and in so doing realize their full, divine nature. For instance, in "On Another's Sorrow," Blake says:

Think not thou canst sigh a sigh,
And thy Maker is not by;
Think not thou canst weep a tear,
And thy Maker is not near.

O! He gives to us His joy
That our grief he may destroy;
Till our grief is fled and gone
He doth sit by us and moan.

Blake means that every sigh and every tear evoke a response from our divine nature and through this are cured and turned to joy. Compassion is part of man's imaginative being, and through it he is able to transform existence. For Blake, God is the divine essence which exists potentially in every man and woman.

The power and appeal of this belief appear in "The Divine Image." The divine image, of course, is man, but man in part of his complex being and seen from a special point of view. Blake speaks quite literally and means to be taken at his word when he says:

> To Mercy, Pity, Peace, and Love
> All pray in their distress;
> And to these virtues of delight
> Return their thankfulness.
>
> For Mercy, Pity, Peace, and Love
> Is God, our father dear,
> And Mercy, Pity, Peace, and Love
> Is Man, his child and care.
>
> For Mercy has a human heart
> Pity a human face,
> And Love, the human form divine,
> And Peace, the human dress.
>
> Then every man, of every clime,
> That prays in his distress,
> Prays to the human form divine,
> Love, Mercy, Pity, Peace.
>
> And all must love the human form,
> In heathen, turk, or jew;
> Where Mercy, Love, and Pity dwell
> There God is dwelling too.

The divine qualities which Blake enumerates exist in man and reveal their divine character through him. Though Blake says of man's imagination that "it manifests itself in his Works of Art," [8] he spread his idea of art to include all that he thought most im-

portant and most living in conduct. In mercy, pity, peace, and
love, he found the creed of brotherhood which is the centre of
his gospel. He knew that by itself love may become selfish and
possessive and needs to be redeemed by other, generous qualities.
It is in the combination of these that man is God. In the state of
innocence, life is governed by these powers, and it is they which
give to it its completeness and security. That is why Blake calls
his *Songs of Innocence* "happy songs" and says that every child
will joy to hear them.

In his prophetic books Blake presents something like the state
of innocence in what he calls Beulah, a kind of lower paradise,
inferior indeed to the highest state of the active imagination
which he calls Eden, but superior to the lower states in which
reason inhibits and kills the imagination. His Beulah has its own
peculiar charm, as of a world of dream:

> There is from Great Eternity a mild and pleasant rest
> Nam'd Beulah, a soft Moony Universe, feminine, lovely,
> Pure, mild and Gentle, given in mercy to those who sleep,
> Eternally Created by the Lamb of God around,
> On all sides, within and without the Universal Man.
> The daughters of Beulah follow sleepers in all their dreams,
> Creating spaces, lest they fall into Eternal Death.[9]

When he wrote that, Blake had already decided that Beulah was
not the highest state. It is not perfect because there is no effort
or struggle in it as there is in Eden, and a full personality can be
realized only if men leave Beulah for a state less confined and less
secure. There can be little doubt that even when he wrote the
Songs of Innocence, Blake had formed some of these ideas. He
saw that though this state of childlike happiness, which he seems
to have enjoyed in his first manhood, is wonderfully charming, it
is not everything, and it cannot last. To reach a higher state man
must be tested by experience and suffering. This is the link between the two sections of Blake's book. Experience is not only a

fact; it is a necessary stage in the cycle of being. It may in many ways be a much lower state than innocence, and this Blake stresses with great power, but it is none the less necessary. The difference between the two states is reflected in the quality of Blake's poetry. Sweet and pure though the *Songs of Innocence* are, they do not possess or need the compelling passion of the *Songs of Experience*. In dealing with innocence Blake seems deliberately to have set his tone in a quiet key to show what innocence really means in his full scheme of spiritual development. He was careful to exclude from the first part of his book anything which might sound a disturbing note or suggest that innocence is anything but happy. That is why he omitted a striking verse which he wrote in the first version of "A Cradle Song":

> O, the cunning wiles that creep
> In thy little heart asleep.
> When thy little heart does wake,
> Then the dreadful lightnings break.

The illusion of childhood and of the human state which resembles it must be kept free from such intruding suggestions, and there must be no hint that innocence is not complete and secure.

From innocence man passes to experience, and what Blake means by this can be seen from some lines in *The Four Zoas*:

> What is the price of Experience? do men buy it for a song?
> Or wisdom for a dance in the street? No, it is bought with the price
> Of all that a man hath, his house, his wife, his children.
> Wisdom is sold in the desolate market where none come to buy,
> And in the wither'd field where the farmer plows for bread in vain.[10]

Blake knew that experience is bought at a bitter price, not merely in such unimportant things as comfort and peace of mind, but in the highest spiritual values. His *Songs of Experience* are the poetry of this process. They tell how what we accept in childlike innocence is tested and proved feeble by actual events, how much that we have taken for granted is not true of the living world, how every noble desire may be debased and perverted. When he sings of this process, he is no longer the piper of pleasant glee but an angry, passionate rebel. In "Infant Sorrow" he provides a counterpart to his "Introduction" and shows that even in the very beginnings of childhood there is a spirit of unrest and revolt:

> My mother groan'd! my father wept.
> Into the dangerous world I leapt:
> Helpless, naked, piping loud:
> Like a fiend hid in a cloud.
>
> Struggling in my father's hands,
> Striving against my swaddling bands,
> Bound and weary, I thought best
> To sulk upon my mother's breast.

At the start of its existence the human creature feels itself a prisoner and, after its first efforts to resist, angrily gives up the struggle.

When experience destroys the state of childlike innocence, it puts many destructive forces in its place. To show the extent of this destruction Blake places in the *Songs of Experience* certain poems which give poignant contrasts to other poems which appear in the *Songs of Innocence*. For instance, in the first "Nurse's Song" he tells how children play and are allowed to go on playing until the light fades and it is time to go to bed. In this Blake symbolizes the care-free play of the imagination when it is not spoiled by senseless restrictions. But in the second "Nurse's Song" we hear the other side of the matter, when experience has set to work:

When the voices of children are heard on the green
And whisp'rings are heard in the dale,
When days of my youth rise fresh in my mind,
My face turns green and pale.

Then come home, my children, the sun is gone down,
And the dews of night arise;
Your spring and your day are wasted in play,
And your winter and night in disguise.

The voice that now speaks is not that of loving care but of sour age, envious of a happiness which it can no longer share and eager to point out the menaces and the dangers of the dark. It sees play as a waste of time and cruelly tells the children that their life is a sham passed in darkness and cold, like one of Blake's terrible prophetic scenes of desolation, as in *The Four Zoas*:

But from the caves of deepest night, ascending in clouds of mist,
The winter spread his wide black wings across from pole to pole:
Grim frost beneath and terrible snow, link'd in a marriage chain,
Began a dismal dance. The winds around on pointed rocks
Settled like bats innumerable, ready to fly abroad.[11]

The first and most fearful thing about experience is that it breaks the free life of the imagination and substitutes a dark, cold, imprisoning fear, and the result is a deadly blow to the blithe human spirit.

The fear and denial of life which come with experience breed hypocrisy, and this earns some of Blake's hardest and harshest words. For him hypocrisy is as grave a sin as cruelty because it rises from the same causes, from the refusal to obey the creative spirit of the imagination and from submission to fear and envy. He marks its character by providing an antithesis to "The Divine Image" in "The Human Abstract." In bitter irony he shows how love, pity, and mercy can be distorted and used as a cover for base or cowardly motives. Speaking through the hypocrite's lips, he goes straight to the heart of the matter by showing how glibly hypocrisy claims to observe these cardinal virtues:

> Pity would be no more
> If we did not make somebody Poor;
> And Mercy no more could be
> If all were as happy as we.

In this corrupt frame of mind, selfishness and cruelty flourish and are dignified under false names. This process wrecks the world. Harsh rules are imposed on life through what Blake calls "Mystery," with its ceremonies and hierarchies and its promise of "an allegorical abode where existence hath never come." [12] It supports those outward forms of religion which Blake regards as the death of the soul:

> Soon spreads the dismal shade
> Of Mystery over his head;
> And the Catterpiller and Fly
> Feed on the Mystery.
>
> And it bears the fruit of Deceit,
> Ruddy and sweet to eat;
> And the Raven his nest has made
> In its thickest shade.
>
> The Gods of the earth and sea
> Sought thro' Nature to find this Tree;
> But their search was all in vain:
> There grows one in the Human Brain. [13]

So Blake re-creates the myth of the Tree of Knowledge or of Life. This tree, which is fashioned by man's reason, gives falsehood instead of truth and death instead of life.

Perhaps the worst thing in experience, as Blake sees it, is that it destroys love and affection. On no point does he speak

with more passionate conviction. He who believes that the full
life demands not merely tolerance but forgiveness and brotherhood finds that in various ways love is corrupted or condemned.
In "The Clod and the Pebble" he shows how love naturally seeks
not to please itself or have any care for itself, but in the world
of experience the heart becomes like "a pebble of the brook" and
turns love into a selfish desire for possession:

> Love seeketh only Self to please,
> To bind another to Its delight,
> Joys in another's loss of ease,
> And builds a Hell in Heaven's despite.

The withering of the affections begins early, when their elders
repress and frighten children. In "Holy Thursday" Blake shows
what this means, how in a rich and fruitful land children live in
misery:

> And their sun does never shine,
> And their fields are bleak and bare,
> And their ways are fill'd with thorns:
> It is eternal winter there.

The horror of experience is all the greater because of the contrast, explicit or implicit, which Blake suggests between it and
innocence. In "The Echoing Green" he tells how the children
are happy and contented at play, but in "The Garden of Love,"
to the same rhythm and with the same setting, he presents an
ugly antithesis. The green is still there, but on it is a chapel with
"Thou shalt not" written over the door, and the garden itself has
changed:

> And I saw it was filled with graves,
> And tomb-stones where flowers should be;
> And Priests in black gowns were walking their rounds,
> And binding with briars my joys and desires.

In the state of experience, jealousy, cruelty, and hypocrisy forbid the natural play of the affections and turn joy into misery.

Blake's tragic appreciation of the restrictions which imprison and kill the living spirit was no purely personal thing. It was his criticism of society, of the whole trend of contemporary civilization. His compassionate heart was outraged and wounded by the sufferings which society inflicts on its humbler members and by the waste of human material which seems indispensable to the efficient operation of rules and laws. In "London" he gives his own view of that "chartered liberty" on which his countrymen prided themselves, and exposes the indisputable, ugly facts:

I wander thro' each charter'd street,
Near where the charter'd Thames does flow,
And mark in every face I meet
Marks of weakness, marks of woe.

In every cry of every Man,
In every Infant's cry of fear,
In every voice, in every ban,
The mind-forg'd manacles I hear.

How the Chimney-sweeper's cry
Every black-ning Church appalls;
And the hapless Soldier's sigh
Runs in blood down Palace walls.

But most thro' midnight streets I hear
How the youthful Harlot's curse
Blasts the new born Infant's tear,
And blights with plagues the Marriage hearse.

The child chimney-sweeper, the soldier, and the harlot are Blake's types of the oppressed — characteristic victims of a system based not on brotherhood but on fear. Each in his own way shows up the shams on which society thrives. The chimney-

sweeper's condemned life is supported by the churches; the soldier's death is demanded by the court; and the harlot's calling is
forced on her by the marriage-laws. The contrasts between truth
and pretence, between natural happiness and unnatural repression, are stressed by Blake in these three examples, and through
them we see the anguish in which he faced the social questions
of his time.

The astonishing thing about the *Songs of Experience* is that,
though they were inspired by violent emotions and have a merci-
less satirical temper, they are in the highest degree lyrical. Indeed, no English poet, except Shakespeare, has written songs of
such lightness and melody. Yet Blake's subjects are not in the
least like Shakespeare's. He writes not about fundamental matters like spring and love and death, but about his own original
and complex views on existence; and the miracle is that in presenting themes which might seem to need comment and explanation, he succeeds in creating pure song. His words have an
Elizabethan lilt, a music which emphasizes their meaning and
conforms exactly to it. Despite his strong emotions and his unfamiliar ideas, Blake keeps his form miraculously limpid and melodious. This success is partly the result of a highly discriminating art.
Blake made many changes in his texts before he was satisfied
with a final version, and these show how well he knew what he
was doing, how clear an idea he had of the result which he
wished to reach. But this art was shaped by a creative impulse so
powerful that it can only be called inspiration. Blake indeed believed that his words were often dictated to him by some supernatural power. As he wrote to Thomas Butts about a prophetic
book, "I may praise it, since I dare not pretend to be any other
than the Secretary; the Authors are in Eternity." [14] In the strange
workings of the creative mind there is a point at which words
come with such force and intensity that they have a more than
human appeal. Though the poet may not receive them all at once
but gradually find, as Blake did, the exact words which he needs,
yet these songs are miracles because their creation cannot be

explained and because with them we feel ourselves in the presence of something beyond the control of man.

Two examples must suffice to illustrate Blake's art of song, and each is equally wonderful. The first is "The Sick Rose":

O Rose, thou art sick!
The invisible worm
That flies in the night,
In the howling storm,

Has found out thy bed
Of crimson joy,
And his dark secret love
Does thy life destroy.

This illustrates in an astonishing way Blake's gift for distilling a complex imaginative idea into a few marvellously telling words. If we ask what the poem means, we can answer that it means what it says, and that this is perfectly clear. It conjures up the vision of a rose attacked in a stormy night by a destructive worm, and so Blake depicts it in his accompanying illustration. But, as in all symbolical poems, we can read other meanings into it and make its images carry a weight of secondary associations. We may say that it refers to the destruction of love by selfishness, of innocence by experience, of spiritual life by spiritual death. All these meanings it can bear, and it is legitimate to make it do so. But the actual poem presents something which is common and fundamental to all these themes, something which Blake has distilled so finely from many particular cases that it has their common, quintessential character. And this Blake sees with so piercing and so concentrated a vision that the poem has its own independent life and needs nothing to supplement it. If we wish to know more about Blake's views on the issues at which the poem hints, we may find them in his prose works and prophetic books. But here he is a poet, and his thoughts are purified and transfigured in song.

My second example is "Ah! Sun-flower!":

Ah, Sun-flower! weary of time,
Who countest the steps of the Sun,
Seeking after that sweet golden clime
Where the traveller's journey is done:

Where the Youth pined away with desire,
And the pale Virgin shrouded in snow
Arise from their graves, and aspire
Where my Sun-flower wishes to go.

This raises questions similar to those raised by "The Sick Rose." Again a complex thought is distilled into two verses, and again what matters is the imaginative presentation which transports us in intense, excited delight. Here Blake's theme is not quite so single as in "The Sick Rose." He has transposed into this song his central ideas and feelings about all young men and young women who are robbed of their full humanity because they are starved of love. Because of this, the youth pines away with desire and the pale virgin is shrouded in snow. It is the pathos of their earth-bound state that the song catches and makes significant through Blake's deep compassion. The central spring of the poem is the image of the sun-flower. The flower which turns its head to follow the sun's course and is yet rooted in the earth is Blake's symbol for all men and women whose lives are dominated and spoiled by a longing which they can never hope to satisfy, and who are held down to the earth despite their desire for release into some brighter, freer sphere. In this poem Blake expresses an idea which means a great deal to him, but he does not explain or elaborate it. He assumes that his poem will do its work by itself, and his reward is that "Ah! Sun-flower" belongs to that very rare and small class of poems in which inspiration carries words to a final enchantment.

The *Songs of Experience* are more powerful and more magical than the *Songs of Innocence* because they are born of a deep anguish, from a storm in the poet's soul. Blake knows that one kind of existence is bright with joy and harmony, but he sees its place taken by another which is dark and sinister and dead. But Blake was not content simply to complain or to criticize. He sought some ultimate synthesis in which innocence might be wedded to experience, and goodness to knowledge. That such a state is possible he reveals in the first poem of *Songs of Experience,* where he speaks with the voice of the bard and summons the fallen soul of earth to some vast apocalypse:

> O Earth, O Earth, return!
> Arise from out the dewy grass;
> Night is worn,
> And the morn
> Rises from the slumberous mass.
>
> Turn away no more;
> Why wilt thou turn away?
> The starry floor,
> The wat'ry shore,
> Is giv'n thee till the break of day.

The world is still wrapped in darkness, but the stars which pierce the night are a sign of other things to come, and the sea of eternity beats on the narrow shore where mankind lives.[15] The "break of day" is Blake's symbol for the new life in which both innocence and experience are transformed, and the soul passes in its cycle to a fuller, more active life in the creative imagination. As Blake says in a note written on a page of *The Four Zoas:*

> *Unorganiz'd Innocence: An Impossibility.*
> Innocence dwells with Wisdom, but never with Ignorance.[16]

The true innocence is not after all that of the *Songs of Innocence,* but something which has gained knowledge from the ugly lessons of experience and found an expanding strength in the unfettered life of the creative soul. Beyond experience Blake foresees this consummation and hints that it will come, even though he is concerned with the dark hither side of it.

Blake knows well that such a consummation will not come simply from good will or pious aspirations and that the life of the imagination is possible only through passion and power and energy. That is why he sometimes stresses the great forces which lie hidden in man and may be terrifying but are none the less necessary if anything worth while is to happen. He sees that the creative activity of the imagination and the transformation of experience through it are possible only through the release and exercise of awful powers. He chooses his symbols for these powers in violent and destructive things, as when in his *Proverbs of Hell* he says, "The wrath of the lion is the wisdom of God," or "The roaring of lions, the howling of wolves, the raging of the stormy sea, and the destructive sword, are portions of eternity, too great for the eye of man." [17] It was in such elemental forces that Blake put his trust for the redemption of mankind, and he contrasted them favourably with the poor efforts of the human intelligence: "The tigers of wrath are wiser than the horses of instruction." The wrath which Blake found in Christ, his symbol of the divine spirit which will not tolerate restrictions but asserts itself against established rules, was the means by which he hoped to unite innocence and experience in some tremendous synthesis.

The poetry of this desire and of what it meant to Blake can be seen in "The Tyger." Here, too, enraptured song conveys in essential vision some themes which Blake presents elsewhere in more detail. This is the pure poetry of his trust in cosmic forces. The images of "The Tyger" recur in the prophetic books, but in the poem, detached from any very specific context, they have a special strength and freedom. The tiger is Blake's symbol for the fierce forces in the soul which are needed to break the bonds of experience. The "forests of the night," in which the tiger lurks, are ignorance, repression, and superstition. It has been fashioned by unknown, supernatural spirits, like Blake's mythical heroes,

Orc and Los, prodigious smiths who beat out living worlds with their hammers; and this happened when "the stars threw down their spears," that is, in some enormous cosmic crisis when the universe turned round in its course and began to move from light to darkness — as Urizen says in *The Four Zoas,* when he finds that passion and natural joy have withered under his rule and the power of the spirit has been weakened:

> I went not forth: I hid myself in black clouds of my wrath;
> I call'd the stars around my feet in the night of councils dark;
> The stars threw down their spears and fled naked away.[18]

If we wish to illustrate "The Tyger" from Blake's other works, it is easy to do so, and it adds much to our understanding of its background and its place in Blake's development. But it is first and last a poem. The images are so compelling that for most purposes they explain themselves, and we have an immediate, overwhelming impression of an awful power lurking in the darkness of being and forcing on us questions which pierce to the heart of life:

> Tyger! Tyger! burning bright
> In the forests of the night,
> What immortal hand or eye
> Could frame thy fearful symmetry?
>
> In what distant deeps or skies
> Burnt the fire of thine eyes?
> On what wings dare he aspire?
> What the hand dare sieze the fire?
>
> And what shoulder, and what art,
> Could twist the sinews of thy heart?
> And when thy heart began to beat,
> What dread hand? and what dread feet?
>
> What the hammer? what the chain?
> In what furnace was thy brain?

What the anvil? what dread grasp
Dare its deadly terrors clasp?

When the stars threw down their spears,
And water'd heaven with their tears,
Did he smile his work to see?
Did he who made the Lamb make thee?

Tyger! Tyger! burning bright
In the forests of the night,
What immortal hand or eye,
Dare frame thy fearful symmetry?

Just as early in the *Songs of Innocence* Blake sets his poem about the lamb, with its artless question,

Little Lamb, who made thee?
Dost thou know who made thee?

so early in the *Songs of Experience* Blake sets his poem about the tiger with its more frightening and more frightened questions. The lamb and the tiger are symbols for two different states of the human soul. When the lamb is destroyed by experience, the tiger is needed to restore the world.

In the *Songs of Innocence and Experience* there are only hints of the final consummation which shall restore men to the fullness of joy. The poems are concerned with an earlier stage in the struggle and treat of it from a purely poetical standpoint. What Blake gives is the essence of his imaginative thought about this crisis in himself and in all men. When he completed the whole book in its two parts, he knew that the state of innocence is not enough, but he had not found his full answer to his doubts and questions. From this uncertainty he wrote his miraculous poetry. Against the negative powers, which he found so menacingly in the ascendant, he set, both in theory and in practice, his gospel of the imagination. Strange as some of his ideas may be to us, the poetry comes with an unparalleled force because of the prodigious release of creative energy which has gone to its making. The prophet of gigantic catastrophes and celestial reconciliations was also a poet who knew that poetry alone could make others share his central experiences. In the passion and the tenderness of these songs there is something beyond analysis, that living power of the imagination which was the beginning and the end of Blake's activity. In *A Vision of the Last Judgment* he says:

"What," it will be Question'd, "When the Sun rises, do you not see a round "disk of fire somewhat like a Guinea?" O no, no, I see an Innumerable company of the Heavenly host crying, "Holy, Holy, Holy is the Lord God Almighty." [19]

Because Blake pierced beyond the visible world to these eternal powers and made them his daily company, he was able to give to his poetry the clarity and the brightness of vision.

III

THE ANCIENT MARINER

WHEN the first signs of the Romantic spirit appeared in the eighteenth century, the time-worn theme of the supernatural took a new character and received a new prominence. The fashionable cult of strangeness turned inevitably to this alluring world of the unknown and exploited it with a reckless carelessness. The result is that ghosts and goblins crowd the Romantic poetry of Germany, and in England the spate of "Gothick" novels spent its none too abundant resources in trying to make the flesh creep with death-pale spectres and clanking chains. The result, it must be admitted, is not very impressive. Instead of creating real horror and dread, this literature tends to be factitious and a little silly. It fails because it has not mastered the lessons of the past on how the supernatural should be treated. Instead of making it a subordinate element in a wider scheme, as Homer and Shakespeare do, the writers concentrate on it to the exclusion of almost everything else, and this over-emphasis spoils a subject which is effective only when it is taken in small doses. In the second place, they do not really believe in the supernatural as the great writers of the past did. It is not an authentic chapter of human experience, but an indulgence, an exercise of ghoulish fancy, and therefore unconvincing and dull. When the Romantic movement came to maturity, this cult was already largely discredited. There are, it is true, traces of its influence in Shelley's love for charnel-houses, and it is not entirely absent from Keats' *Lamia*, but these are no more than legacies from a past generation. It meant nothing to Blake or to Wordsworth, for whom it was at once too unreal and too foolish. But with Coleridge it was different. It appealed to him with a special power and was responsible for his finest work.

In 1797, being then twenty-five years old, Coleridge suddenly found the full scope of his genius. The outburst of creation lasted for about two years and then began to fail, but not before he had written the first part of "Christabel," "The Ancient Mariner," and "Kubla Khan." He had already composed good poetry, and in the long years afterwards he was to compose it again. But in 1797 and 1798 he wrote three poems which no one else could have written and which he himself was never again to equal or approach. At this time something set all his powers to work and brought to the surface all the hidden resources of his conscious and unconscious self. The dreamer was able to give a concrete form to his dreams, the omnivorous reader to fuse the heterogeneous elements of his reading into magical combinations, and the critic to satisfy his own exacting ideas of what a poem ought to be. In his later years Coleridge too often wrote with only a part of himself and was unable to speak from his full experience or to use the whole range of his powers, but into the three great poems he put all that he had. Why this happened we cannot say. We can do no more than note that here was a young man who suddenly found a voice new and strange and indisputably his own. But we can at least say what was not responsible for this. It is wrong to connect the flowering of Coleridge's genius with the formation of the opium habit; for though he had begun to take opium, it was not yet a habit, and as yet he took it only at intervals to get rest and sleep. It certainly does not explain the prodigious outburst of energy needed to create his unique poems. On the other hand, it is possible that his new acquaintance with the Wordsworths helped to unloose his hidden strength. Coleridge was always a prey to doubts and afterthoughts and rambling speculations, but Wordsworth encouraged and sustained him and kept him to his task. And though Coleridge had a remarkable sensibility to physical nature, it is abundantly clear that this was enhanced by the quiet and delicate observation of Dorothy Wordsworth. Nevertheless, the genius was Coleridge's own, and, whatever set it to work, it is the genius that counts. Coleridge's supreme contribution to poetry was the three poems, and of all English Romantic masterpieces they are the most unusual and the most romantic.

All three poems are concerned with the supernatural. "Kubla Khan," it is true, is less directly concerned than "Christabel" or "The Ancient Mariner," but into its wild magnificence the supernatural has found its way, whether in the "woman wailing for her demon-lover" and the "ancestral voices prophesying war," or in the magical music of its close when the poet seems to break the bounds of human kind and become a wild spirit of song. In "Christabel" the whole scheme is based on the supernatural. The evil spirit who haunts the body of Geraldine and tries to ruin the innocent happiness of Christabel is in the true tradition of vampires, and Coleridge infuses a mysterious dread into her. In her we see an embodiment of evil powers from another world and realize how helpless ordinary human beings are against them. It is the last, and indeed the only, triumph of the "Gothick" taste for the phantoms bred by darkness and fear, and it succeeds because Coleridge believes so much in his subject that he relates it to life and to living experience. Both "Kubla Khan" and "Christabel" are fragments, and we can only imagine what they might have been. "The Ancient Mariner" is complete. In it Coleridge did what he set out to do and showed what his powers could be. It too deals with the supernatural, on a large scale and in a generous sense. From what divers sources it came may be read in the pages of John Livingston Lowes' *The Road to Xanadu,* which shows the strange alchemical process of its creation. To that superb work of scholarship there is nothing to add. What we have to consider is not how "The Ancient Mariner" came into existence, but what it is and what it means.

Coleridge intended to introduce "The Ancient Mariner" with an essay on the supernatural.[1] Like so many of his projects, this was never realized, and though Coleridge seems to have lectured on the subject in 1818,[2] we do not know what he said or what his views were. Perhaps it is as well, since when Coleridge began to theorize on literary matters, he was apt to forget his own practice or at least to make it out to be more elaborate than it was. We have therefore to deduce his theory from his practice and to look at what he actually did. His first idea came from a Mr. John Cruikshank, who, according to Wordsworth, had a dream about "a person suffering from a dire curse for the commission of some crime" and "a skeleton ship with figures in it." [3] Coleridge spoke of this to Wordsworth, who saw that it was a subject well suited to Coleridge's genius and would fit into the part allotted to him in the plan of the *Lyrical Ballads*. Wordsworth was to take the subjects "chosen from ordinary life," and Coleridge another class in which

the incidents and agents were to be, in part at least, supernatural; and the excellence aimed at was to consist in the interesting of the affections by the dramatic truth of such emotions, as would naturally accompany such situations, supposing them real.[4]

On a walk in the Quantock Hills on November 20th, 1797, the plan of "The Ancient Mariner" was formed.[5] Wordsworth contributed not only one or two phrases but the part played by the albatross and the navigation of the ship by dead men.[6] The rest is the work of Coleridge, and on March 23rd, 1798, he brought the finished text to the Wordsworths at Alfoxden.

In taking the supernatural for his province, Coleridge must at the start have had to face a certain degree of prejudice. The subject was outmoded in the view of good judges, and any attempt to revive it might be greeted with suspicion. On the surface, "The Ancient Mariner" belonged to a class of poetry which provoked adverse comment. Even Hazlitt, who regards it as Coleridge's "most remarkable performance," adds less kindly that "it is high German, however, and in it he seems to 'conceive of poetry but as a drunken dream, reckless, careless, and heedless, of past, present, and to come.' " [7] Charles Lamb responded with greater sympathy, but he too had his doubts about the use of the supernatural and said: "I dislike all the miraculous part of it, but the feelings of the man under the operation of such scenery dragged me along like Tom Piper's magic whistle." [8] Coleridge set himself a difficult task. To succeed in it he must do a great deal more than reproduce the familiar thrills of horrific literature: he must produce a poetry of the supernatural which should in its own way be as human and as compelling as Wordsworth's poetry of everyday things. Coleridge saw these difficulties and faced them courageously. Though his poem has a supernatural subject, its effect is much more than a thrill of horror. He lives up to his own program and interests the affections by the dramatic truth of what he tells.

The triumph of "The Ancient Mariner" is that it presents a series of incredible events through a method of narration which makes them not only convincing and exciting but in some sense a criticism of life. No other poet of the supernatural has quite done this, at least on such a scale and with such abundance of authentic poetry. In his conquest of the unknown, Coleridge went outside the commonplace thrills of horror. Of course, he evokes these, and his opening verses, in which the Mariner stays the Wedding-Guest, suggest that at first Coleridge followed familiar precedents in appealing to a kind of horrified fear. But as he worked at his poem, he widened its scope and created something much richer and more human. To be sure, he chose his subject well. The weird adventures of his Mariner take place not in the trite Gothic setting of a mediaeval castle, which Coleridge used once and for all in "Christabel," but on a boundless sea with days of pitiless sun and soft nights lit by a moon and attendant stars. Nor are his "machining persons" of the same breed as his Geraldine. They are spirits of another sort, who may have their home in some Neo-Platonic heaven, but are transformed by Coleridge into powers who watch over the good and evil actions of men and requite them with appropriate rewards and punishments. The new setting and the new persons with which Coleridge shapes the supernatural give to it a new character. Instead of confining himself to an outworn dread of spectres and phantoms, he moves over a wide range of emotions and touches equally on guilt and remorse, suffering and relief, hate and forgiveness, grief and joy. Nor has his creation the misty dimness commonly associated with the supernatural. What he imagines is indeed weird, but he sees it with so sharp a vision that it lives vividly before our eyes. At each point he anticipates the objection that his is an outmoded kind of composition, and does the opposite of what his critics expect.

The first problem for any poet of the supernatural is to relate it to familiar experience. So long as it was accepted as part of the scheme of things, there was no great difficulty in this. No doubt Homer's audience accepted the ghost of Odysseus' mother because they believed in ghosts and saw that they must be like this and behave in this way. But Coleridge could not rely on his readers' feeling at home with his unfamiliar theme. He must relate it to something which they knew and understood, something which touched their hearts and imaginations, and he did this by exploiting some of the characteristics of dream. Here was something which would appeal to them and through which they could be led to appreciate the remoter mysteries which he keeps in reserve. No doubt Coleridge did this because his first impulse to "The Ancient Mariner" came from Mr. Cruikshank's dream, but, once he saw this, he made full use of it and shaped his poem in accordance with it. Dreams can have a curiously vivid quality which is often lacking in waking impressions. In them we have one experience at a time in a very concentrated form, and, since the critical self is not at work, the effect is more powerful and more haunting than most effects when we are awake. If we remember dreams at all, we remember them very clearly, even though by rational standards they are quite absurd and have no direct relation to our waking life. They have, too, a power of stirring elementary emotions, such as fear and desire, in a very direct way, though we do not at the time ask why this happens or understand it, but accept it without question as a fact. It is enough that the images of dreams are so penetrated with emotional significance that they make a single and absorbing impression. Coleridge was much attracted by their strange power. In "Christabel" he speaks of

> such perplexity of mind
> As dreams too lively leave behind,

and "The Ancient Mariner" bears the marks of such a liveliness. On the surface it shows many qualities of dream. It moves in abrupt stages, each of which has its own single, dominating character. Its visual impressions are remarkably brilliant and absorbing. Its emotional impacts change rapidly, but always come with an unusual force, as if the poet were haunted and obsessed by them. When it is all over, it clings to the memory with a peculiar tenacity, just as on waking it is difficult at first to disentangle ordinary experience from influences which still survive from sleep.

In the criticism of "The Ancient Mariner" which Wordsworth added to the edition of *Lyrical Ballads* published in 1800, he complained that "the events, having no necessary connection, do not produce each other." Now no one expects the events of dream to have the kind of necessary connection which we find in waking life, and Wordsworth's criticism is beside the mark. Indeed, he is less than fair to Coleridge, who gives to the world of his poem its own coherence and rules and logic. Things move indeed in a mysterious way, but not without some connecting relations which may reasonably be called causal. When in a fit of irritation or anger the Mariner shoots the albatross, he commits a hideous crime and is punished by the doom of "life-in-death," which means that, after being haunted by the presence of his dead comrades, he carries a gnawing memory to the end of his days. His shipmates, too, are the victims of the same laws when they are doomed to death as accomplices in his crime for saying that he was right to kill the bird. In such a system it is no less appropriate that when the Mariner feels love gushing from his heart at the sight of the water-snakes, he begins to break the first horror of his spell, and the albatross falls from his neck. Once we accept the assumption that it is wrong to kill an albatross, the rest of the action follows with an inexorable fatality. It is true that this assumption is perhaps the hardest which "The Ancient Mariner" demands of us, but of that Wordsworth was in no position to complain, since it was he who suggested the idea to Coleridge.

This imaginary world has its own rules, which are different from ours and yet touch some familiar chord in us. Nor, when we read the poem, do we really question their validity. Indeed, they are more convincing than most events in dreams, and we somehow admit that in such a world as Coleridge creates it is right that things should happen as they do. It is not too difficult to accept for the moment the ancient belief that spirits watch over human actions, and, once we do this, we see that it is right for them to interfere with men and to do extraordinary things to them. Both the figures on the skeleton ship and the spirits who guide the Mariner on his northward voyage have sufficient reality for us to feel that their actions are appropriate to their characters and circumstances. Nor is it absurd that, when the ship at last comes home, it sinks; it has passed through adventures too unearthly for it to have a place in the world of common things. It and its stricken inmate bear the marks of their ordeal, and it is no wonder that the Pilot's boy goes mad at the sight or that the only person able to withstand their influence is the holy Hermit. Coleridge makes his events so coherent and so close to much that we know in ourselves that we accept them as valid in their own world, which is not ultimately very dissimilar from ours. Because it has this inner coherence, "The Ancient Mariner" is not a phantasmagoria of unconnected events but a coherent whole which, by exploiting our acquaintance with dreams, has its own causal relations between events and lives in its own right as something intelligible and satisfying.

Coleridge knew that he must make the supernatural convincing and human. In the *Biographia Literaria,* after saying that such poetry must interest the emotions and have dramatic truth, he adds that his aim is

to transfer from our inward nature a human interest and a semblance of truth sufficient to procure for these shadows of imagination that willing suspension of disbelief for the moment, which constitutes poetic faith.[9]

We may connect these words with what Coleridge said in 1818 in a lecture on dreams:

In ordinary dreams we do not judge the objects to be real; — we simply do not determine that they are unreal.[10]

It is clear that Coleridge felt about the creations of his imagination something similar to what he felt about dreams. He assumes that while we have them we do not question their reality. "The Ancient Mariner" lives in its own world as events in dreams do, and, when we read it, we do not normally ask if its subject is real or unreal. But this is due to a consummate art. Each action, and each situation, is presented in a concrete form in which the details are selected for their appeal to common experience. Coleridge exercises an imaginative realism. However unnatural his events may be, they are formed from natural elements, and for this reason we believe in them. We may even be at home with them because their constituents are familiar and make a direct, natural appeal. Once we have entered this imaginary world, we do not feel that it is beyond our comprehension, but respond to it as we would to actual life.

In other words, though Coleridge begins by appealing to our experience of dreams, he so uses it as to present something which is more solid and more reasonable and more human than the most haunting dreams. He uses the atmosphere of dreams to accustom us to his special world, and then he proceeds to create freely within his chosen limits. At each step he takes pains to see that his eery subject is real both for the eye and for the emotions, that it has both the attraction of visible things and the significance which belongs to actions of grave import. His natural background, for instance, could have been fashioned only by a man who had learned about nature from loving observation and shared the Wordsworths' devotion to it. Amid all these strange happenings nature remains itself, and its perseverance in its own ways sometimes comes in ironical contrast to what happens on the ship, as when, at the moment when the Mariner is haunted by the look in his dead comrades' eyes, the moon continues her quiet, unchanging course:

> The moving Moon went up the sky,
> And no where did abide:
> Softly she was going up,
> And a star or two beside.

Even when nature breaks into more violent moods, it is still itself, and each touch of description makes it more real, as when Coleridge sketches a storm with something of Turner's delight in wild effects of sky and cloud:

> The upper air burst into life!
> And a hundred fire-flags sheen,
> To and fro they were hurried about!
> And to and fro, and in and out,
> The wan stars danced between.

In such scenes there is no indeterminacy of dream. Each detail comes from the known world and gives a firm background to the supernatural events which accompany it.

This realistic treatment of the setting is matched by the appeal which Coleridge makes to our emotions in handling his human persons. The Mariner and his comrades are hardly characters in any dramatic sense. They lack lineaments and personality. But perhaps this is well, since what touches us in them is the basic humanity of their sufferings. They are more types than differentiated human beings, and for this reason their agonies are simply and universally human. We feel that what happens to them might in similar circumstances happen to anyone, and we respond readily to their pathos and their misery. And these Coleridge conveys with a masterly directness. He portrays the helpless agony of thirst in the crew becalmed at sea:

> And every tongue, through utter drought,
> Was withered at the root;
> We could not speak, no more than if
> We had been choked with soot.

When at last the rain comes, and the Mariner's thirst is slaked as he sleeps, Coleridge makes no less an appeal to elementary human and physical feelings, as with a striking economy of words he shows how this happens and what a wonderful relief it is:

> My lips were wet, my throat was cold,
> My garments all were dank;
> Sure I had drunken in my dreams,
> And still my body drank.

Of course, physical sensations play a large part in dreams, but Coleridge describes them as we know them in a waking state, and the lively way in which he handles them creates a powerful emotional effect.

What is true of physical sensations in "The Ancient Mariner" is no less true of mental states. The Mariner passes through an ordeal so weird and so fearful that it might seem impossible to make it real for us. We shrink from asking what such suffering means in conditions so unfamiliar and so hideous as those in the poem. To rise to such an occasion and to give a persuasive and moving account of what the Mariner endures demands a powerful effort of the imagination. Coleridge rises to the full claim of his subject and by concentrating on elementary human emotions makes the most of them. His Mariner is indeed in a fearful plight, alone on a ship, surrounded by the dead bodies of his comrades, and Coleridge conveys the full implications of his state by drawing attention to his sense of utter helplessness and solitude:

> Alone, alone, all, all alone,
> Alone on a wide wide sea!
> And never a saint took pity on
> My soul in agony.

That is the authentic anguish of a man who feels himself abandoned both by God and man and faced with the emptiness of his guilty and tormented soul. Conversely, when the ship at last comes to land, the Mariner sees angels standing by the dead bodies and feels an infinite relief. The very silence of the celestial presences fills him with hope and joy:

> This seraph-band, each waved his hand,
> No voice did they impart —
> No voice; but oh! the silence sank
> Like music on my heart.

Coleridge understood the extremes of despair and of joy, and he distilled them into these brief moments. Because his poem moves between such extremes it has a certain spaciousness and grandeur and reflects through its variations the light and the shadow of human life.

Coleridge expects us to suppose that his situations are real, and to have some kind of human feelings about them. This is no doubt easy enough when they belong to ordinary experience, but when the supernatural takes command it demands a more unusual art. Then Coleridge makes it look as natural as possible because, however strange it may be, he forms it from elements which are in themselves familiar. The paradoxical nature of the Mariner's voyage from England to the Southern Pacific, from the known to the unknown, from the familiar to the impossible, is conveyed in a verse which begins with something delightfully friendly and then, without ado, breaks into an uncharted, spell-bound world:

> The fair breeze blew, the white foam flew,
> The furrow followed free;
> We were the first that ever burst
> Into that silent sea.

There is perhaps nothing fundamentally strange in the silence of this sea, and yet after the bustle of the waves and the wind it comes with a magical surprise. When dreadful and unnatural things happen, the same art shows how they would look and what impression they would make. When the albatross first begins to be avenged, the sea changes its appearance, and horrible things are seen on it:

> The very deep did rot: O Christ!
> That ever this should be!
> Yea, slimy things did crawl with legs
> Upon the slimy sea.

Though this is seen by a man in the last agonies of thirst and has some qualities of delirious hallucination, it is poignantly real. It has the right degree of exactness for such an occasion, and it is well that the "slimy things" are not described more precisely. But when exactness is needed, Coleridge uses it with a masterly economy. When the dead men stir and begin to do again in death what they used to do in life, Coleridge epitomizes the weird situation in one highly significant action:

> The body of my brother's son
> Stood by me, knee to knee:
> The body and I pulled at one rope,
> But he said nought to me.

No more is needed than these very simple words. The habitual, perfunctory action, now conducted by a dead man and a living man together, has an extraordinary horror.

Coleridge's realism is of course much more than an art of circumstantial details. It is a special form of poetry, the reflection of his love for the sensible world and his sensitiveness to its lights and shades and colours and sounds. He possessed to a high degree that cardinal quality of poetry which he calls "the power of exciting the sympathy of the reader by a faithful adherence to the truth of nature." [11] And he has more than "faithful adherence." He is by no means photographic or merely descriptive. His eye for nature is for its more subtle charms and less obvious appeals. In his choice of details we can see his affinity with the Wordsworths, but there is much that is indisputably his own, especially in the richer and more luxurious pleasure which he takes in some natural things. Nature was no moral teacher for Coleridge; he preferred to bask in its favours and enjoy them without any ulterior satisfaction that it was doing him good. Moreover, he was bolder than Wordsworth in describing scenes which he himself never saw, like the icebergs around the ship or the single sudden stride of the tropical night. Wordsworth was perhaps capable of doing this, but he was too conscientious to try. Coleridge, for whom the contents of books had a vivid reality, was able to see with the mind's eye, as if objects were literally in front of him. More, too, perhaps than Wordsworth, he evokes the magical associations of sound, whether it be an angel's song or the pleasant noise of the sails:

> A noise like of a hidden brook
> In the leafy month of June,
> That to the sleeping woods all night
> Singeth a quiet tune.

The Romantics knew how to use their senses, and Coleridge, despite his love of metaphysical abstractions, was in this respect a true member of their company. He used nature to give colour and music, solidity and perspective, to his creations, and it is one of the chief means by which he sustains the enchantment of his poem.

Most of us, when we read "The Ancient Mariner," are content to respond to its magic and to ask no questions about any ulterior purpose or symbolical significance that it may have. It lives so fully by its own rules in its own world that it seems impertinent to ask for more. And in this attitude Coleridge himself seems to support us. So far from agreeing with the worthy Mrs. Barbauld that his poem has not a sufficient moral, he said that its moral is too emphatically expressed; and so far from allowing that the action has some secondary meaning, he said that it has no more than may be found in a tale of the *Arabian Nights*.[12] Worse even than this, he seems to rule out any attempt to explain his practice by his theories when he says: "For my part, I freely own that I have no title to the name of poet, according to my own definition of poetry." [13] Nor can any justification for a symbolical purpose be found in what Coleridge says about the kind of poetry which he was to write in the *Lyrical Ballads*. The "willing suspension of disbelief" is hardly a state in which we look for ulterior meanings and concealed mysteries. Even in his later years, Coleridge seems to have been satisfied if readers of "The Ancient Mariner" supposed his situations to be real and responded to their dramatic truth with appropriate emotions. He must have known that he was successful in doing what he set out to do and that he had carried out his bargain with Wordsworth. It is therefore not surprising that most readers of "The Ancient Mariner" are quite happy that it should be a story of supernatural events and do not wish it to be anything else.

And yet, though this position is natural and reasonable, we cannot but feel doubts about it. How are we to accommodate a poem, which is no more than a work of fancy, to all that Coleridge says about the imagination and its relation to truth and reality? If "The Ancient Mariner" is no more than a glittering fairy-tale, why did Coleridge not take account of this in his many elaborate statements about the nature of poetry? It is of course true that most of these statements were made at a considerable distance of time from his wonderful creative years, and that in the interval he may have changed his views or at least have fitted them not to the poetry which he had written but to that which he vainly hoped to write. Yet it is clear that, even when he wrote "The Ancient Mariner," Coleridge believed in the imagination as a vehicle of truth. Both some of his early poems[14] and his own account of the effect which Wordsworth had on him[15] indicate that, if he had not yet formed his full, mature doctrine of the imagination, he had already made up his mind on some fundamental points. It is therefore all the more strange if in writing "The Ancient Mariner" Coleridge did not put some of his theories into practice.

However much we may enjoy "The Ancient Mariner," we must surely feel that there are moments when it breaks beyond illusion and calls to something deep and serious in us. It has after all a moral, and though Mrs. Barbauld thought it inadequate and Coleridge too emphatic, it cannot be dismissed:

> He prayeth best, who loveth best
> All things both great and small;
> For the dear God who loveth us,
> He made and loveth all.

Now, whatever its faults may be, this states something which is clearly serious and must be heard. It is not enough to treat it as an archaism, a piece of mediaeval simplicity which Coleridge introduces to complete a poem which has already many old-world themes and phrases. The important thing is that Coleridge thought it necessary to include this moral and did not exclude it, as he did many other verses, when he revised the poem in later life. Of course, it is true that he was unhappy about it in later years and would have liked it to be less emphatic. This means not that he disapproved altogether of it, but that he was not satisfied with the way in which he had stated it. In other words, he still felt that the poem needed a moral, and there is no warrant for thinking that, whatever its form might have been, he intended its substance to be other than what it is. And this is surely of great importance. Coleridge, who thought that the "secondary imagination," with which poetry is concerned, is itself concerned with eternal values, slips into his poem his notion of the values which it represents. It is an all-embracing theory of love between living creatures, and that in some way the poem illustrates.

If we keep these considerations in mind, we see that there is much in the poem which is more weighty and more serious than the actual episodes demand. We may begin by asking, as others have, why there is all this "pother about a bird," but we end by seeing that, whatever the pother may be, it involves grave questions of right and wrong, of crime and punishment, and, no matter how much we enjoy the poetry, we cannot avoid being in some degree disturbed and troubled by it. Now this is surely the effect which Coleridge wished to produce. Through his concrete story he reaches to wider and vaguer issues, and his poem is symbolical in the sense which he gives to the word:

A symbol . . . is characterized by a translucence of the special in the individual, or of the general in the special, or of the universal in the general; above all by the translucence of the eternal through and in the temporal.[16]

For Coleridge a symbol is something which presents the eternal in a temporal, individual shape, and since by "eternal," he means belonging to the world of absolute values, a symbol's task is to present in poetry an instance of a universal truth. This is what "The Ancient Mariner" does. Its story, presented and enriched with the appeal of high poetry, passes beyond its immediate purview to something vague and remote and yet intimate and important.

In other words, "The Ancient Mariner" is a myth. It presents in an unusual and lively form certain issues with which we are all familiar and forces us to look afresh at them. It is the advantage of such a myth that it first dissociates certain ideas and then gives a new appeal to them by setting them in new associations. By this means it gives a fresh emphasis to much that we know and takes us to the heart of many matters to which custom has dulled us. By creating an impossible story in impossible conditions, "The Ancient Mariner" draws attention to neglected or undiscovered truths. And this is what Coleridge believed to be the task of poetry. Because through creation the poet reveals the secrets of the universe, especially in the sphere of absolute values, he is often forced to work through myths. They enable him to rearrange familiar material in such a way that we see fundamental issues in their right proportions and in their true nature because of the vivid illumination which the imagination gives to them. To be sure, the myth is only one kind among many kinds of poetry, but it is specially adapted to Coleridge's outlook because it can deal with supernatural issues. It is an extension of the use of symbols. Just as Blake has special symbols for the many mysterious powers which he saw at work in the universe, or Shelley for his far-ranging prophecies, so too Coleridge has his for the mysterious issues which excite him. In "The Ancient Mariner" he shapes these symbols into a consistent whole and subordinates them to a single plan, with the result that his poem is in the first place a story which we enjoy for its own sake, but in the second place a myth about a dark and troubling crisis in the human soul.

Reduced to its lowest terms in the dry language of abstraction, "The Ancient Mariner" is a tale of crime and punishment. It falls into seven sections, and each section tells of a new stage in the process. In each, of course, what counts is the imaginative and poetical effect, the emotional impression which the words make on us. It is this which illuminates the relentless progress from the commission of a crime to its last results. Coleridge puts into his myth the essential qualities which make crime and punishment what they are and shows what they mean to the conscience when it is sharpened and clarified by the imagination. He goes to the heart of the matter in its universal character, and he

is able to do this because his myth is so striking that we pay special attention to it. The first section tells of the actual crime. To
us the shooting of a bird may seem a matter of little moment, but
Coleridge makes it significant in two ways. First, he does not say
why the Mariner kills the albatross. We might infer that it is in
a mood of annoyance or anger or mere frivolity, but these are
only guesses. What matters is precisely the uncertainty of the
Mariner's motives; for this illustrates the essential irrationality of
crime, which we may explain by motives but which is in many
cases due to a simple perversity of the will. Secondly, this crime
is against nature, against the sanctified relations of guest and
host. The bird, which has been hailed in God's name "as if it had
been a Christian soul," and is entirely friendly and helpful, is
wantonly and recklessly killed. There is no need to argue that
Coleridge was at this time obsessed by Neo-Platonic ideas of the
brotherhood of all living things. Perhaps he was, but it does not
matter. What matters is that the Mariner breaks a sacred law of
life. In his action we see the essential frivolity of many crimes
against humanity and the ordered system of the world, and
we must accept the killing of the albatross as symbolical of
them.

In the second section the Mariner begins to suffer punishment for what he has done, and Coleridge transfers to the physical world the corruption and the helplessness which are the common attributes of guilt. The world which faces the Mariner after
his crime is dead and loathsome. The ship has ceased to move
and the sailors are tortured by thirst, while the only moving
things in the hideous scene are the slimy creatures on the sea and
the death-fires which dance at night. The immediate results of
crime are portrayed in the image of a universe dying of thirst and
haunted by menacing phantoms. The third section shows how the
guilty soul becomes conscious of what it has done and of its isolation in the world. The Mariner first begins to realize the consequences of his action for himself when he sees the phantom ship
which decides his doom:

The Night-mare LIFE-IN-DEATH was she,
Who thicks man's blood with cold.

The night in which the Mariner's companions die symbolizes the
darkness in the soul when it suddenly finds itself alone and robbed
of familiar ties. In the fourth section this sense of solitude is
elaborated. The guilty soul is cut off not merely from human
intercourse but from the consoling friendship of nature which
mocks it with majestic detachment. Then a turn comes for the
better. When the Mariner, albeit unaware, blesses the water-
snakes, he begins to re-establish relations with the world of the
affections. This is not much, and it is by no means the end, but
it opens the way to the future. Instead of being dead, the spirit
shows some small signs of that love which holds life together.

The fifth section continues the process of the soul's revival.
The ship begins to move, and celestial spirits stand by the bodies
of the dead men. The Mariner hears heavenly music in the air
and is comforted by it. Before he can be fully healed, he must
establish relations not merely with men but with God, and this,
faintly and feebly, he begins to do. When the music flows into his
soul and delights him, he is on the way to recovery. But much
awaits him. He has still his penance to do, but he is ready for it.
In the sixth section the process of healing seems to be impeded.
The Mariner is haunted by the presence of his dead comrades
and feels that he is pursued by some fearful power of vengeance:

Like one, that on a lonesome road
Doth walk in fear and dread,
And having once turned round walks on,
And turns no more his head;
Because he knows, a frightful fiend
Doth close behind him tread.

In the figure of the Mariner haunted by memories and fears Coleridge gives his special symbol of remorse. But because remorse
brings repentance and humility, the section closes with the vision

of angelic forms standing by the dead sailors. The forgiveness of God awaits even the most hard-hearted sinners if they will only be ready to receive it. In the last section the end, such as it is, comes. The guilty man has been shriven and restored to a place among living men. Most of the visible traces of his crime have been obliterated, but the punishment of "life-in-death" is still at work. Since he has committed a hideous act, the Mariner will never be the man that he once was. He has his special past and his special doom. At times the memory of what he has done is so insistent that he must speak of it:

> Since then, at an uncertain hour,
> That agony returns:
> And till my ghastly tale is told,
> This heart within me burns.

The need for confession is to be found in most criminals, and the Mariner's need to speak is specially appropriate, because by forcing others to listen to him he regains some of that human converse of which his crime has robbed him. Coleridge does not tell the end of the story, but leaves us to suppose that the Mariner's sense of guilt will end only with his death. The poem is a myth of a guilty soul and marks in clear stages the passage from crime through punishment to such redemption as is possible in this world.

"The Ancient Mariner," then, is a myth of guilt and redemption, but of course it is also much more. Its symbolical purpose is but one element in a complex design. Though Coleridge has his own poetry of a guilty soul, it is not comparable in depth or in insight with the poetry of some other men who have given the full powers of their genius to writing about crime and the misery which it engenders. None the less, Coleridge's introduction of this theme into "The Ancient Mariner" gives to it a new dimension. What might otherwise be no more than an irresponsible fairy-tale is brought closer to life and to its fundamental issues.

The myth of crime and punishment provides a structure for the supernatural events which rise from it but often make their appeal irrespective of it. Much of the magic of "The Ancient Mariner" comes from its blend of dark and serious issues with the delighted play of creative energy. Coleridge had good reasons for fashioning his poem in this way. In the first place, the combination of different themes responded to his own complex vision of existence. For him life had both its dark and its bright sides, its haunting responsibilities and its ravishing moments of unsullied delight. He saw that the two were closely interwoven and that, if he were to speak with the full force of his genius, he must introduce both into his poem. In the second place, he saw life not analytically but creatively, and he knew that any work of creation must itself be an extension and an enhancement of life. He must preserve the mystery and the enchantment which he knew in his finest moments, and for him these came alike from the beauty of the visible world and the uncharted corners of the human soul. The shadow cast by the Mariner's crime adds by contrast to the brilliance of the unearthly world in which it is committed, and the degree of his guilt and his remorse serves to stress the power of the angelic beings which watch over humankind. The result is a poem shot with iridescent lights. It appeals to us now in this way, now in that, and there is no final or single approach to it.

In creating "The Ancient Mariner" in this way Coleridge obeyed the peculiar and paradoxical nature of his genius. In him the poet and the metaphysician were uneasily blended, and the creative spirit, which was capable of such rapturous flights, worked most freely when it was free from metaphysical speculations. His three great poems owe nothing to his study of philosophy or his own conscious theories about the universe. But to attain and enjoy this freedom and to allow his creative gifts to work unhindered, Coleridge needed subjects remote from his ordinary existence. Only when he was free from the topics which engaged his philosophic curiosity was he able to release all his imaginative powers. That is why his unequalled successes were secured with subjects so unusual as those of "Christabel" and "Kubla Khan" and "The Ancient Mariner." In these poems he was able to fling the whole of his poetical self into a subject which had no connection with metaphysical abstractions and to concentrate on the particular effects of which he was a master, but which would have been ruined if he had allowed himself to speculate about them. In "The Ancient Mariner" he does indeed treat a subject of universal interest, about which philosophers have had something to say, but he succeeds in making it poetry just because he keeps at some distance from his habits of abstract thought. Once Coleridge had set his theme in this strange world, he was able to give to it a special life and to make each element tell. The great advantage of a myth is that it enables a poet to concentrate on the issues which really concern him and, despite an apparent remoteness from life, to convey in a vivid form some fundamental truths which may be fogged or lost in a more literal treatment.

We may well ask why, in all his three great poems, Coleridge felt the attraction of the supernatural, and why he used it for his myth in "The Ancient Mariner." We might suppose that if guilt and punishment were his theme, he could have treated them more realistically in some subject closer to ordinary experience and have found some crime more immediately hideous than the killing of an albatross. But this would not have suited Coleridge. What touched his genius to its finest issues was his sense of mystery at unknown forces at work in life, and to keep this mystery intact he needed some subject which was in itself mysterious. Like Blake, he saw strange powers behind the visible world, and he believed that men were moved and directed by them. To show what he really saw in them he needed characters and circumstances in themselves strange and arresting. By introducing us to a world of dream and fantasy, he suggests how mysterious is the experience which concerns him. Once he had found a subject of this kind, his creative imagination set freely to work and built its own system. There was nothing to hamper the

free play of his gifts, and he felt at home in the incredible and
the unknown. What Wordsworth found in a world of vision,
Coleridge found in the supernatural. It clarified his ideas for him
and enabled him to present in concrete shapes many feelings and
apprehensions which were not less haunting because they were
undefined. He was both fascinated by the unknown and in some
sense afraid of it. This helped him to make "The Ancient Mariner." It gave him the thrill of excitement which he needed before
he could concentrate his mind on a subject, and through it he
sharpened his vision and purified his mind of many disturbing
and distracting elements.

Like all great poetry, "The Ancient Mariner" suggests prospects and possibilities beyond its immediate subject. Indeed, it is
a great poem largely because it does this. In creating this imaginary world Coleridge offers an alternative to familiar existence
which is at the same time an illuminating commentary on it. Both
in the main plan of the Mariner's crime and in the spiritual
forces who battle over him, Coleridge emphasizes the state of
man between persecuting horrors and enchanting beauties. Such
a state was no doubt his own. He, whose genius in Hazlitt's
words "had angelic wings, and fed on manna," [17] was destined to
know many dark and guilty hours of sloth and regret. "The Ancient Mariner" is his greatest poem because he put most of himself into it and in it spoke most fully from his inner being. The
brilliant reality which he gives to this invention of his imagination comes from his prophetic insight into himself. He was to
suffer, as few poets have suffered, from the discordant contrast
between reality and dream, between blissful confidence and bitter, broken hopes, between the warmth of human ties and the
cold solitude of the haunted soul. It was from some foretaste or
premonition of these contrasts and these struggles that Coleridge
made his poem, and they provide its relation to life. He was too
modest when he said that all he wished to secure was "that willing suspension of disbelief for the moment, which constitutes

poetic faith." His poem creates not a negative but a positive condition, a state of faith which is complete and satisfying because it is founded on realities in the living world and in the human heart.

IV

ODE ON INTIMATIONS
OF IMMORTALITY

WHEN Wordsworth arranged his collected poems for publication, he placed the Ode entitled "Intimations of Immortality from Recollections of Early Childhood" at the end, as if he regarded it as the crown of his work and his last word on the central problems of his creative life. There is no need to dispute the honour in which by common consent it is held, but it has a special interest as a personal document. Wordsworth began it at the height of his genius, in the middle of the splendid ten years between 1797 and 1807, when he had recovered his balance after the failure of his hopes in the French Revolution and had not yet begun to suffer from that desiccation of powers which came with early middle age. The poem was started in the spring of 1802, and by summer the first four stanzas seem to have been completed [1] and the main design conceived; it was finished from two to four years later.[2] The delays in composition have made no difference to its unity. It is built on a simple but majestic plan. The first four stanzas tell of a spiritual crisis, of a glory passing from the earth, and end by asking why this has happened. The middle stanzas (v–viii) examine the nature of this glory and explain it by a theory of reminiscence from a pre-natal existence. Then the last three stanzas show that, though the vision has perished, life has still a meaning and a value. The three parts of the Ode deal in turn with a crisis, an explanation, and a consolation, and in all three Wordsworth speaks of what is most important and most original in his poetry.

That Wordsworth believed himself to be attempting an unusual task in the Ode is clear from the form which he gave to it.

His usual odes are not like this, but more formal and more regular. Only here does he build an ode not in repeated stanzas of a fixed form, and it must be of this that Hazlitt was thinking when he said of Wordsworth: "The Ode and Epode, the Strophe and the Antistrophe, he laughs to scorn." [3] In fact, the great Ode is a development of what the poets of the seventeenth century called a "Pindarick." The form, created on a false analogy with Pindar, fell easily into English poetry because it was ultimately not very different from those adaptations of the Italian *canzone* which Spenser made in *Prothalamion* and Milton in *Lycidas*. It differs from these not in kind but in degree. It has a greater variety of structure and takes greater risks with the length of its lines, but otherwise it belongs to the same family. When Wordsworth wrote his Ode, the form was well established. It had been used with accomplished skill by Gray, and, if we do not like to think that Wordsworth owed anything to Gray, we know that he read Dryden and may have learned something from the adroit technique of "Alexander's Feast." The ode was thought appropriate to great occasions and sublime subjects, and in his choice of it Wordsworth shows how seriously he treated his theme. He was more at home with a strict and narrow form like that of his "Ode to Duty," and there are passages in the "immortal ode" which have less than his usual command of rhythm and ability to make a line stand by itself, as if he were not quite sure how to use the liberties at his disposal. But these are unimportant. The whole has a capacious sweep, and the form suits the majestic subject with which Wordsworth deals.

The Ode's unusual form is matched by its unusual language. It is perhaps unfair to charge Wordsworth with departing in it from his famous principle that poetry should be written "as far as possible in a selection of language really used by men"; for the words of the Ode are on the whole such a selection. It is not so much its vocabulary which surprises as what it says and the way in which it says it. It shows no trace of that Wordsworthian quality of which Coleridge complained to Hazlitt: "a something corporeal, a *matter-of-fact-ness,* a clinging to the palpable, or often to the petty." [4] These words are true of much that Wordsworth wrote even in his best years, but they are not true of the Ode. Its tone is set in what is for him an unusually lofty key, and it is remarkable that the author of "The Idiot Boy" and "We Are Seven" should have written such lines as:

> The cataracts blow their trumpets from the steep;
> No more shall grief of mine the season wrong;
> I hear the Echoes through the mountains throng,
> The Winds come to me from the fields of sleep.

The whole poem is written, not indeed at this level of accomplishment, but at least in this tone. The stately metrical form is matched by a stately use of words. Wordsworth seems to have decided that his subject was so important that it must be treated in what was for him an unusual manner, and for it he fashioned his own high style.

Because the Ode lies outside Wordsworth's usual range, it does not perhaps always realize its ambitious aims. There are moments when we suspect Wordsworth of trying to say more than he means, or of losing himself in an unaccustomed and not always convincing grandeur. This was at least what Coleridge thought when he claimed that the seventh stanza is an instance of *"mental* bombast" or "thoughts and images too great for the subject." [5] The criticism is hard but not entirely unjust, and it throws some light on Wordsworth's mind when he wrote the Ode. In his account of a crisis which he believes himself to have surmounted, he is determined to stress the positive gains and refuses to admit defeat. At the end he claims that though he has lost something irreplaceable, he has still something else consoling and satisfying. That undoubtedly he believed. But perhaps the crisis was more severe than he realized. It lay in the centre of his creative life. He, who had known moments of visionary splendour, found that he knew them no more, and that is a loss which no poet can take lightly, or, however comforting his consolations may be, accept in a calm, philosophic spirit. But Wordsworth was so determined not to surrender to circumstances that he made his Ode more confident than was perhaps warranted by the mood which first set him to work. As he passed further from his crisis and worked at his poem, he found a cheerfulness which cannot have been his when he received his first shock. Though the completed Ode tells of a crisis surmounted, we cannot doubt that the crisis was grave and that Wordsworth was severely shaken by it.

The gravity of the situation which called the Ode into being is clear from the first two stanzas. If we take them as they stand without considering what follows, we see the degree of Wordsworth's dismay. Each of them ends on a similar note, the first saying:

> Turn wheresoe'er I may,
>   By night or day,
> The things which I have seen I now can see no more;

and the second:

> But yet I know, where'er I go,
> That there hath past away a glory from the earth.

There is something close to anguish in these words, and, though we may forget it as we read the rest of the poem, they warn us at the outset to treat seriously the situation which Wordsworth describes, and to listen to every word that he says about it. He naturally cannot make his meaning very precise, but has to speak in image and metaphor. What he has lost is variously called "celestial light," "visionary gleam," "the glory and the freshness of a dream." But despite the lack of exactness, it is clear that Wordsworth has lost something very special in his whole approach to nature and his relations with it. On a spring morning he finds that something of the greatest importance is missing. The familiar scene, the tree and the field and the flower at his feet, which have played so large a part in his life, are suddenly changed. He cannot but ask:

> Whither is fled the visionary gleam?
> Where is it now, the glory and the dream?

The Ode was conceived in this questioning, troubled mood. At the height of his creative career Wordsworth discovered that nature, in which he had put an unquestioning trust as the inspiration of his poetry, seemed to have abandoned him and deprived him of his most cherished strength.

When Wordsworth began to compose the Ode, the main problem with which it deals was not an entirely new discovery. For some time he had been conscious of the waning of his youthful vision. When four years earlier, in 1798, he wrote "Tintern Abbey," he distinguished between the blessed time of his seventeenth year:

> For nature then . . .
> To me was all in all,

and the years after it when this all-absorbing vision was lost:

> That time is past,
> And all its aching joys are now no more,
> And all its dizzy raptures.

"Tintern Abbey" anticipates the Ode in distinguishing between two periods in Wordsworth's life. In his youth he throve on a visionary power which worked through nature; later he found a living presence which inspired him with devotion and was the "soul of all his moral being." This difference and this contrast run through the Ode. Wordsworth seems, after a period of years, to have reverted to what he had known for some time and to have found a new challenge in it. At first sight we might think that this reversion to an old theme is characteristic of the way in which Wordsworth worked. He needed time and tranquillity to absorb his experiences and transform them into poetry. But, when we look at the circumstances in which the Ode was begun, we see that something had recently happened to Wordsworth and that an old problem had developed a new seriousness and insistence.

Dorothy Wordsworth records that on March 22nd and 25th, 1802, "William worked at the Cuckow poem," and this is "To the Cuckoo," in which Wordsworth tells how he hears the cuckoo and wonders if it is not more than a bird, and this wonder rises from recollections of childhood when the cuckoo opened worlds of the imagination to him. He finds that it still does this, and he connects the present with the past and discovers that he has not after all quite lost his visionary power:

> O blessed bird! the earth we pace
> Again appears to be
> An unsubstantial faery place
> That is fit home for thee.

For the moment Wordsworth regained his old power, and this gave him joy and confidence. But this episode must be connected with something that happened immediately after it. In the Ode Wordsworth says:

> To me alone there came a thought of grief:
> A timely utterance gave that thought relief,
>   And I again am strong.

We can hardly doubt that Wordsworth's "thought of grief" is connected with his fear that nature has somehow lost its magic for him, and the "timely utterance" is the poem on the rainbow which he wrote on March 26th, the day after he finished "To the Cuckoo." The lines on the rainbow provided Wordsworth with a motto for the Ode and are much to the point:

The Child is father of the Man;
And I could wish my days to be
Bound each to each by natural piety.

That, after all, is the gist of the doctrine with which Wordsworth consoles himself in the Ode. The conjunction of these two poems with the Ode, which Wordsworth began on March 27th, the day after he wrote the lines on the rainbow, suggests two considerations. First, it is clear that despite the emphatic statements of "Tintern Abbey" Wordsworth had not entirely lost his youthful vision of nature, but was at intervals revisited by it, as he was when he heard the cuckoo. Secondly, though he had this visitation and was for the moment much exalted by it, it did not save him from a gnawing anxiety about his relations with nature. The "thought of grief" came to him when he thought that all was well, and he was able to subdue it only by his trust in nature as a source of moral strength.

In other words, Wordsworth began the Ode at a time when he was exercised by two different ideas about nature. In the first place, the fitful returns of his youthful vision made him ask why they were not more frequent and more secure. This made him anxious and uneasy, and prompted the first stanzas of the Ode. In the second place, he believed that in the moral inspiration of nature he had found something to take the place of his visions, and this discovery gave to the Ode its positive and consoling character. Such, no doubt, was his state of mind when he conceived the outline of the Ode. But we may ask why this issue was forced so powerfully on Wordsworth in the spring of 1802, since he was aware of it when he wrote "Tintern Abbey" four years before. No doubt in the interval he found that his visionary gift was not so dead as he had thought, but still at times returned to him. No doubt, too, he saw more clearly how much comfort was to be found in his moral conception of nature. None the less, something must have happened to press the issue on him with a new and inescapable insistence. Why was Wordsworth, after feeling such delight in the message of the cuckoo, assailed on the very next day by painful doubts? And why was he so comforted when in the rainbow he saw a sign of the power of natural piety?

In the spring of 1802 Wordsworth was the victim of an inner crisis. He was thirty-two years old and found that his inspiration was not what it had once been, that it did not work so readily or come in the same way as of old. That is no doubt a familiar enough experience among poets. But in Wordsworth's case the problem took a special form. He built his poetry on nature. It was the source of his creative strength and opened worlds of the imagination to him. It was therefore a matter of anxious concern when he realized that this source was in some ways drying up. He had been conscious of this for some time, but he had had his answer to it. Nature might fail him in one way but it still supported him in another, and he was more than content with that. This he still believed, but he now saw that the problem was more complex than he had realized and that he must face it fully and fairly. Something had forced the issue on him with a new emphasis, and it seems likely that this was his discovery that his crisis was not confined to himself but afflicted Coleridge in an even more poignant manner. The two friends shared their innermost thoughts so freely with each other and with Dorothy that they were indeed three persons with one soul, and it is often hard to say where the thought of one ends and that of another begins. In 1802 the long and dismal afterlife to which Coleridge was doomed had begun its course. Soon after finishing the second part of "Christabel" in 1800, he saw that things were going wrong with him. He was listless and depressed. Much of his sad state was due to the failure of his marriage; and his consciousness that he was tied to a woman who understood nothing of his inner life was made the more bitter when he fell in love with Sara Hutchinson, who had all the qualities which his wife lacked. He wrote freely of his troubles to the Wordsworths, and more than one entry in Dorothy's journal shows how distressed she and her brother were by them. The root of the trouble was deep and affected much more than Coleridge's happiness. He knew that something catastrophic had happened to him, and he was afraid that his creative gifts were ruined. He put the blame on his lack of happiness, but he knew that, whatever the cause might be, the results were grave indeed.

In facing his own crisis Wordsworth could not but think about Coleridge's. Their cases were on the face of it similar, and we may surmise that even at the beginning of the Ode Wordsworth had Coleridge in mind. In the preceding year Coleridge had written *The Mad Monk,* a short, melodramatic piece in Mrs. Radcliffe's spirit. But despite its histrionic airs, it is a personal document which reveals his own distress of soul. It begins with some lines which are too weighty for the remote and unreal subject and suggest that Coleridge was forced to speak from his heart on a matter which concerned him deeply:

> There was a time when earth, and sea, and skies,
> The bright green vale, and forest's dark recess,
> With all things, lay before mine eyes
> In steady loveliness:
> But now I feel, on earth's uneasy scene,
> Such sorrows as will never cease; —
> I only ask for peace;
> If I must live to know that such a time has been!

When Wordsworth began his Ode, he must have had these lines in mind — lines which seemed to anticipate something deep in himself — and, whether consciously or unconsciously, he echoed them in his opening verse:

> There was a time when meadow, grove, and stream,
> The earth, and every common sight,
>   To me did seem
>   Apparelled in celestial light,
> The glory and the freshness of a dream.

It is not now as it hath been of yore; —
    Turn wheresoe'er I may,
      By night or day,
The things which I have seen I now can see no more.

If he was moved by his sympathetic understanding of Coleridge, his sympathy was the more powerful because he understood his friend's situation through his knowledge of his own.

Wordsworth, then, seems to have begun his Ode because of some deep trouble which had been brought to the surface by his affection for Coleridge. Coleridge's case was indeed hard, but Wordsworth saw that it was a counterpart to what he himself had for some time felt and had recently realized with peculiar acuteness. The problem which concerned both friends was that of poetical inspiration. Each felt that his hold on it was precarious and asked why this was so. Wordsworth faced the problem in the first three stanzas of the Ode and then abandoned it for at least two years; Coleridge, slower perhaps to start but quicker once he had started, told of his crisis in the poem which he afterwards called "Dejection." The interrelations of this with Wordsworth's Ode repay attention. Wordsworth began the Ode on March 27th. On the 28th he and Dorothy went to Keswick for a few days, where Coleridge had begun to write his poem, and they seem to have seen parts of it. They then went back to Grasmere, and on April 21st Dorothy wrote in her journal:

William and I sauntered a little in the garden. Coleridge came to us, and repeated the verses he wrote to Sara. I was affected with them, and . . . in miserable spirits. The sunshine, the green fields, and the fair sky made me sadder; even the little happy, sporting lambs seemed but sorrowful . . . I went to bed after dinner, could not sleep.

The "verses to Sara" were the first, full version of "Dejection," [6] which Coleridge addressed to Sara Hutchinson and in which he spoke of some private matters omitted from the printed text of the poem. In the following months Coleridge pruned and altered it. He brought the final version to the Wordsworths on May 6th and printed it in the *Morning Post* on October 4th, Wordsworth's wedding-day. The poem is a cry from Coleridge's heart to his most intimate friends, and though he abridged and altered it, it keeps its essential substance. Long before Wordsworth completed his Ode, Coleridge had given full and powerful voice to his own crisis, and Wordsworth could not but take heed of it. Wordsworth's Ode, at least in its eight last stanzas, is a kind of answer to Coleridge's "Dejection." From one angle it may be regarded as a poem of comfort and encouragement, but it is much more than that. It is a declaration of belief, intended to counteract the searching doubts and melancholy fears which Wordsworth saw in Coleridge and had felt to a lesser degree in himself. The two poems are concerned with central problems in the Romantic outlook and show to what different conclusions two men could come who shared their innermost thoughts, and followed, as they believed, very similar aims.

At the outset we notice a great contrast of temperament between the two poets. Both find themselves in somewhat similar situations, and it is no accident that in the first text which he sent to Sara Hutchinson Coleridge more than once has a conscious echo of Wordsworth. When Wordsworth says

The things which I have seen I now can see no more,

and Coleridge says

But oft I seem to feel and evermore I fear
They are not to me now the Things which once they were,

we see that both poets share a common crisis. But each interprets it characteristically in his own way. When Coleridge examines himself and speaks with fearful candour of his inner being, he sees nothing but an empty, lifeless depression:

A grief without a pang, void, dark, and drear,
  A stifled, drowsy, unimpassioned grief,
  Which finds no natural outlet, no relief,
    In word, or sigh, or tear.

Perhaps at some moment which the Ode has left behind Wordsworth felt something like this, but he has conquered and sup-
pressed it. In the Ode, almost as if in answer to Coleridge, he
stresses his own confidence and the delight which he still takes
in nature, despite his loss of something most valuable:

My heart is at your festival,
  My head hath its coronal,
The fulness of your bliss, I feel — I feel it all.

There was in Wordsworth something tough and bellicose which
Coleridge lacked. Coleridge's sensitiveness was part of a gentle,
in some ways passive, nature. When things went wrong with
him, he did not know what to do and was prone to lament defeat.
Wordsworth was made of sterner stuff and sought for a new
scheme of life to replace the old.

The difference between the two men is well illustrated by the
different scenes which they describe. While Wordsworth speaks
of a fine morning in spring, Coleridge speaks of a stormy night
with the moon shining between clouds. What should fill him
with inspiring joy leaves him cold:

And those thin clouds above, in flakes and bars,
That give away their motion to the stars;
Those stars, that glide behind them or between,
Now sparkling, now bedimmed, but always seen:
Yon crescent Moon, as fixed as if it grew
In its own cloudless, starless lake of blue;
I see them all so excellently fair,
I see, not feel, how beautiful they are!

If there was one thing which, more than another, touched Coleridge to poetry, it was the moon. He, whose metaphysics Carlyle rudely described as "bottled moonshine," knew all the enchantments of the moon and saw in it almost a symbol of the poet's power to transform the material world into a world of the imagination. In "Christabel" the hidden moon serves to emphasize the helpless state of the heroine, and in "The Ancient Mariner" the moon increases the mystery of a spirit-haunted world. Coleridge was drawn to the moon because of the magic half-light with which it invests the too emphatic forms of things. It is appropriate that he should use it to illustrate his dejected state. It is no less appropriate that Wordsworth should speak of a spring morning. His poetry was inspired not by vague forms and indefinite contours, but by the stirring of light and life, the budding of flowers, and the sunshine on the meadows. While Coleridge was at his best among dimly descried shapes, Wordsworth moved happily and confidently among solid forms. The contrast shows the more delicate nature of Coleridge's genius and illustrates why, when his crisis came, it was more fearful and more final than Wordsworth's.

The differences of personality which are illustrated by the Ode and by "Dejection" are enhanced by differences of outlook on the task of poetry and the place of the imagination in life. Indeed, these differences show what a variety of outlook was possible under the apparently homogeneous body of Romantic doctrine. In the first place, the double crisis shows how differently Coleridge and Wordsworth reacted to the external world. Whatever relics of Locke's universe Coleridge may have kept in his philosophical opinions, as a poet he was an idealist who believed that the mind fashions the universe for all purposes that really matter. His present grief has come because he feels that he has lost his power to create through the imagination, that he can no longer shape experience into beauty and impose his will on nature:

> O Lady! we receive but what we give,
> And in our life alone does Nature live:
> Ours is her wedding garment, ours her shroud!

Because he has lost his inner joy, he has lost his gift of imaginative creation, and he cannot but lament the circumstances which are responsible for this:

> But now afflictions bow me down to earth:
> Nor care I that they rob me of my mirth;
>   But oh! each visitation
> Suspends what nature gave me at my birth,
>   My shaping spirit of Imagination.

For Coleridge, who believes that the imagination is the primary instrument of all spiritual and creative activities, this is indeed a bitter confession. He has lost not only his poetical gift but what makes life worth living.

With Wordsworth it is quite different. For him nature exists independently and needs only to be used and interpreted. Even in the first three stanzas of the Ode, when the memory of his crisis is still fresh, Wordsworth sees nature as not merely living its own life but full of beauty and joy:

> The Rainbow comes and goes,
> And lovely is the Rose,
> The Moon doth with delight
> Look round her when the heavens are bare;
>   Waters on a starry night
>   Are beautiful and fair.

As he develops his poem, Wordsworth stresses this independence and this essential joyfulness of nature. Whereas Coleridge puts all his trust in his own imagination and is in despair when it fails him, Wordsworth continues to believe that nature stands outside himself and has still much to give him, if he will only be ready to receive it.

A second point of contrast revealed by the two poems is between the different ways in which Coleridge and Wordsworth were inspired to write poetry. The creative genius is so wayward in its comings and goings that it is impossible to say what will provoke it, but in some poets certain moods provoke it more than others, and though they cannot be summoned at will, they can, when they come, be marked and recorded. On his own experience Coleridge is emphatic. For creation he needs joy. It may not be all that he needs, but, so far as it goes, it is indispensable.

> Joy, virtuous Lady! Joy that ne'er was given,
> Save to the pure, and in their purest hour,
> Life, and Life's effluence, cloud at once and shower,
> Joy, Lady! is the spirit and the power,
> Which wedding Nature to us gives in dower
>   A new Earth and new Heaven,
> Undreamt of by the sensual and the proud.

This pure joy is the "strong music in the soul" which enables Coleridge to create, and this is what he has lost. Without it he feels helpless and miserable. Now on this point Wordsworth might at one time have agreed with him, and indeed in the opening stanzas of the Ode it looks as if the "glory" which he no longer finds in nature were indeed his delight in it. Of course, this delight is of a special kind and brings special rewards, but it is none the less joy, and Wordsworth sees it at work in nature. But, as he develops the Ode, he implicitly corrects this notion and gives his own version of what the creative spirit is. When he, who has known such rapturous hours with nature, looks back on them, especially as he knew them in childhood, he gives thanks, not so much for "delight and liberty,"

> But for those obstinate questionings
> Of sense and outward things,

Fallings from us, vanishings;
Blank misgivings of a Creature
Moving about in worlds not realised,
High instincts before which our mortal Nature
Did tremble like a guilty Thing surprised.

What stirred Wordsworth's creative energy was not joy, as Cole-ridge describes it, but something more complex. Nature might delight him, but it also did something else. It woke hidden powers in him by a process which was not always enjoyable.

Though such experiences might at the time be frightening, in retrospect they became matter for gratitude. For Wordsworth, beauty and awe were closely mingled in any keen appreciation of natural things, and each contributed to his conception of his task. When he says of his childhood,

Fair seedtime had my soul, and I grew up
Fostered alike by beauty and by fear,

he gives a correct account of his spiritual development. If he was sometimes assailed by fear, it was not a deadening emotion but something which enriched his nature through the awe with which it struck him. Wordsworth saw that some kinds of fear are good and that a man does well to be afraid before the mysteries of life and death. How liable he was to such attacks can be seen from the occasion, soon after he came to Grasmere, when, on hearing bad news of Coleridge, he went for a walk in John's Grove. Later in the evening Dorothy found him there and re-corded her impressions:

He had been surprized and terrified by a sudden rushing of winds, which seemed to bring earth sky and lake together, as if the whole were going to enclose him.[7]

Fear bred surprise, and from surprise Wordsworth derived a spe-cial exaltation, a sense of enhanced life, a keener vision and a greater power to create. His childhood had moments of anguish and terror, and he was more grateful for them than for its hours of happiness. In retrospect, when he wrote the Ode, he saw that his moments of awful vision were responsible for the best things which he did or knew. In comparison with the strange workings of Wordsworth's creative faculty, those of Coleridge were indeed frail, since they were founded in a joy which he lost early and never regained.

A third point of comparison between Coleridge and Wordsworth turns on their conception of the world which the imagination finds beyond the senses. On this point Coleridge does not say much in "Dejection," but what he says is to the point. He insists that from the soul must issue

> A light, a glory, a fair luminous cloud
> Enveloping the Earth.

We know what he means. Through the exercise of the imagination the "inanimate cold world" is transformed into something real and living. The imagination creates reality by absorbing the given into the world of spirit. This is the only reality for Coleridge, but it is not what Wordsworth sought or found. There were moments when by some mysterious and magnificent process he passed beyond the visible world into some other order of being, vaster and more wonderful. In *The Prelude* he speaks of times when

> the light of sense
> Goes out in flashes that have shewn to us
> The invisible world.   (VI, 600–602)

To this experience Wordsworth's poems bear eloquent witness. Instead of examining nature with a close, observant eye and extracting all that he could from it, he found himself unaccountably transported into another sphere of being, shapeless and frightening and beyond the reach of exact words. He seemed then to lose all ties with common life and to be absorbed in something much wider and more majestic. Physical nature ceased to count for its own sake and became the entry into another world (*The Prelude,* VII, 632–634). So in his lines on going through the Simplon Pass, Wordsworth tells of the overwhelming effect which the wild scenery made on him and how the different elements in it

> Were all like workings of one mind, the features
> Of the same face, blossoms upon one tree,
> Characters of the great Apocalypse,
> The types and symbols of Eternity,
> Of first and last, and midst, and without end.   (VI, 636–640)

While Coleridge seeks to transform the given world through the imagination, Wordsworth knows moments when he passes beyond it to something else, and he believes that this task is essentially one of the imagination. He has known it often enough in the past, and he believes that it still comes to him, as it came when he heard the cuckoo and was transported to another world as in childhood. When he speaks of this, Wordsworth thinks not of Coleridge but of himself. This is his special problem and the central concern of his present crisis.

The Ode, then, is a kind of answer to Coleridge's "Dejection," or at least to the doubts and anxieties which prompted it. But of course it is much more than this. In setting out his positive beliefs for the comfort of his friend, Wordsworth could not but think about his own case and try to lighten his own burden. This must have been heavy enough. He lived not only with but on nature, and what he prized most in it was its capacity to open to him another world through vision. It is this which he has lost, perhaps not entirely, but enough to cause him a deep anxiety. It is idle to ask too closely what Wordsworth means by "the visionary gleam" or "the glory and the dream." If it were simple, he would probably have expressed it in simple words, but because it is complex and unfamiliar, he uses image and symbol. We may however distinguish three elements in it. First, there is Words-worth's conviction that at times he was in another world which was more real than that of the senses, a world not of sight but of vision. Secondly, his entries into this world were closely con-nected with his creative and imaginative faculties. It was the justification of his poetry, and he believed that his acquaintance with it was due to his imagination, which, in creating, had mo-ments of visionary clairvoyance. Thirdly, when he had this ex-perience, he felt that he had passed outside time into eternity. He was then so unaware of the common ties of life that he had a timeless exaltation. The three notions are closely allied, though they are distinct enough on analysis. Wordsworth saw them as a single experience and felt a need to explain them.

To make his meaning clear, Wordsworth devotes stanzas v–viii to his special idea of childhood as a time when "the vision splendid" is normally with us, and to his explanation of this by a theory that a child has memories, which he gradually loses, of a blessed state in another world before birth. Of course, he has his own childhood in mind, and, though in *The Prelude* he says little or nothing along these lines, there is no need to question his truthfulness. Now, on looking back over the years, he sees what childhood was and finds in it an explanation of his early visions. Indeed, we can almost see why his mind turned to childhood and children in this way. In the Ode he has a single, living child in mind:

> Behold the Child among his new-born blisses,
> A six years' Darling of a pigmy size!
> See, where 'mid work of his own hand he lies,
> Fretted by sallies of his mother's kisses,
> With light upon him from his father's eyes!

This child is Hartley Coleridge, who was born in 1796 and could fairly be described as "a six years' Darling" in 1802. He seems to have been a delightfully imaginative little boy, who made an irresistible appeal to all who knew him. Coleridge, in the second part of "Christabel," speaks of him and his lively play:

> A little child, a limber elf,
> Singing, dancing to itself,
> A fairy thing with red round cheeks,
> That always finds, and never seeks,
> Makes such a vision to the sight
> As fills a father's eyes with light.

In 1803 Coleridge wrote to his friend, Poole:

> Hartley . . . is a strange strange Boy — *"exquisitely wild"*! An utter Visionary! like the Moon among thin Clouds, he moves in a circle of Light of his own making — he alone, in a Light of his own.[8]

The child, Hartley, captivated Wordsworth and became one of the chief figures in the Ode. It is his games of make-believe which are described in the seventh stanza, and he who illustrates Wordsworth's theory that children trail "clouds of glory" from another world. In the attention which he pays to Hartley, Wordsworth again speaks intimately to Coleridge. For in the first version of "Dejection," Coleridge complained that his children had become for him a cause for regret and anxiety which only made his situation more painful:

> Those little Angel Children (woe is me!)
> There have been hours when feeling how they bind
> And pluck out the Wing-feathers of my Mind,
> Turning my Error to Necessity,
> I have half-wish'd they never had been born.

In answer to this, Wordsworth puts forward his belief that in childhood we see a celestial state which explains much that we most value in ourselves. He seems almost to pick up Coleridge's complaint and to say that, instead of children being an occasion for lamentation, they should be an occasion for joy.

In childhood Wordsworth sees the imagination at work as he has known it himself in his finest, most creative moments. To explain the presence of this power in childhood and its slow disappearance with the coming of maturity, he advances his account of recollections from a celestial state before birth. In later years Wordsworth tried to explain away the theory which inspires so much of the Ode, or at least to minimize its importance:

It is far too shadowy a notion to be recommended to faith, as more than an element in our instincts of immortality . . . I took hold of the notion of pre-existence as having sufficient foundation in humanity for authorizing me to make for my purpose the best use of it I could as a poet.[9]

No doubt when he wrote this, Wordsworth was troubled by the criticism of some pious souls who argued, correctly enough, that the notion of pre-existence has no warrant in Holy Writ. No doubt, too, in later years as he grew more orthodox, he himself ceased to believe in it; but that he believed it when he wrote the Ode is surely beyond all question. His words speak for their authenticity:

> Our birth is but a sleep and a forgetting:
> The Soul that rises with us, our life's Star,
>   Hath had elsewhere its setting,
>   And cometh from afar:
>   Not in entire forgetfulness,
>   And not in utter nakedness,
> But trailing clouds of glory do we come
>   From God, who is our home.

Wordsworth was not a man to put ideas into poetry merely because they were suitable for it, nor was he capable of saying as a poet what he did not believe as a man. When he said a thing, he did so because he believed it to be true and to need saying. It is impossible to read the Ode without seeing that, when he wrote it, Wordsworth was convinced of pre-existence and of recollections from it in childhood.

The theory of recollection goes back to Plato, but Wordsworth did not take it from him, nor is his application of it Plato's. His sources are Coleridge and Henry Vaughan. Coleridge had played with the idea of pre-existence as an explanation of a feeling that we have in a previous existence done something or been somewhere. He expresses it in a sonnet which he wrote in 1796 on hearing the news of Hartley's birth:

> Oft o'er my brain does that strange fancy roll
> Which makes the present (while the flash doth last)
> Seem a mere semblance of some unknown past,
> Mixed with such feelings, as perplex the soul
> Self-questioned in her sleep; and some have said
> We lived, ere yet this robe of flesh we wore.

Wordsworth picked up the idea because it helped him to explain his own visionary moments. But of course the actual experience of which he speaks is different from Coleridge's. It is not an isolated moment but a process in which the visionary power, at its most powerful in childhood, slowly declines. And this decline was what Wordsworth found in Vaughan's poem, "The Retreate." Vaughan recalls and regrets the days of his "Angell-Infancy," and tells how the vision of celestial things has grown weaker with passing years. But this idea, too, changes in Wordsworth's handling. He is concerned with the loss not of imagination but of innocence. From Coleridge Wordsworth took the idea of pre-existence and from Vaughan that of a slow decline in celestial powers, and from this combination formed his own original theory.

Wordsworth's theory of recollection enabled him to put into a single consistent form the three matters which most concerned him. In the first place, he had known a vision of another world, and he could not but believe that this was both real and divine.

He saw that his moments of intimacy with it were close to something which he had enjoyed in childhood and which other children enjoyed. It is this to which he refers when he addresses the
child of his poem and says:

> Thou, over whom thy Immortality
> Broods like the Day, a Master o'er a Slave,
> A Presence which is not to be put by.

In the child's vision of another world Wordsworth saw something
very like his own visions, and he could not but connect the one
with the other. Secondly, Wordsworth knew that this visionary
power was closely connected with the imagination and the creative process. Indeed, he hardly distinguishes between the two,
so convinced is he that the act of creation in the highest sense involves a special insight into the nature of things. In children he
sees this creative power in its purest form. The child fashions his
own little worlds of the mind because he is divinely inspired by
heavenly memories:

> See, at his feet, some little plan or chart,
> Some fragment from his dream of human life,
> Shaped by himself with newly-learned art.

The child's "whole vocation" seems to be "endless imitation"
because his creative spirit is still unsullied and unhampered.
Thirdly, through vision Wordsworth found what he called eternity. The idea is too vast for analysis, but we can at least say that
when he felt himself in its presence Wordsworth believed both
that he had transcended his temporal being and that he was at
the heart of reality. And this is what he sees in the child:

> Thou best Philosopher, who yet dost keep
> Thy heritage, thou Eye among the blind,
> That, deaf and silent, read'st the eternal deep,
> Haunted for ever by the eternal mind.

Wordsworth found his explanation of imaginative power in the capacity of children to create and to imagine and, while doing so, to have no sense of time or of the limitations of our human state. He wished to explain something very special, and the best way in which he could make himself clear was to point to the example of childhood.

Wordsworth speaks, as indeed do most apostles of such recollection, as if it took place in time, and our mortal state were preceded temporally by a celestial state of which we retain memories. No doubt he meant this, but he also meant something else which is not inconsistent with it. The relation of time to the timeless is not easily put into words, and Wordsworth perhaps did not distinguish very clearly between a purely temporal process and another process in which we pass from time to the timeless. Yet some passages in the Ode show that he had this in mind and saw some of its implications. He is in fact not so much concerned with events in time as with a timeless condition which we can attain even in this life. Just as in the Simplon Pass he saw "types and symbols of eternity," so in the Ode he still believes that he can have glimpses of it, if not by himself, at least as it is reflected in children:

> Hence in a season of calm weather
> Though inland far we be,
> Our Souls have sight of that immortal sea
> Which brought us hither,
> Can in a moment travel thither,
> And see the Children sport upon the shore,
> And hear the mighty waters rolling evermore.

In the visionary experience which Wordsworth once knew so well and now knows only rarely and fitfully, he feels that he passes to eternity, and this is what his theory expresses. That is why in December 1814 he wrote to Mrs. Clarkson:

The poem rests entirely upon two recollections of childhood, one that of a splendour in the objects of sense which is passed away, and the other in an indisposition to bend to the law of death as applying to our case.[10]

In fact, the two themes are one. Wordsworth believed himself to be immortal because through the objects of sense he had known a lofty exaltation in which he passed beyond time.

In this way Wordsworth sets forth his crisis. The "glory and the dream" which he has lost is the visionary power which made his finest poetry. Perhaps it still came back to him at intervals, but he could not be sure of this and placed no hopes in it. He preferred to put his trust in something else and believed that this was more than an adequate consolation. In the last stanza he gives his solution for his crisis and begins with a declaration of his trust that nature will still sustain him:

> And, O, ye Fountains, Meadows, Hills, and Groves,
> Forebode not any severing of our loves!
> Yet in my heart of hearts I feel your might;
> I only have relinquished one delight
> To live beneath your more habitual sway.

The "one delight" is the old visionary power, and the "habitual sway" is that companionship with nature which Wordsworth had always enjoyed and now believed to be more lasting and less intermittent than his visions. It had indeed done much for his poetry. In the presence of nature his human emotions were stirred and enhanced in a peculiar way. His feeling for the fellowship of natural things was so instinctive and so powerful that he was almost more at home with them than with human beings, and among human beings he preferred on the whole those who were closest to nature. He believed that life in towns corrupts and deadens the finer instincts of men and that they find their true selves only in the presence of natural things. He, whom Carlyle rhetorically described as "a cold, hard, silent, practical man . . . a man of an immense head and great jaws like a crocodile's," found it hard to release his feelings except with a very few intimate friends and-relations. But in the presence of nature his feelings were set free, and he felt no shyness afterwards in writing of them. In him nature awoke especially those emotions of sympathy and affection which he felt for his sister and his wife and a few chosen friends. Under his impenetrable exterior he concealed a real need for giving and receiving affection, and, when he was among his mountains and trees and flowers, he allowed this to rise to the surface and express itself in poetry.

It is because Wordsworth believed that nature inspires the affections that he ended the Ode in the confidence that he still has much to comfort and sustain him:

> Thanks to the human heart by which we live,
> Thanks to its tenderness, its joys, and fears,
> To me the meanest flower that blows can give
> Thoughts that do often lie too deep for tears.

In analysing his creative powers, Wordsworth distinguished between his moments of vision and the more enduring effect which nature had on his affections. This, he believed, remained with him, when the visions had departed. He was in his thirties, and he had settled in the countryside where he felt at home and which he was to make indissolubly his own. In the autumn he was to marry Mary Hutchinson and to build that family life which meant so much to him. The quiet tenor of his long later years presents a notable contrast to Coleridge's broken efforts and pathetically helpless dreams. Nor need we doubt that much of Wordsworth's happiness came from living close to nature. In it he found a calm and a contentment. He had years of work before him, and, even when his powers began to fail, he was still at times able to regain some of his old rapture. At a first glance

Wordsworth's optimism seems to be justified. He who had once put his trust in visions now put it in a religion of nature and thought that all would be well with him.

Yet all was not so well as he hoped. Before long it was clear that the religion of nature was not enough, and Wordsworth abandoned it for a more orthodox faith. When in 1818 he wrote his lines on "An Evening of Extraordinary Splendour and Beauty" and gave his later, revised version of much that he had said in the Ode, he had transferred his allegiance to another, more respectable creed. In truth, Wordsworth's belief in natural religion began to wane soon after the completion of the Ode. Its decay almost inevitably followed his loss of visionary power. When something snapped in his sensibility to nature and he no longer knew his old raptures, his whole outlook was affected. The sights which had absorbed his boyhood and then brought him visions of another world began to move him so little that even his human affections ceased to be stirred by them. When he wrote the Ode, Wordsworth hoped that nature would continue to inspire him. No doubt in his own life all was well. He was happy and contented in the habitual round of his routine. Nor is it quite fair to speak, as W. B. Yeats does, of "Wordsworth, withering into eighty years, honoured and empty-witted." [11] His mind was vigorous enough, and in his intimate circle he inspired warmth and security. But what mattered most in him was gone — the creative imagination which carried him beyond the bounds of space and time into some vast order of things, where, in almost losing his individuality, he saw in impassioned vision the power which sustains the universe and gives meaning to life. And when he lost this, it was not long before he lost his secondary but hardly less remarkable gift of feeling himself so close to nature that in its presence he was able to understand the tenderer movements of the human heart and to enter into full sympathy with them.

V

PROMETHEUS UNBOUND

AMONG the Romantic poets, Shelley is peculiar for the hold which abstract ideas had on him. It is of course true that they abound in Wordsworth and may be found in Keats, but, whereas Wordsworth and Keats derived them from an accumulation of particular experiences, Shelley seems first to have formed his ideas and then to have interpreted experience through them. Among the chief springs of his creative activity were ideas which most men would find remote and impersonal, but which had for him a peculiarly vivid appeal. He was enough of a philosopher not merely to enjoy ideas for their own sake but to make them a starting-point for bold speculations in which he found the thrills of a wild adventure. Whether he derived his notions from Plato or from Godwin, he was equally enthralled by them, and much of his inspiration came from them. The result is that his poetry moves in its own metaphysical world. It is concerned hardly with ordinary things or with living men and women, but with vast conceptions which are indeed related to people and things but not immediately or in the first place. Even in *Adonais* there is less personal grief for Keats, whom after all Shelley did not know at all well, than indignant protest against the persecution of genius and triumphant confidence in the eternity of great art. Indeed, most of Shelley's longer poems seem to have been inspired by some great abstract idea which filled him with a wild excitement and moved him to express it as fully and as powerfully as he could. For him the creations of the mind were more real than the sensible world, and though this means that his poetry is sometimes almost inhuman in its remoteness, it is none the less the source of his most characteristic successes.

This is undeniably true of *Prometheus Unbound*. Into no poem did Shelley put so much of himself or of what he thought most important. He wrote it in what were perhaps the happiest months of his life, when he had escaped from the trials and frustrations of England to the freer air of Italy. He was at last able to give himself up almost without hindrance to that special kind of imaginative thought which was the centre of his being and to forget immediate cares in the contemplation of tremendous causes and radiant ideals. In the spring at Rome, among the ruins of the Baths of Caracalla, he found something awaking in himself, and the result was a poem which presents with an almost intoxicated excitement the ideas on which he shaped his own life and which he believed could change the world. When he finished *Prometheus Unbound,* in the late summer of 1819, he was twenty-seven years old, and, though he had had his full share of disappointments and defeats, he was still at heart the same confident, dogmatic young man whose career at Oxford had come to so abrupt an end eight years before. Though Shelley matured and modified his youthful ideas, he was still concerned with the same problems. He was still occupied with nothing less than the whole destiny of man and still approached it with the far-ranging assurance of philosophical youth. The germs of *Prometheus Unbound* may be found in *Queen Mab,* but they have grown from didactic rhetoric into poetry — poetry, it is true, of a peculiar kind and not to everybody's taste, but undeniably and always poetry.

Such ideas as obsessed Shelley are not easily turned into poetry. Just because they are abstract, they do not lightly fall into the particular shapes which poetry demands. Most philosophical poets have solved this difficulty in the same way. They present individual characters in an individual setting and convince us that they are real and related to the familiar world. Having done this, they are able to make them embody and represent wide issues and show what these issues mean. That Shelley was capable of this is clear from *The Cenci,* which raises powerful and impelling issues but is none the less a drama about human beings.

But he did not do the same for the ideas which fermented in his mind in the spring of 1819, and we can see why. This time the ideas were so important to him that he could not confine them in too concrete a form. He wished to show how wonderful they were in their very vagueness and vastness, to present them with all the attractions and enchantments which he himself found in them, to keep their intellectual nature and not to reduce them to shapes which would rob them of much which was essential to them. Because he enjoyed ideas for their own sake, he could not, in writing what he believed to be his best poem, deprive them of the peculiar appeal which, as an imaginative philosopher, he found in them.

Shelley solved this problem with bold originality. To make his ideas vivid and persuasive, he evolved a system of coherent symbols which would appeal as poetry and yet take away nothing from the metaphysical character of his subject. In him the philosopher and the poet were so closely blended that he saw general ideas almost as particular objects of devotion, and he felt for them the kind of regard which Plato felt for his ideal Forms which are at once universal realities and perfect particulars. As a poet Shelley was able to keep so close a relation with his ideas that they developed a special individuality for him, and it is this which he turned into poetry. He presented his abstract thoughts in a myth derived from the Greeks and was thereby able to make them lively. In his *Prometheus Bound* Aeschylus had written the first of three plays on the conflict between Prometheus, the friend of man and the pioneer of civilization, and Zeus, the upstart tyrant of the universe. This presents only one stage in the conflict, and it was fortunate for Shelley that the other two plays are lost, though we know something about the second, in which Prometheus was delivered. Shelley was able to start at the point where Aeschylus ends his first play, to make use of the myth and to give to it a new meaning and a new character. He dismissed the solution which he knew Aeschylus to have found, and presented his own high argument on a new plan.

Aeschylus provided Shelley with the material for his myth, but not with very much more. By some process not fully known to us, Aeschylus reconciled Prometheus with Zeus, but Shelley would have none of this. As he says in his Preface, "I was averse from a catastrophe so feeble as that of reconciling the Champion with the Oppressor of mankind." No doubt Aeschylus would hardly accept this as a fair account of what he did, since his Zeus is far from being merely the oppressor of mankind and, even if he were, Greek religious realism would still think that a divine power should be regarded with humility and awe. Once he had found a suitable vehicle for his ideas, Shelley had to go his own way just because they were not Greek. This he was fully entitled to do, and he chose his myth well. He gave shape to huge modern issues through a story which was familiar enough for his readers to approach it without such misgivings as they might have felt if he had invented a new myth, as, for instance, Blake did for his even bolder speculations. From Aeschylus Shelley took the struggle between Prometheus and Zeus. He does not recapitulate what Aeschylus says, but starts where the *Prometheus Bound* finishes. Aeschylus provides an introduction to what Shelley has to say, but that is entirely his own, and he presents it in his own way, not through any attempt to revive the archaic form of Attic tragedy but in a lyrical drama, with a variety of characters and scenes and songs, in the manner of the Romantic age.

There is a profound gulf between the Greek myth and Shelley's use of it. For the Greeks the ancient stories about which they wrote their incomparable poetry were not allegorical or symbolical but concerned with what they believed to be real persons, whether divine or human, existing in a real world. For Aeschylus both Zeus and Prometheus exist, and their conflict belongs to history. Of course, he uses their story to present far-reaching metaphysical issues, but every dramatist is entitled to do that, and it does not detract from the reality of his presentation. But with Shelley it is different. His Prometheus is not a real person in whose individual existence he believes, but a figure who symbolizes a great abstract idea. What matters in him is not a personal destiny but something universal. He is not really a character, and indeed there are in this sense no characters in *Prometheus Unbound*. The *dramatis personae* belong to no actual world, nor even to a world of the imagination which wears the appearance of the actual world. What matters is not what they are in themselves but what they represent. They are incarnate ideas, and perhaps they are not very incarnate but still have some relics of their intellectual origin about them. They are not symbols such as Blake uses to present visionary experience, but ideas presented in visible shape, principles made more attractive through the lineaments which Shelley gives to them, forces of the human soul translated to a special setting which makes them more vivid and more convincing. Shelley was at home with abstractions and able to give to them at least a local habitation and a name.

The persons of *Prometheus Unbound* have Greek or Latin names which suggest that they possess some kind of individuality. But their reality is not personal, and the names are delusive. Prometheus himself is the embodiment, if that is not too strong a word, of something which Shelley greatly valued, and is described in the Preface as "the type of the highest perfection of moral and intellectual nature, impelled by the purest and truest motives to the best and noblest ends." Prometheus is all that. He stands for the desire in the human soul to create harmony through reason and love, and for this he displays an unequalled courage and endurance. He is what Shelley regarded as the noblest force in the human self, the desire for the good and the willingness to make any sacrifice for it. Prometheus' ideal nature is both intellectual and moral and devoted equally to truth and to goodness. His companions are the daughters of Ocean — Panthea, Ione, and Asia — who are in effect Faith, Hope, and Love, those forces in the soul which inspire and sustain the reason and set it to work in the best possible way. Pitted against them is Jupiter, who represents the brutal forces in human nature which obstruct and persecute its noble desires. He is in the first place a figure of tyranny, of that lust to rule others which uses fear and superstition to its base ends and produces cruelty and ignorance. But he is more than this. He is the incarnation of all that Shelley regards as evil, of those destructive forces which take many forms but all arise from the denial of the good. The conflict with which the poem begins is between Prometheus and Jupiter, between the principle of reason and love and the principle of tyrannous destructiveness which hates and harasses the good but is unable to destroy it.

On this balance of forces Shelley arranges his plot. It too is quite simple. The age-long struggle between Prometheus and Jupiter must come to an end, and for this Shelley adapts a theme from Aeschylus. In Aeschylus Prometheus is eventually delivered because he reveals a secret, known to him alone, that if Zeus has a child by Thetis, he will be overthrown by him. Shelley disdains the notion that Prometheus should ever come to terms with Jupiter, and ingeniously makes Prometheus refuse to divulge his secret, which is that Jupiter will inevitably be overthrown by his son. In making this change Shelley was able to accommodate his myth to his beliefs. To him it was both intolerable and impossible that reason should come to terms with evil. It must act on the highest motives of love for the good, and evil must perish through its own progeny. So Prometheus refuses either to help Jupiter or to harm him. Evil must be defeated by itself, and this happens when Jupiter is overthrown by his own offspring. Shelley takes a theme from Aeschylus and gives it an entirely new shape and meaning consonant with his own moral ideas.

The son who overthrows Jupiter is Demogorgon. Shelley found the name in Spenser and Milton, and his choice of it is peculiar, if not a little perverse. For in these poets Demogorgon is a principle of chaos and disorder, who haunts the darkness of the abyss. No doubt Shelley chose his name because he liked to think of him as some kind of opponent to Milton's God, a superior Satan, who is no less opposed to the supreme power but, being less familiar than Satan, lacks Satan's familiar faults. In any case, Demogorgon has a mysterious and resounding name, and that is perhaps enough to justify Shelley's introduction of him. He receives a new character and a new role. He is the son whom Jupiter has begotten and who is to overthrow him. But we may well ask what Shelley means to present in him, why he has gone out of his way to find a character alien to his Greek myth, and what part Demogorgon plays. These questions are not easy to answer because they concern points on which Shelley had powerful but not very precise ideas. Demogorgon's part in *Prometheus Unbound* is central, but it requires examination before we see what it means.

In Act III Demogorgon appears before Jupiter, who asks him his name. He answers:

Eternity. Demand no direr name.

This does not make things much clearer. "Eternity" is too ambiguous a word to provide an exact clue, and the hint of a "direr name" suggests that Demogorgon stands for more than at the moment he is willing to say. If we take "eternity" to mean endless time, the words must signify that in the course of time evil will be destroyed, and such an idea would certainly have appealed to Shelley in his youth when he believed in the automatic amelioration of human life. But we may doubt if he still believed in this when he wrote *Prometheus Unbound,* and anyhow "eternity" is not a way to speak of a period of time which, however long, is none the less finite. If, on the other hand, we take "eternity" to mean those eternal things which are always present in the full scheme of being, the words are more to the point. In that case, Shelley suggests that there are indestructible forces in the universe which will, sooner or later, overcome evil. What these forces are may be seen from Act II, scene 3, when Asia and Panthea come to a pinnacle of rock among the mountains, and Panthea says:

Hither the sound has borne us — to the realm
Of Demogorgon, and the mighty portal,
Like a volcano's meteor-breathing chasm,
Whence the oracular vapour is hurled up
Which lonely men drink wandering in their youth,
And call truth, virtue, love, genius, or joy,
That maddening wine of life, whose dregs they drain
To deep intoxication; and uplift
Like Mænads who cry loud, Evoe! Evoe!

Demogorgon is in some sense the spirit of life, and especially of
that spiritual energy which is displayed in "truth, virtue, love,
genius, or joy." No wonder that it is hard to find, and that Shelley
makes the search for it more mysterious through the voices which
sing to Asia and Panthea of the deep downward path which they
must take to it. Indeed, Shelley's imagery of a journey into the
bowels of the earth hints that this spirit lies at the centre of being
and can be found only by devotion and inspiration. Asia and
Panthea, who are Love and Faith, are able to find it because they
hold the keys to the mystery of life.

The power which dethrones the principle of evil is the principle of life which asserts itself and breaks its imprisoning bonds.
In this conception Shelley uses certain ideas which meant much
to him. In the first place, he believed that in the end evil is conquered because it breeds its own opposite. In Act I he shows what
this means. As Prometheus hangs in chains on his rock, he is
deeply troubled by the images of cruelty and evil which have
attacked him. He hears Spirits singing, and they comfort him
with the reminder that, though dark forces may be in the ascendant, the human soul is not quenched but remains faithful to its
heroic endeavours:

From unremembered ages we
Gentle guides and guardians be
Of heaven-oppressed mortality.

Then the four Spirits sing in turn of soldiers who die for some high cause on the battlefield, of sailors drowned in saving the lives of others, of the sage studying at night, and of the poet who creates "forms more real than living man." These are examples of the living forces which not only refuse to submit to evil but are even brought into action by opposition to it. They illustrate the "deep intoxication" which men find in Demogorgon's cave from the spirit which is the spirit of life because in it life is more active and more abundant than in any other manifestation. When Demogorgon dethrones his father, Jupiter, the spirit of life conquers the spirit of destruction, to which it largely owes its existence.

In the second place, Shelley had absorbed from Plato the idea of a world-soul. So far from thinking that the sum of things can be divided into spirit and matter, he held that matter does not exist and that spirit is the only reality: that nature is no less alive than man and has, like him, a soul. For Shelley the earth and everything in it are alive and directed by an immanent principle of life. That is why the persons of *Prometheus Unbound* include not merely embodiments of human forces but natural things like Earth and Ocean, who speak their own appropriate words and take part in the action. Just as the Greeks saw living spirits in the physical world and had their gods of earth and sea, so Shelley believes that everything that exists is alive and manifests the influence of some central directing power. His Demogorgon rises from this belief. He lives at the centre of the world because he is the principle of the life which extends beyond human beings to all existing things. A power so vast cannot be defined closely; it must be understood through the imagination, and that is why Shelley stresses its mystery and its invincible strength. When Asia and Panthea go in search of it, they hear a Semichorus of Spirits singing of a power which draws all after it, and themselves follow the irresistible summons:

> There those enchanted eddies play
> > Of echoes, music-tongued, which draw,
> > By Demogorgon's mighty law,
> > With melting rapture, or sweet awe,
> All spirits on that secret way;
> > As inland boats are driven to Ocean
> Down streams made strong with mountain-thaw.

The "mighty law" which draws the spirit along unknown paths comes from the living soul of the universe and its commands cannot but be obeyed.

Prometheus Unbound dramatizes the defeat of evil by the spirit of life. Shelley was not shy of so enormous a subject and was ready with his own solution for the problems which it raises. This is, as we might expect, quite simple: evil is subdued through love. The idea is developed with elaborate poetry and is responsible for much that is most attractive in the poem. In Act I it is introduced when Prometheus sees the vision of Christ, the type of all who suffer for love, but is hardly able to endure the sight because of all the evil that has been committed in Christ's name:

> Remit the anguish of that lighted stare;
> Close those wan lips; let that thorn-wounded brow
> Stream not with blood; it mingles with thy tears!
> Fix, fix those tortured orbs in peace and death,
> So thy sick throes shake not that crucifix,
> So those pale fingers play not with thy gore.
> O, horrible! Thy name I will not speak;
> It hath become a curse.

Prometheus, who at this stage is unable to face what Christ's sufferings have brought to man, represents the spirit which is unable to understand the true nature of love because of the false associations attached to it. In this scene Shelley puts something from his own experience. In his youth he denounced not only Christianity but Christ, whom in *Queen Mab* he calls a "malignant soul." In *Prometheus* he has passed beyond that and found in Christ a type of those who suffer because they love. He shows how Prometheus, who represents human reason at its noblest, begins by being unable to understand what love really is.

The hint thus given is soon developed. In the same scene the First Spirit, which sings of death on the battlefield, closes the song with the words:

> And one sound, above, around,
> One sound beneath, around, above,
> Was moving; 'twas the soul of love
> 'Twas the hope, the prophecy,
> Which begins and ends in thee.

Other examples of loving sacrifice are presented, and then the whole Chorus draws the conclusion:

> In the atmosphere we breathe,
> As buds grow red when the snow-storms flee,
> From spring gathering up beneath,
> Whose mild winds shake the elder brake,
> And the wandering herdsmen know
> That the white-thorn soon will blow:
> Wisdom, Justice, Love, and Peace,
> When they struggle to increase,
> Are to us as soft winds be
> To shepherd boys, the prophecy
> Which begins and ends in thee.

The words are addressed to Prometheus; in him the prophecy is to begin and end, and the prophecy is of love. Once human goodness is aware of love and touched by it, marvellous things may happen, and this is the directing idea of Act I. After this, love awakes in Asia, or rather awakes again after many years. Her love for Prometheus begins with a dream of him and ends in a splendid scene in which she sings of the power which carries her off to the music of unseen spirits. And this is the signal and the occasion for the release of the forces which are to dethrone evil. The moment when Asia realizes her love for Prometheus is the moment when spirits set forth in chariots drawn by winged horses to conquer the sky. This is the crisis to which Shelley gives an almost mystical significance. When love and reason are united, evil is doomed.

In love Shelley finds much more than a power which sets reason to work. When Asia and Panthea question Demogorgon about the government of the world, though he answers that "the deep truth is imageless" and cannot be told, he adds:

> For what would it avail to bid thee gaze
> On the revolving world? What to bid speak
> Fate, Time, Occasion, Chance, and Change? To these
> All things are subject but eternal Love.

This is Shelley's revised version of his old belief that everything is governed by mechanical laws. These laws indeed exist, but love is outside them and above them. It stands in its own category and is a principle of action subject to nothing but itself. This is of course much more than even Plato attributed to love. It is Shelley's mature conception of the force which he had once seen at work in the physical universe and now saw at work in the realm of spirit. This is the "Life of Life" of which a Voice sings when Asia prepares to join Prometheus — the central, creating, inspiring principle which sustains all life and without which even goodness is not enough. It is not surprising that, when Shelley wishes to celebrate it, he finds hard to express in precise words its meaning for him, but, as Tennyson said of him, "seems to go up and burst." Yet this song, which is given pride of place at the main crisis of the poem, has its own mysterious splendour and shows what Shelley felt about this vision which provided him with all that was most important in his philosophy:

Child of Light! thy limbs are burning
 Thro' the vest which seems to hide them;
As the radiant lines of morning
 Thro' the clouds ere they divide them;
And this atmosphere divinest
Shrouds thee wheresoe'er thou shinest

Fair are others; none beholds thee,
 But thy voice sounds low and tender
Like the fairest, for it folds thee
 From the sight, that liquid splendour,
And all feel, yet see thee never,
As I feel now, lost for ever!

When Shelley tried to reduce his most essential convictions to order, he found that it was almost impossible. He could do no more than hint at a radiance so dazzling that he could hardly look at it.

The material which Shelley put into *Prometheus Unbound* requires a special kind of treatment. The abstract ideas which meant so much to him and had for him an almost personal existence could be presented only in symbols and images. On this he has something to say in his Preface:

The imagery which I have employed will be found, in many instances, to have been drawn from the operations of the human mind, or from those external actions by which they are expressed.

He goes on to claim the precedents of Dante and Shakespeare and above all of the Greek poets. It is easy to illustrate what he means from many passages in the *Prometheus*. For instance, when Asia addresses the spring she compares a physical event to mental events and their manifestations:

From all the blasts of heaven thou hast descended:
Yes, like a spirit, like a thought, which makes

Unwonted tears throng to the horny eyes,
And beatings haunt the desolated heart,
Which should have learnt repose.

This is in its way comparable to what Homer does when he says that a ship is "swift as a thought." But it is difficult not to see more in Shelley's claim than this and not to connect his reference to the example of Greek poets with some words which Mary Shelley records from a manuscript book of his:

In the Greek Shakespeare, Sophocles, we find the image,

πολλὰς δ' ὁδοὺς ἐλθόντα φροντίδος πλάνοις.

A line of almost unfathomable depth of poetry, yet how simple are the images in which it is arrayed,

Coming to many ways in the wanderings of careful thought.[1]

. . . What a picture does this line suggest of the mind as a wilderness of intricate paths, wide as the universe, which is here made its symbol; a world within a world, which he, who seeks some knowledge with respect to what he ought to do, searches throughout, as he would search the external universe for some valued thing which was hidden from him upon the surface.[2]

The line of Sophocles, in which Shelley finds so rich a meaning, illustrates the other side of the process illustrated by Asia's speech. Just as she compares visible things to invisible, so Sophocles compares invisible to visible and thereby gives them a far greater cogency and clarity. And this is what Shelley himself does. Just as Sophocles suggests that the mind of Oedipus is a universe, so Shelley presents his own thoughts as a universe. It is true that he attaches great importance to them and expects all men to accept them, but his method is none the less what he praises in Sophocles. He gives to his mental world a more or less visible form and at the same time makes it clear that it is still mental. In *Prometheus Unbound* Shelley tried to provide his radiant ideas with a particular shape no less radiant. In this he set himself a task such as no other poet of his time did on anything like the same scale, and his efforts to surmount the difficulties of such an enterprise are an illuminating commentary on its nature.

In the first place, since Shelley embodies abstract ideas in his figures and events, we are apt to press every detail of what he says and to relate everything to his main theme. Nor is this always wrong. Many of his details are indeed relevant to his main themes in that they increase their poetical appeal. Take for instance the lines which Asia speaks at the end of Act II:

> My soul is an enchanted boat,
>   Which, like a sleeping swan, doth float
> Upon the silver waves of thy sweet singing;
>   And thine doth like an angel sit
>   Beside a helm conducting it,
> Whilst all the winds with melody are ringing.
>   It seems to float ever, for ever,
>   Upon that many-winding river,
>   Between mountains, woods, abysses,
>   A paradise of wildernesses!

The theme is the progress of the soul in love, and it is presented in a highly imaginative way. Of course, we must not examine the details separately as if each stood for some special stage or element in the experience, but the whole idea of the enchanted journey is apt and illuminating. The impression of enchanting music and of irresistible motion is essential to the picture. The intellectual idea has been fused with the images, and the result is that the idea has a new appeal.

Shelley, however, could not always do this, or at least his imagery is not always so close to the point. There is in *Prometheus Unbound* much description of natural scenery, and we might think that Shelley indulges his love of it for its own sake, with the justifiable excuse that it adds to the beauty and the reality of his poem. He is hardly to be blamed if not all the details are equally relevant to his directing ideas. Yet when we look more closely, we see that on the whole Shelley does more than this, that his descriptions are in fact relevant because they set a tone or create an atmosphere. A good example comes from Act II when Asia speaks of the dawn:

> The point of one white star is quivering still
> Deep in the orange light of widening morn
> Beyond the purple mountains: thro' a chasm
> Of wind-divided mist the darker lake
> Reflects it: now it wanes: it gleams again
> As the waves fade, and as the burning threads
> Of woven cloud unravel in pale air:
> 'Tis lost! and thro' yon peaks of cloudlike snow
> The roseate sun-light quivers: hear I not
> The Æolian music of her sea-green plumes
> Winnowing the crimson dawn?

This is a perfectly real dawn and may be enjoyed as such, but it is also symbolical. The dawn is in the world and in the soul, and it has the same character in both. To show what it means for the soul, Shelley uses the language appropriate to a visible scene, and we should not attempt to interpret each detail allegorically but respond to the whole effect and see what the awakening of the soul means.

A second problem which Shelley had to face was that of relating his abstract ideas to human experience and human feelings. For him, of course, the vast causes which obsessed him were the causes of humanity, and his belief in them was accompanied by a real compassion for the dark condition of man. But since he lived so much among abstractions and found so celestial a glory in them, there was a danger that his poetry would lose touch with life and confine itself to a Platonic heaven. Nor does Shelley always avoid this. There are moments when his ideas are so diaphanous that they elude us, at least as real experience. But at other times Shelley's compassion takes control and gives a warm humanity to his poetry, and it is interesting to note that when this happens he tends to abandon symbols and becomes almost realistic in his presentation of actual facts. He does indeed indulge in wide generalities, but he could hardly do otherwise, since the whole of history is his subject; but his strong convictions make these generalities live. His compassion for the persecuted and the oppressed inspires some of the finest lines which he ever wrote, as when Prometheus tells the Fury of the doom which befalls the wise and the just:

> Some hunted by foul lies from their heart's home,
> An early-chosen, late-lamented home;
> As hooded ounces cling to the driven hind;
> Some linked to corpses in unwholesome cells:
> Some — Hear I not the multitude laugh loud? —
> Impaled in lingering fire: and mighty realms
> Float by my feet, like sea-uprooted isles,
> Whose sons are kneaded down in common blood
> By the red light of their own burning homes.

In this passage, and in others like it, Shelley shows the human feelings implicit in his abstract notions. The deliverance of humanity was for him a real and urgent question which aroused his finest emotions. Such passages may stand out with a particular emphasis in the general texture of the poem and have a different kind of appeal from the rest, but because Shelley's human feelings are intimately related to his ideas, the two kinds of poetry are not discordant but combined in a single harmony.

A third problem which such a poem as the *Prometheus* raises is how much should be put into it. Shelley evidently believed that he was writing a great philosophical poem and poured into it all his most imaginative and daring speculations. His main scheme is clear and simple, but there are moments when his originality has led critics to think that he has gone too far and allowed his interest in philosophy or science to carry him away from his main theme. A signal case of this is alleged in Act IV, when Ione and

Panthea see bewildering forms in a forest, and these are thought to represent Shelley's scientific notions. One is a crescent chariot, and its driver is described in detail as having a white face, white feathers, a white body, and white hair:

> yet its two eyes are heavens
> Of liquid darkness, which the Deity
> Within seems pouring.

The second is more complex:

> A sphere, which is as many thousand spheres,
> Solid as crystal, yet through all its mass
> Flow, as through empty space, music and light:
> Ten thousand orbs involving and involved,
> Purple and azure, white and green and golden,
> Sphere within sphere.

These two visions are certainly mysterious, and it is something of a relief to be told that in the first Shelley depicts electricity and in the second Davy's theory of the "dance of matter." If, however, this is the whole truth, Shelley has wandered far from his ideal subject and involved himself in not very relevant topics. But this is not necessarily the complete answer. Shelley was interested in scientific speculations, and no doubt makes use of them here. But he transforms them to suit his own system. They concern, in his view, not matter but spirit. He brings into his poem not physical phenomena but spiritual forces at work in the living world. For him even electricity was an activity of the world-soul.

On the other hand, the kind of poetry which Shelley wrote sometimes raised technical problems for which he found no complete solution. In the first place, the task of translating abstract ideas into images is full of traps, and Shelley did not always see all the dangers. One reason for this was that, perhaps despite himself, he had certain notions fixed in his mind which warred with those which are important in his poem. A special case is his attitude towards Jupiter. In the main scheme Jupiter is the power of evil in the world and especially in the human soul. How evil he is Shelley shows by many moving passages on the misery caused to humanity by hatred, ignorance, cruelty, and fear. For such a principle Shelley had nothing but hostility, but his presentation of it is clouded by something else. In his youth he had claimed that God is evil, and this conviction is not quite absent from *Prometheus Unbound*. At times Jupiter appears to be not an ultimate and hideous principle of evil but a deity who has to be fought as a personal enemy. Thus, in Act I, Prometheus withdraws his curse on Jupiter, and in so doing shows his generous character and foreshadows the ultimate triumph of love. His reasons for this are that the only way to treat an enemy is to forgive him. No doubt Shelley believed that this was right, but he was wrong to apply this belief to an enemy who is not a person but the very principle of evil. This, as Shelley well knew, should not and will not be defeated by forgiveness. In making his myth dramatic, Shelley has for the moment forgotten what his Jupiter really represents, and the result is a confusion in the scheme of the poem.

A second difficulty in *Prometheus Unbound* is that sometimes it is not clear whether Shelley speaks literally or symbolically. Though most of the action is symbolical, the actual consummation which he foresees takes place in the familiar world. Shelley clearly wishes to be taken literally when the Spirit of the Hour foretells the brotherhood of free men, or when Asia describes the limitless possibilities which are now open to human endeavour. But there are other times when we are uncertain whether events which take place on earth are intended to be taken literally or not. He makes Earth foresee a change in her actual condition, when there will be everlasting spring, and all noisome and dangerous things will lose their power to harm. Nor is this expressed vaguely, as if it were a hint of a new spirit in man, but with a definiteness of detail which suggests an actual change in physical nature, as when the Spirit of the Earth tells how she has seen birds eating deadly nightshade without being harmed. Now, if this is symbolical, it fails in its effect; for we inevitably feel that it is intended to be real. It is at least possible that Shelley intended it to be taken literally and foresaw a change in the conditions of life, because in his view all physical things are really spiritual. It is not necessary to criticize the validity of this belief, but it remains true that in presenting a matter of this kind he should have put his meaning beyond doubt.

A third difficulty rises from the nature of Shelley's subject and the form in which he presented it. No one would expect a lyrical drama to be as rich in thrills and action as other kinds of drama, but at least we expect it to be in some sense dramatic, to portray actions which are in themselves exciting and which make us respond to the expectations and anxieties that belong to drama. In his own way Shelley sometimes does this, but not always. Indeed, the greatest failure in the poem is the scene which might have been the most dramatic, the actual dethronement of Jupiter by Demogorgon. An event of such wide import and such dramatic possibilities might, we may well think, have been enriched with more than a short colloquy which leads to the immediate collapse and surrender of Jupiter. But it looks as if this method were forced on Shelley by his metaphysical plan. Since Jupiter must inevitably succumb to the spirit of life, no real conflict is possible, and his fall must have this undramatic character. All that Shelley can do is to draw a fine picture of the fate which awaits Jupiter after his fall, and this is not drama but description. Again, the whole of Act IV is nothing but a series of magnificent songs accompanied by no action, and for all dramatic purposes the action closes with the end of Act III. Yet Act IV is necessary to Shelley's design if he is to say all that he has in mind about the various spiritual forces which govern life. *Prometheus* is so much a drama of ideas that it has no very great place for action and the dramatic interest is continually sacrificed to other, more urgent needs.

The events of *Prometheus Unbound* take place in so rarefied and so unfamiliar an atmosphere that we hardly relate them to historical time or ask when the consummation which Shelley describes is going to take place. Indeed, the question might well have meant little to him. None the less, it is reasonable to ask whether Shelley believed that such a consummation was likely or possible. In his early years Shelley, under Godwin's influence, believed in the perfectibility of man. In *Queen Mab* he assumes that reason must triumph and that it will bring wealth and liberty, abolish hunger and poverty, make the earth supply all human needs, and assuage the sting of death. In *Prometheus Unbound* this mechanical process has been discarded, and whether things get better or not depends on the finer forces of human nature and especially love, as Mary Shelley says in her notes:

The prominent feature of Shelley's theory of the destiny of the human species was, that evil is not inherent in the system of the creation, but an accident that might be expelled . . . Shelley believed that mankind had only to will that there should be no evil, and there would be none.[3]

There is no reason to doubt that Mary Shelley reports her husband's views faithfully, but she leaves the most important question unanswered. Of course Shelley thought that mankind had only to will that "there should be no evil," but did he think this at all likely? In other words, is *Prometheus Unbound* a prophecy of something which is likely to happen, or is it a summons to men to destroy evil by exerting reason and love? The two interpretations are quite different, and our acceptance of the one or the other will determine our view of Shelley's purpose in writing the poem.

The answer is to be found in the closing scene. After wild visions of an increased life and a greater unity between man and nature, after the songs of Spirits and Hours about the new world which awaits men, after the love-duet of the Moon and the Earth which tokens a greater harmony in the world-soul, Shelley comes down again to something more like fact and makes Demogorgon address Prometheus and deliver a solemn warning. He hints that not only is there no end to evil but that evil is even necessary to create goodness, and the highest goodness lies in an unending struggle. There can be no doubt about the importance of these words, coming as they do at the very last and addressed as they are by the principle of life to the principle of goodness:

> Gentleness, Virtue, Wisdom, and Endurance,
> These are the seals of that most firm assurance
>   Which bars the pit over Destruction's strength;
> And if, with infirm hand, Eternity,
> Mother of many acts and hours, should free
>   The serpent that would clasp her with his length;
> These are the spells by which to re-assume
> An empire o'er the disentangled doom.
>
> To suffer woes which Hope thinks infinite;
> To forgive wrongs darker than death or night;
>   To defy Power, which seems omnipotent;
> To love, and bear; to hope till Hope creates
> From its own wreck the thing it contemplates;
>   Neither to change, nor falter, nor repent;
> This, like thy glory, Titan, is to be
> Good, great and joyous, beautiful and free;
> This is alone Life, Joy, Empire, and Victory.

It is true that in the context Shelley suggests that this reappearance of evil is a possibility in a remote future, but the strength and sincerity of his words leave no doubt that this struggle is both what he knows in the existing world and what he expects to continue in it, since through it man achieves the highest perfection of which he is capable.

Prometheus Unbound is not a prophecy but a challenge. It is concerned not with events in time but with the eternal situation of man and the universe. Shelley was always seeking for a single abiding reality behind the multiplicity of transient things, and his mind turned naturally to the universal and the permanent whose faint reflections he saw in the phenomenal world. For him poetry was the only way in which to grasp this ultimate reality, because it must be understood not through the intellect but through the imagination. It follows that in nearly all his poetry, but above all in *Prometheus Unbound,* we are brought into close touch with what Shelley means by the imagination, the inspired insight into "the very image of life expressed in its eternal truth" and "those forms which are common to universal nature and existence." [4] Because he believed this, Shelley wrote as he did, not merely refusing to polish his texts, because they represented for him the uncontaminated messages of inspiration, but placing his main emphasis on that eternal sphere in which his spirit was at home. Few men share to the full the philosophy which Shelley made part of his being. For most of us the world of abstractions is duller and dimmer than the visible world, and what is true of most men is true also of poets. Mystics have indeed the gift of making their transcendental experience real to us through the intensity of their vision. But Shelley was not a mystic. He was a metaphysician, and that is the secret both of his strength and of his limitations. At times he seems to pass into spheres so rarefied that we cannot follow him and to become

> The loftiest star of unascended heaven,
> Pinnacled dim in the intense inane.

But that is not so much his fault as ours. His triumph is that at other times, through the enchantment which his poetry sets on us, we are able to explore regions of which he is the discoverer and almost the only denizen, and to know in his company the delights of a condition in which the old quarrel of poetry and philosophy is healed and the pallid abstractions of analytical thought take on the glow and the glory of visible things.

VI

ODE ON A GRECIAN URN

APRIL and May 1819 were perhaps the most remarkable period of Keats' creative life, remarkable not so much for the quantity of his work as for its quality. In these months he wrote "La Belle Dame sans Merci," the "Ode to Psyche," the "Ode to a Nightingale," and the "Ode on a Grecian Urn." In these poems he found his true voice and the perfection which he had been seeking. It was an astonishing outburst, and it came all the more unaccountably since, in the preceding months of February and March, Keats had written very little. In February he temporarily abandoned *Hyperion* because, as he wrote to his brother George, "to tell the truth I have not been in great cue for writing lately," [1] and he left "The Eve of St. Mark" unfinished. When his inspiration returned in April, it was not a case of continuing something already begun. The great odes were a new venture unlike anything that Keats had hitherto done, and he conducted it in a new spirit. As he says of the "Ode to Psyche," "This I have done leisurely — I think it reads the more richly for it and will I hope encourage me to write other things in even a more peaceable and healthy spirit." [2] If the "Ode to Psyche" was the first of the odes to be written, Keats' hopes were realized. The odes which follow certainly "read the more richly" for the care which has gone to their composition and for the selection and concentration of imaginative experience in them. In them Keats carries out the prescription for poetry which he gave to Shelley[3] and loads every rift of his subject with ore.

This sudden flowering of genius is of course inexplicable, but at least it shows how strange are the reactions of the creative spirit to circumstances. In the spring of 1819 Keats had received more than his fair share of blows from fortune. He was only twenty-three years old, and his happiness was menaced from several quarters. In the preceding June his brother, George, who had been "more than a brother" to him and his "greatest friend," [4] had emigrated with his wife to America. In December his other brother, Thomas, whom he loved no less than George, died. On Christmas Day Keats had indeed become betrothed to Fanny Brawne, but, however we may judge her feelings for him and his feelings for her, it is clear enough that their relations were not a source of strength and encouragement to him. And lastly, the symptoms of his fatal illness, which had appeared in the preceding September, returned in February and were with him intermittently in the spring and summer of 1819. Though as yet he had no suspicion of their deadly menace, they cannot but have depressed his spirits and lowered his vitality. In such conditions Keats might not be expected to start on a new form of poetry and to give to it an unprecedented richness. Yet this is what happened, and it is only another example of the unaccountable ways in which the creative spirit works. Perhaps something is due to the famous walk and talk which Keats had with Coleridge on April 11th, when Coleridge spoke, among other topics, of "Nightingales, Poetry — on Poetical Sensation — Metaphysics." [5] Mr. H. W. Garrod has persuasively argued that this talk contained the first germ of the "Ode to a Nightingale," [6] and if that is so, the other odes may indirectly trace their descent from it. But the talk can have done no more than set Keats' genius to work. He was ready for a new venture, and, once the creative fit began, he owed little to Coleridge.

The "Ode on a Grecian Urn" invites special consideration among Keats' odes for two reasons. First, it is his maturest, almost final word on the vision of Hellas which he first discovered through Lemprière's Classical Dictionary, Chapman's Homer, and the Elgin marbles. Secondly, alone among the odes it has been interpreted in quite different ways. It is true that Keats himself thought that poems should explain themselves without comment, but in this case he did not succeed in his aim. The "Ode on a Grecian Urn" calls for comment because its meaning and its purpose have been variously interpreted and variously judged. For this Keats is not entirely responsible. Most of us know the Ode so well that we do not trouble to ask carefully what it means, and, if we do ask, we try to force its meaning to fit our own convictions. What was perfectly clear to Keats is not so clear to us because we do not share all his ideas, and in our conceit we assume that his most pondered conclusions about his life-work must somehow agree with our own.

The title of the Ode suggests that Keats had in mind a particular work of Greek art, which he first describes, then interprets. But no Greek urn has been discovered which corresponds with that which Keats describes. We must look at his words and see what he had in mind. His description is quite clear. His urn is of marble, and we may infer that the scenes on it are carved in relief:

> with brede
> Of marble men and maidens overwrought.

These scenes are two and separate. The one, described in the first three stanzas, is of a "mad pursuit," in which a youth pipes under a tree while another youth pursues a maiden. The other scene is of a sacrificial procession, in which a priest leads a garlanded heifer to a "green altar" and is followed by a company of pious worshippers. The two scenes may be complementary, but they are not united. Their spirit and their temper are different, and in them Keats anticipates Nietzsche's famous analysis of the Greek genius into the Dionysian and the Apollonian elements, ecstatic excitement and luminous order. Now it is clear that, if Keats describes a marble vase, it must be of the neo-Attic kind which had so wide a vogue in the Greco-Roman world. Marble vases of the earlier periods are very rare, and it is most unlikely that Keats ever saw one. But the difficulty arises that these neo-Attic marble vases portray not two separate scenes, as do black-figured and red-figured vases of the classical age, but a single scene which goes round the circumference and makes a continuous design. Keats indeed seems to have known this peculiarity of Greek marble vases and to have touched on it in his "Ode on Indolence," when he says of three figures which haunt him,

> They pass'd, like figures on a marble urn,
>   When shifted round to see the other side;
>   They came again; as when the urn once more
> Is shifted round, the first seen shades return.

The word "return" suggests a circular pattern going round the vase. But this is not what Keats has in mind in the "Ode on a Grecian Urn." His marble urn has two separate scenes. Such an object cannot have been known to him, and the Urn of his Ode must in some sense be an invention of his fancy.

We are fortunate in being able to identify some of the elements from which Keats constructed his imaginary Urn. His friend, Charles Wentworth Dilke, told his grandson, Sir Charles Dilke, that a tracing of a marble urn had been made by Keats. This survives in Rome in the house on the Piazza di Spagna where Keats died. It was made from a book, published in 1804 by F. and P. Piranesi, called *Les Monuments antiques du Musée Napoléon,* with engravings by Thomas Piroli. The engraving which Keats copied is of one side of a marble vase made by the sculptor Sosibios and still to be seen in the Louvre. In the frieze on this vase the central point is an altar which is approached from each side by four figures. The nearest to the altar on the left brings or drags a kid. Behind it are a woman playing the lyre and a man playing the flute. On the right side are an old man, a young man, and two female figures. In general, the scene bears some resemblance to that of the sacrifice in the Ode. The various figures may have suggested to Keats the "pious folk" who come from the little town, and there are undeniably an animal and an

altar. But the resemblances cease at this point. The kid is not a
heifer and is not so much led as dragged; its flanks are dressed
with no garlands; it is dragged not by a priest but by a female
with a bow, presumably a goddess; and the altar is not in any
sense green or even rustic, but an architectural construction of
stone or marble. Though Keats knew this vase and may have derived some ideas from it, it cannot have been his only source, and
his poem is far from being a description of it.

A second vase, also in the Louvre, may have performed a
similar service for Keats' scene of pursuit and revelry. It too is
of marble and of the same type as the vase of Sosibios. Keats may
have seen a picture of it in G. B. Piranesi's book on vases, can-
delabra, and so forth, published in 1778. This vase shows a Dionysiac scene of ten figures, and among them are some relevant
to Keats' Ode — a man playing the flute, a woman with a timbrel,
a nearly naked man laying hold of a woman's dress as he pursues
her. The general temper certainly agrees with Keats' words:

> What men or gods are these? What maidens loth?
> What mad pursuit? What struggle to escape?
> What pipes and timbrels? What wild ecstasy?

The vase also provides sufficient justification for the trees under
which Keats' flute-player stands, in the pattern of a vine which
surmounts the whole carved company. There are, it is true, other
figures of whom Keats says nothing, but the three essential figures
of the flute-player, the lover, and the pursued maiden are present.
If Keats derived some elements of his sacrifice from the Sosibios
vase, he may have derived part of his revelry from this other vase.
In his ideal Urn he kept the two scenes apart both in design and
in spirit, and created an imaginary work of art which goes beyond
the limitations of the marble vases which he knew from the
illustrations of the Piranesis.

If these two neo-Attic marble vases provided Keats with the
first crude material for his imaginary Urn, he treated them with
considerable freedom. He retained certain themes which ap-

pealed to him and discarded the rest. Nor is it perhaps foolish to think that in his selection of themes Keats was guided by his instinct for Hellenic things away from the Greco-Roman world to the art of Athens in the fifth century B.C. If the groups of figures which he imagines have an affinity with the designs of Attic artists of the great age, it is not entirely an accident. Keats, as a famous sonnet shows, was well acquainted with the Elgin marbles, and it is unlikely that in creating an imaginary work of Greek art he did not, consciously or unconsciously, owe something to these relics of "Grecian grandeur." The balance and the harmony of their design are beyond the reach of Sosibios or any other neo-Attic sculptor, and it is tempting to think that Keats, with his unfailing eye for a beautiful object, was inspired by this Phidian art to simplify the scenes of revelry and sacrifice which he knew from the Piranesis' illustrations. Indeed, at one point we can almost see how the process worked. Keats says:

> To what green altar, O mysterious priest,
>> Lead'st thou that heifer lowing at the skies?

On the Sosibios vase there is, as we have seen, no priest, and the sacrificial kid can hardly be said to be led or to be lowing. Keats seems to have fused two impressions into one: the dragged kid of the vase and the lowing oxen led by priests on the southern frieze of the Parthenon. For that these oxen are intended to be lowing is indicated by their upturned heads. Keats may have marked this, and then the alchemy of creative genius transmuted two visual memories into one perfect effect.

The memories which Keats retained of these Greek monuments were gradually refined and changed until they found their final form in the "Ode on a Grecian Urn." Mysterious as the process is by which a poet stores his impressions and slowly matures them, we can in this case discern some of the steps in Keats' progress from his first knowledge of these Greek works of art to his presentation in the Ode of themes drawn from them. In Book

I of *Endymion* there is an elaborate account of a rustic sacrifice conducted by a "venerable priest" and attended by shepherds and country maidens. It is possible that Keats misinterpreted the figure on the right of the altar on the Sosibios vase and thought that what is really Mercury with his wand was a shepherd with his crook. Be this as it may, the scene of sacrifice was already lively in Keats' mind in the spring of 1817. In *Endymion* he gives to it the crowded activity which he found on the Sosibios vase and later excluded from the Ode. He still operates on a wide stage with a large number of characters. Even so, some of the details have already begun to be transformed. For instance, though the altar on the Sosibios vase is unadorned, in *Endymion*

> There stood a marble altar, with a tress
> Of flowers budded newly.   (I, 90–91)

A year later the whole picture is greatly simplified in Keats' mind. In his poetical epistle to J. H. Reynolds, written in March 1818, he meditates on the ugly visions which haunt him and thinks of other more fortunate men who see visions of more charming scenes, among which is a sacrifice which points forward to the fourth stanza of the "Ode on a Grecian Urn":

> The sacrifice goes on; the pontiff knife
> Gleams in the Sun, the milk-white heifer lows,
> The pipes go shrilly, the libation flows.

In the Ode even this has been reduced, and little remains except the lowing heifer, and even that is not said to be milk-white. The knife and the libation have disappeared, and the pipes are transferred to the other scene.

This other scene has also left traces of its history in Keats' work. The frenzied activity and Dionysiac revel can be seen in Book IV of *Endymion*, where the Indian Maid sings of the coming of Bacchus and tells of music and dancing and revelry.

The earnest trumpet spake, and silver thrills
From kissing cymbals made a merry din —
    'Twas Bacchus and his kin!
Like to a moving vintage down they came,
Crown'd with green leaves, and faces all on flame;
All madly dancing through the pleasant valley
    To scare thee, Melancholy!

When Keats wrote the "Ode on a Grecian Urn," he seems to have had at the back of his mind either this passage or its originating experience. For in *Endymion* the revellers are asked:

Why have ye left your bowers desolate,
    Your lutes, and gentler fate?

and in the Ode this idea is expanded and enriched and given a new appeal to the imagination:

And, little town, thy streets for evermore
    Will silent be; and not a soul to tell
        Why thou are desolate, can e'er return.

That such a reminiscence is almost unconscious can be seen from Keats' transference of the idea from a scene of revelry to his new scene of solemn sacrifice. His treatment of it illustrates how certain conceptions were associated in his mind and, after lying untouched in it, emerged together in new relations. Another small point in the Ode shows how Keats advances from his earlier vision to something more austere, and then feels that he has gone too far and retraces part of the way. In the Ode there is no word of Bacchus who plays so lively a part in *Endymion,* and the scene of pursuit has a less defined character. But at one place Keats had second thoughts which suggest a suspicion that he had refined too much. In the manuscript of the first stanza we read

What love? What dance? What struggle to escape?

but in the printed text this has been changed to

What mad pursuit? What struggle to escape?

The change intensifies the impression of revelry and brings the Ode closer again to the song of the Indian Maid.

In the wild scene on his Urn, Keats gives a special prominence to a lover in pursuit of a maiden. The beginnings of this idea may perhaps be found in the second vase of which we have spoken, but the idea gathered force in Keats' mind, and what was originally a man pulling at a woman's dress became for him a man in amorous pursuit. Perhaps this picture was helped by scenes of Bacchic revelry depicted on Greek marbles which Keats saw in the British Museum. But the idea, once formed, matured and developed and took different shapes. In the early poem, "I stood tip-toe," Keats recalls some ancient stories, especially one

> Telling us how fair, trembling Syrinx fled
> Arcadian Pan, with such a fearful dread.
> Poor Nymph, — poor Pan.

Soon afterwards, in "Sleep and Poetry," Keats returns to this idea of pursuit when he muses on what imaginary nymphs can do for him and says:

> Another will entice me, on and on
> Through almond blossoms and rich cinnamon;
> Till in the bosom of a leafy world
> We rest in silence, like two gems upcurl'd
> In the recesses of a pearly shell.

However shy Keats may have been as a lover in actual life, he countered his modesty with dreams of wild pursuit, until in the Ode he pictures his ideal bold lover on the verge of kissing the maiden whom he chases.

The main figures whom Keats imagines on the Urn had been treasured by him from the time when he first made his acquaintance with Greek vases through the publications of the Piranesi.

The "Ode on a Grecian Urn" gives his final selection from this material and organizes his various themes into a single poem. Keats imposes a pattern on the whole which has escaped the notice of most critics and led to false judgements on his achievement. There is a tendency to think that the poem contains a single static idea, and that it does no more than amplify and illustrate this. So Robert Bridges says:

> The thought as enounced in the first stanza is the supremacy of ideal art over Nature, because of its unchanging expression of perfection; and this is true and beautiful; but its amplification in the poem is unprogressive, monotonous, and scatter'd, the attention being call'd to fresh details without result . . . which gives an effect of poverty in spite of the beauty.[7]

In other words, Bridges saw no development in the poem but merely the amplification of a theme stated at the start. We might well complain that this theme is not in fact stated at the start, but even if it were, could we honestly say that there is nothing but amplification? Are all the stanzas concerned with the same idea as the first? And is there really no change of tone, no introduction of new ideas? When we read the poem, we surely have the impression that it does more than amplify a single theme, and, when we look closely at it, we see that this impression is justified.

The "Ode on a Grecian Urn" is built on a neat and recognizable plan in three parts: introduction, main subject, and conclusion. The first stanza gives the introduction, the second, third, and fourth stanzas the main subject, and the fifth the conclusion. The introduction presents the Urn in its mystery and shows what questions it poses to the poet. The main subject consists of the scenes on the Urn, not as a casual observer might notice them, but as Keats sees them with the full force of his imaginative insight into the metaphysical problems which they raise and their hint of another life different from that which we ordinarily know. The conclusion relates the experience gained from the Urn to its special order of reality and answers the questions which the poem has raised. The poem has what Aristotle would call a beginning, a middle, and an end; it asks questions and answers them; it evokes a special state of mind and relates this to ordinary life; it moves from eager curiosity to delighted amazement, exalted rapture, and devout solemnity; it closes on a note akin to revelation and summarizes its message in words of astonishing, paradoxical clarity. This ideal world of the imagination is given an unexpected strength by the comparison made between it and love as Keats actually knows it:

> That leaves a heart high-sorrowful and cloy'd,
>   A burning forehead, and a parching tongue.

The poem has more than a direct line of development; it has its contrasts of height and depth, and the richness which these add to it.

The structure of the "Ode on a Grecian Urn" has a close parallel in that of its contemporary, the "Ode to a Nightingale." The "Ode to a Nightingale," with its eight stanzas, is longer, but has the same kind of plan and development. The first verse provides the introduction, in which the poet, feeling like one numbed or drugged, hears the nightingale singing of summer. No comment is made, and, though no explicit questions are asked, the contrast between the lethargy of the poet and the rapturous song of the bird is itself a question and provokes what follows. In the second to seventh verses, Keats develops the main subject, which is the effect of the nightingale's song on him. He wishes in turn to fade away with the bird, to dissolve and forget his fever and his fret, to cease upon the midnight; and then he rises to a more positive theme. He sees that the bird's song belongs to a timeless order of things, and the climax comes at the end of the seventh stanza with its recognition that song like this is beyond the grasp of death. The eighth stanza brings the conclusion, in which Keats returns to reality and relates his enrapturing experience to it, recognizing that he cannot for long share the ecstasy of the bird's song. He has come back to where he started, but something has happened which makes him unsure of himself, asking whether he is awake or asleep. Yet the implicit questions of the first stanza have been answered. Keats has understood the bird's rapture and entered into it, and he sees more clearly than before the ambiguous nature of his relations to all such experiences. And, just as in the "Ode on a Grecian Urn" Keats deepens the significance of his poem by his contrasts between ideal beauty and actual life, so in the "Ode to a Nightingale" he passes from his contemplation of the bird's unaging happiness to a world in which beauty perishes. In these two poems Keats created a pattern which allowed his poetry to develop the full implications of a subject and yet to keep the clean outlines of a work of art.

At each stage of the "Ode on a Grecian Urn" Keats transmutes into poetry thoughts to which he had given prolonged attention and which are very much his own. The first verse sets out a situation, not indeed directly as in the "Ode to a Nightingale," but more mysteriously and more provokingly. The opening lines are a challenge to our attention:

> Thou still unravish'd bride of quietness,
>   Thou foster-child of silence and slow time.

In calling the Urn an "unravish'd bride of quietness," Keats goes to the heart of the experience which concerns him. In a noisy, changing world here is something beyond sound and beyond change. The note for the poem is set at the start by these daring words. We are brought at once into an order of things remote from our usual lives. The poet asks that we should see the Urn in all the mystery of its unchanging silence. Nor is this all. He chooses his words with careful precision. The Urn is an "unravish'd bride" because it stands in a special, sacred relation to a special kind of existence and keeps this relation immaculate and intact. The Urn is a concrete symbol of some vast reality which can be reached only through a knowledge of individual objects which share and reflect its character.

The Urn is also the "foster-child of silence and slow time." It is not their actual child, because they have not created it. But they have kept and preserved it, and that is why it is called their "foster-child." Keats felt strongly the appeal of the uncalendared past and saw in the Urn a repository of the wisdom of the ages. But he saw more than that. It is not for nothing that he couples silence with slow time. In this line he concentrates a thought which meant much to him and to which he had given fuller expression elsewhere. It concerns what he calls "ethereal things." In a letter to Bailey, written on March 13th, 1818, Keats advances the view that

every mental pursuit takes its reality and worth from the ardour of the pursuer — being in itself a nothing — Ethereal things may at least be thus real, divided under three heads — Things real — things semireal — and no things.[8]

In other words, ethereal things are real because they mean so much to us and because we pursue them so ardently. We may well conclude, though Keats does not say so in this letter, that things which have been pursued and loved through many generations are more than usually "ethereal." And that Keats believed this is clear from a passage in Book III of Endymion, in which, after attacking those people who are unable to see the true splendours of existence, Keats states his own case for them. So far from being unreal, he says in effect, they are remote and sublime realities, sought with effort and attained only by patient devotion:

Are then regalities all gilded masks?
No, there are thronèd seats unscalable
But by a patient wing, a constant spell,
Or by ethereal things that, unconfin'd,
Can make a ladder of the eternal wind,
And poise about in cloudy thunder-tents
To watch the abysm-birth of elements.

The phrase "ethereal things" occurs here as in the letter to Bailey and shows that Keats is still thinking about the same problem. They are, as we now see, not the end but the means to some remoter and sublimer end, to those "thronèd seats" which are despised by many but mean everything to Keats.

The relevance of this passage in *Endymion* to the "Ode on a Grecian Urn" is manifest. Just as in the Ode Keats passes beyond the music and the lovers, who are surely "ethereal things," to something else, so in *Endymion* he sees that through his cult of such things he comes to something else and feels at one with the secret powers of nature. But this passage has more in common with the Ode. For Keats goes on to say something which contains the germ of what was to become the Ode:

> Aye, 'bove the withering of old-lipp'd Fate
> A thousand Powers keep religious state,
> In water, fiery realm, and airy bourne;
> And, silent as a consecrated urn,
> Hold spherey sessions for a season due.

There are, he says, beyond the reach of fate, some things which deserve a religious respect and devotion and belong to the essential elements of the world. These things are "silent as a consecrated urn." They do not speak directly to us, but, like an urn, have a message which we feel to be holy. There are times marked in the natural order of the universe — "spherey sessions" — when these powers keep state, and it is then that we must get into touch with them and see what they have to reveal. That, in rude paraphrase, is the meaning of Keats' lines in Book III of *Endymion*, and they take us to the heart of the "Ode on a Grecian Urn." The Urn is the "foster-child of silence" not merely because it is itself dumb, but because it is related to this mysterious hierarchy of supernatural powers which are hidden until we learn how to enter into their presence. Already at this date Keats had found in the idea of an urn a symbol for something central to his outlook. A little later, in a letter written to his brother George, on

March 19th, 1819, Keats shows that this symbol was still active in his mind. He speaks of his detachment from active interests and says:

Neither Poetry, nor Ambition, nor Love have any alertness of countenance as they pass by me: they seem rather like three figures on a Greek vase — a Man and two women whom no one but myself could distinguish in their disguisement.[9]

The symbol of the urn begins by standing for some remote, sublime reality, and then becomes more definite and more intimate, as Keats uses it to mark a peculiar aspect of his experience.

The first stanza of the Ode sets out the situation with which Keats begins. The Urn is an "ethereal thing" which raises and invites questions. At the start the questions do not look very difficult, but, as Keats develops his theme, we see that they have a special point. He does not wish to know who the figures on the Urn are, but what they are, and what they mean. In the next three stanzas he shows how much there is in these questions and in what relation they stand to his themes of quietness and silence. Silence is emphasized at the start of the second stanza, when Keats challenges our curiosity by a paradox expressed with a simplicity which makes it all the more striking:

Heard melodies are sweet, but those unheard
      Are sweeter; therefore, ye soft pipes, play on;
Not to the sensual ear, but, more endear'd,
      Pipe to the spirit ditties of no tone.

This unheard music, this melody of silence, is what Keats finds in the flute-player on the Urn, and the passage from *Endymion* proves that this is no ingenious trope. The music which we do not hear but only imagine is sweeter than any music actually heard because it is the ideal of what music ought to be, the kind of music which we may conceive in fancy but which will never strike the "sensual ear." In all the arts men reach towards such an ideal and know that, though they cannot ever attain it, it provides a standard and a criterion for what art they have. That is why Keats is within his rights when he develops the idea and says:

> And, happy melodist, unwearied,
>   For ever piping songs for ever new.

The ideal song beyond all existing songs has an eternal freshness because it is not actual song but the essence of song presupposed in any music which we make or hear.

The truth is that in his conception of this unheard music Keats expresses with great force something which lies close to the centre of all truly creative experience. Great as was his physical sensibility and his appreciation of everything that came through his senses, he knew in the very moment of enjoying it that it was not everything and not enough. Anything so vivid and yet so transient must be related to some larger reality which, being permanent and complete, gives a satisfying basis to it. We may legitimately call this reality an ideal world, if by that we mean an order of things which gives substance and significance to the gifts of the senses. And that Keats believed this is clear from the lines quoted from Book III of *Endymion*. His ideal world was not a scheme of abstractions but a source of living powers beyond the senses, and therefore silent, but more real than the most entrancing gifts of the senses through the devotion which it commands and the assurance with which he believes that it endures for ever. Nor is this belief irrational. Great art cannot but suggest something beyond its immediate or even its remoter meanings, an indefinable "other," which is the most important thing it has to give. In our apprehension and enjoyment of this, we almost forget the details of an actual work of art and pass beyond them into a state which may be called silence because it speaks not to the ear but to the spirit. If we feel this in reading poetry, we can imagine how much more keenly Keats felt it in writing. In his inspired moments of composition, he sought to give expression in audible and musical words to that other indefinite and yet more powerful music which makes poetry what it is.

Keats' notion of silence is combined with his notion of time, which indeed receives fuller attention, as if it were even more important; and so perhaps it is. The paradox of all art is that it gives permanence to fleeting moments and fixes them in an unchanging form. With this idea Keats is in part concerned. His ideal Urn embodies it. Preserved and sanctified by time, it keeps its original freshness and appeal. Nor is its permanence cold and inhuman. The work of art has its own life, which is more vivid than the actual life on which Keats touches in the third stanza. The paradox of the Urn, as of all true works of art, is that it transcends time by making a single moment last for ever and so become timeless. Nor is this due simply to the material in which the artist works. The timelessness of his achievement is a true reflection of something known to artists when they work at the highest pitch of inspiration. The three stanzas in which Keats tells of the timeless moments depicted on the Urn arise from his own knowledge of what creation is. In the act of creation, when all faculties are harmoniously at work together, time does not so much stand still as vanish. The artist is not conscious of it because he is caught in an activity so absorbing that it is complete in itself, with no sense of before and after. It is this experience which gives a special power to Keats' stanzas about the figures on the Urn. The pursuit and the sacrifice have a peculiar appeal, as Keats presents them, because they embody this sense of timeless rapture. Bridges was right up to a point when he said that the "Ode on a Grecian Urn" deals with "the supremacy of ideal art over nature, because of its unchanging expression of perfection." But the Ode deals with more than that. It shows the meaning to human beings of the mood in which such an art comes into existence, and takes us beyond the actual work of art to the creative vision which has made it and gives life to it.

The main subject of the "Ode on a Grecian Urn" is the creative ecstasy which the artist perpetuates in a masterpiece.

In the three middle stanzas, Keats shows the full meaning of the hints which he has thrown out at the beginning. He has up to a point answered the questions posed at the end of the first stanza. The "leaf-fring'd legend" which haunts about the shape of the Urn is seen to be something very special and wonderful, and yet ultimately not unfamiliar. But Keats is not content to leave his subject at that. He feels compelled to reach some conclusion, to make explicit what this experience means. Just as in the "Ode to a Nightingale" he closes by showing the relation of the bird's rapture to his own life, so in the "Ode on a Grecian Urn" he tries to express the meaning of this timeless rapture to beings who live in time. This is the purpose of the last stanza. Addressing the Urn, Keats says:

> Thou, silent form, dost tease us out of thought
> As doth eternity.

This does not mean that the question of the timeless raised by the Urn is a philosophical problem beyond Keats' reach. No doubt it was, and he would have been the first to admit it. But he is not thinking of that. He means that works of art like the Urn seduce us from the ordinary life of thought into the extraordinary life of the imagination. We must relate the words of the Ode to those in Keats' epistle to Reynolds in which he rejects philosophy:

> Oh, never will the prize,
> High reason, and the love of good and ill,
> Be my award! Things cannot to the will
> Be settled, but they tease us out of thought.

Here Keats expresses his unwillingness to leave his own special approach to experience through the imagination for something like philosophy, and his refusal is based on the belief that the mystery of things cannot be mastered by an act of will but forces us "out of thought," that is, from ordinary ways of thinking into the approach of the imagination. By thought he means the dis-

cursive, puzzled, analytical activity of the intellect. The words in
the Ode represent a similar view. The Urn belongs to an order of
things which is beyond such thought. It is as remote as the eternity which in its timeless existence it represents. Nor is it only
outside thought. It is also outside the ordinary emotions, and
that is why its story is a "cold pastoral." Though in the picture
of the empty town there is a momentary hint of pathos at its desolation, this is only a hint and is intended to remind us that our
ordinary existence is different from that of the Urn. The desolation is transcended in the absence of any human being to speak
of or to feel it:

> and not a soul to tell
> Why thou art desolate, can e'er return.

In the last resort, art reaches beyond the emotions to something
impersonal and absolute.

In this it would be wrong to detect a note of complaint. Keats
does not resent the fact that the Urn stops him from thinking
or bears no relation to his ordinary existence. On the contrary,
the reality of the timeless world attainable through art is a comfort and a solace not merely to him but to future men and
women:

> When old age shall this generation waste,
>   Thou shalt remain, in midst of other woe
> Than ours, a friend to man.

We have already some inkling of what Keats means. In the perfect enjoyment of scenes like those on the Urn, we have indeed
a sense of security and happiness. But he is not content to leave it
at that. The Urn has its final message, which sums up the meaning of its existence and completes the poem in the last two famous lines. Views on these lines have been various. If for Robert
Bridges they redeem an otherwise not very distinguished work,
for Quiller-Couch they are "an uneducated conclusion," and for

Mr. T. S. Eliot "a serious blemish on a beautiful poem." Apart from these differences of taste, which are after all only differences of taste, there are more serious differences of interpretation. What do the lines mean, and what is their relevance to the rest of the poem?

At the start there is a textual difficulty. In his Oxford text, Mr. Garrod prints the lines in the familiar form:

> Beauty is truth, truth beauty, — that is all
> Ye know on earth, and all ye need to know.

In support of this, the editor can claim not only Keats' own autograph but the transcripts made by his friends, Brown, Woodhouse, and Dilke. The text printed in *Annals of the Fine Arts* in January 1820 is substantially the same, though it makes "That is all" begin a new sentence after a full stop. This is formidable authority, but when the poem appeared in the volume which Keats published in June 1820, there was an important difference. The words "Beauty is truth, truth beauty" are placed in inverted commas, while what follows is not. These differences of text have led to two interpretations. The one, based on the manuscript and the transcripts, assumes that the whole two lines are the message of the Urn; the other assumes that only five words constitute the message, which Keats himself then endorses and approves in very emphatic language. The first view presents no difficulty so far as Keats' opinions, as expressed elsewhere, are concerned; the second is at variance with much that he says about the importance of human activities and relations. If this is his deliberate conclusion, he sets himself up as a more ruthless aesthete than he ever admits in his letters.

Now it is quite clear that the text of the 1820 volume must represent Keats' final choice of how the words should be printed. He would not have added the inverted commas if he had not felt them to be necessary. But it does not follow that this text has been correctly interpreted, nor need we admit that the last words are Keats' independent comment on the message of the Urn. For it is surely clear that in these words it is not Keats but the Urn who speaks. This follows from the use of the word "ye." Keats does not usually address his readers in this way, and it is inconceivable that he should so address them when in the preceding line he has spoken of "other woe than ours." If he had meant to speak for himself, he would have said not "ye" but "we." We may therefore dismiss the view that these last words are Keats' comment on the Urn's message. They are part of that message, and in a sense the Urn's own comment on something more impersonal and universal. They amplify the doctrine that "beauty is truth, truth beauty," which is placed in inverted commas because it is a kind of text or motto or challenge, a piece of doctrine implicit in all art and therefore different from the Urn's own words which follow and emphasize it. The poem, which has been concerned with the Urn, ends with a lesson which all artists have to learn and to which it gives its special commendation.

The meaning of this message is beyond dispute. Mr. Garrod rightly paraphrases it, "there is nothing real but the beautiful and nothing beautiful but the real." Keats uses "truth," as others do, to mean "reality." He then adds, through the Urn, that this is the only knowledge that we possess and that we need no other. It is the Urn that speaks, and it speaks for a unique kind of experience, of which it states the central essence. The words which Keats gives to the Urn are derived from his own meditations on the nature of his art. He knew that this art was not everything, but so far as it concerned him, he was quite consistent about it. Five passages from his letters show how the problem obsessed him and to what conclusions he came:

November 22nd, 1817, to Benjamin Bailey:
I am certain of nothing but of the holiness of the Heart's affections and the truth of Imagination — What the Imagination seizes as Beauty must be truth — whether it existed before or not.

December 21st, 1817, to George and Thomas Keats:
The excellence of every art is its intensity, capable of making all

disagreeables evaporate, from their being in close relationship with Beauty and Truth.

January 30th, 1818, to John Taylor (of *Endymion*):
When I wrote it it was a regular stepping of the Imagination towards a Truth.

May 3rd, 1818, to J. H. Reynolds:
Axioms in philosophy are not axioms until they are proved upon our pulses.

December 1818, to George and Georgiana Keats:
I never can feel certain of any truth but from a clear perception of its Beauty.

These passages were all written before the "Ode on a Grecian Urn" and show how deeply Keats was concerned with the relations of truth and beauty, and how he developed his own theory about them.

This theory may be expressed in something like the following form. Truth is another name for ultimate reality, and is discovered not by the reasoning mind but by the imagination. The imagination has a special insight into the true nature of things, and Keats accepts its discoveries because they agree with his senses, resolve disagreeable discords, and overwhelm him by their intensity. He is convinced that anything so discovered is true in a sense that the conclusions of philosophy are not. Keats calls this reality "beauty" because of its overpowering and all-absorbing effect on him. In fact, he substitutes the discovery of beauty through the imagination for the discovery of facts through the reason, and asserts that it is a more satisfactory and more certain way of piercing to the heart of things, since inspired insight sees more than abstract ratiocination ever can. Keats' concern is with the imagination in a special sense, and he is not far from Coleridge in his view of it. For him it does much more than imagine in the ordinary sense; it is an insight so fine that it sees what is concealed from most men and understands things in their full range and significance and character. The rationale of poetry is that through the imagination it finds something so compelling in its intensity that it is at once both beautiful and real. The theory which Keats puts forward piecemeal in his letters receives its final form in the last lines of the "Ode on a Grecian Urn."

This is not a complete philosophy of life, nor did Keats intend it to be. It is a theory of art, a doctrine intended to explain his own creative experience. He was increasingly conscious that art is not everything, and in his last two years he became more uneasy about the detachment from life which his work imposed on him. In "The Fall of Hyperion" Moneta suggests that the poet is but a "dreaming thing" and must hold a lower place than those who are moved by human suffering. When he wrote the "Ode on a Grecian Urn," Keats had not gone so far as to think that the truth which he sought through the imagination was a dream. It was still a very important truth for him as a poet — but only as a poet. The Ode is his last word on a special activity and a special experience. Within its limits it has its own view of life, and that is what Keats expresses. The belief that "Beauty is truth, truth beauty" is true for the artist while he is concerned with his art. It is no less true that, while he is at work, this is all that he knows for certain and all that he needs to know for the proper pursuit of his special task. Unless he believes this, he is in danger of ruining his art. The "Ode on a Grecian Urn" tells what great art means to those who create it, while they create it, and, so long as this doctrine is not applied beyond its proper confines, it is not only clear but true.

VII

DON JUAN

IN THE history of the English Romantics, Byron has a peculiar place. From a European point of view, he is the chief exponent and most renowned figure of the whole movement, the man who summed up in himself its essential qualities and by his inspiring example imposed them on the civilized world. From the usual English point of view, he is hardly a Romantic at all, but a survival from the eighteenth century and an enemy of much that the true Romantics thought most holy. His European reputation was already great in his lifetime and has not been seriously shaken since. Just as Goethe regarded him as "the greatest genius of the century" and said: "He is not antique and not modern; he is like the present day," so Mazzini said: "He gave a European role to English poetry. He led the genius of England on a pilgrimage through Europe."

This reputation was matched by an influence no less remarkable. There was hardly a country whose leading poets in the thirties and forties of the nineteenth century were not in some sense Byronic, in their rejection of established systems, their aggressive self-assertion, their love of liberty, and their cult of love. When Russian poetry found its first full strength about 1820, Byron was its chief model and its most powerful inspiration. To him Pushkin owed not only the ideas and the form of such poems as *The Prisoner of the Caucasus* and *Poltava*, but intended his *Evgeny Onegin* to be a Russian counterpart of *Don Juan*; and if there was ever a case of nature imitating art, it can be seen in the startling resemblances between Lermontov and the Byronic heroes. From Byron, Lermontov learned to speak of himself as he really was, in his strange contradictions of affection and hatred, of delight and boredom, of sentiment and irony, of love of society and love of solitude. Throughout Europe poets looked to Byron because he had given voice to something which they recognized and prized in themselves. Of course, his fame was all the greater because he was thought to be a victim of English hypocrisy and because he died heroically for the liberation of Greece. But that was fortuitous. What mattered was that he put into poetry something that belonged to many men in his time, and that he was a pioneer of a new outlook and a new art. He set his mark on a whole generation, and his fame rang from one end of Europe to another.

In his own country Byron's reputation has been quite different. In his lifetime he was not admired by his reverend seniors. Wordsworth not only thought his style very slovenly, but regarded him as "a monster . . . a Man of Genius whose heart is perverted." [1] Though Coleridge did not scruple to enlist Byron's support in getting his plays acted, he had no high opinion of his work and thought his later poetry "Satanic." [2] Even Keats, who was much less prejudiced than Wordsworth and Coleridge, dismissed *Don Juan* as "Lord Byron's last flash poem," [3] and was outraged by its description of a storm at sea:

This gives me the most horrid idea of human nature, that a man like Byron should have exhausted all the pleasures of the world so compleatly that there was nothing left for him but to laugh and gloat over the most solemn and heart rending [scenes] of human misery.[4]

Blake was less violent and seems to have felt some tenderness for Byron because he was a rebel and an outcast. That is perhaps why, in 1822, he dedicated *The Ghost of Abel* "To Lord Byron in the Wilderness." Yet he too felt that something was wrong with Byron, that he was an erring, if not a lost, soul, and that he had surrendered to the false lures of naturalism. *The Ghost of Abel* is an answer to Byron's *Cain* and shows how far apart the two poets were in their convictions. In return, Byron felt no regard for the poets who criticized him. He thought Wordsworth a bore, and says so more than once in *Don Juan*. Apart from "Christabel," he had a low opinion of Coleridge's work, and thought the man himself "a shabby fellow." [5] Nor did Shelley's advocacy of Keats persuade Byron to think well of him. Some of Byron's remarks in his letters about Keats are too indecent to be printed, and though he recanted somewhat after Keats' death, his epitaph on him shows no more than a contemptuous pity:

> 'T is strange the mind, that very fiery particle,
> Should let itself be snuffed out by an article.[6]

Of Blake, Byron says nothing, and the probability is that he never heard of him.

In both the European and the English views of Byron there is a mixture of truth and error. Goethe, Mazzini, Pushkin, and others were right to see in Byron the representative of a new age. When the French Revolution broke the equilibrium on which the civilization of the eighteenth century had rested, a new type of man came into existence, and Byron was the supreme example of it in his rejection of established ties, his cult of the self, his love of adventure, and his ironical distrust of his own emotions and beliefs. He was an aristocratic rebel when aristocrats were leaders of new movements and new ideas; in him the poet became a man of action because the creative spirit, long discouraged and constricted, found that words alone were not enough for it and that it must display itself in generous gesture and gallant risk. At the same time, Byron's Continental admirers did not distinguish the false from the true in his work or his personality. They were so fascinated by his early poems that they continued to prize them even when he had begun to compose in a different and more truly creative spirit. The dream-worlds of escape in his early romances answered a dissatisfaction in many men, who accepted as great poetry what was in fact often false or feeble. Until he left England for the second and last time, Byron lacked the experience which alone could make his subjects convincing, and though he dallied with Romantic notions, he did not really believe in them and for that reason was not master of them. Much of Byron's earlier poetry is deficient both in art and in truth. It did indeed open new prospects, and it is extraordinary what the passionate sincerity of a great genius like Pushkin could make of them. But many others were so entranced by Byron's poses that they were content to write a poetry of pose, and it is this, more than anything else, which is so disturbing in much that was written in Latin countries during the Romantic age. The Byronic affectations were ubiquitous, but they are usually neither attractive nor convincing, and even when they are embodied in a man of real talent, they remain an obstacle to our full enjoyment of his work.

Byron's English critics misjudged him in a different way. If Wordsworth and Coleridge were so shocked by his morals that they were blind to the merits of his poetry, the same cannot be said of Keats. Keats condemned Byron because their conceptions of poetry were different, and the chief difference lay in their opposite views of the part to be played by the imagination. In September 1819, Keats wrote to his brother George:

You speak of Lord Byron and me — There is this great difference between us. He describes what he sees — I describe what I imagine. Mine is the hardest task. You see the immense difference.[7]

This is a fair comment, and Keats was not the only man to make it. In dedicating *The Ghost of Abel* to Byron, Blake says:

What doest thou here, Elijah? Can a Poet doubt the Visions of Jehovah? Nature has no Outline, but Imagination has. Nature has no Tune, but Imagination has. Nature has no supernatural and dissolves: Imagination is Eternity.[8]

In Blake's view, Byron's error is to follow nature instead of the imagination. With this Byron would not have quarrelled. For, as he wrote in his first letter on Bowles's *Strictures on Pope*:

It is the fashion of the day to lay great stress upon what they call "imagination" and "invention," the two commonest of qualities: an Irish peasant with a little whisky in his head will imagine and invent more than would furnish forth a modern poem.[9]

On the central article of the Romantic creed, the importance of the imagination, Byron was regarded as a heretic by such good judges as Keats and Blake, and he would not have denied the accusation. It is not surprising that among his contemporaries he was treated as an undesirable alien in the world of English poetry. But he worked by different standards and would not have been troubled by such criticisms. In rejecting the imagination he obeyed a deep conviction, and this rejection inspired his best work and won him a special place among the poets of his time.

In this chorus of disapproval there is one distinguished exception. Shelley liked Byron as a man and admired him as a poet. It is true that the two men were drawn together by circumstances. They belonged to the same social class and had alike come into conflict with it and suffered from it. But there was no call for Shelley to admire Byron's poetry unless he really thought it good, and that, with some reservations, he sincerely did. Shelley met Byron soon after he had left England and begun to discover where his real gifts lay. Even so, Shelley distinguished between the better and the worse poems. When Byron showed him *The Deformed Transformed*, Shelley saw where the faults lay and said so frankly. But when Byron began *Don Juan*, Shelley gave unqualified praise. He saw "the power and the beauty and the wit" of the poem and admired the portraiture of human nature "laid on with the eternal colours of the feelings of humanity." [10] At a time when poets and critics alike poured abuse on *Don Juan* as slovenly and immoral, Shelley saw that it was the great poem which Byron alone could write, and that it was the sincere reflection of his complex nature and alive with human feelings.

Don Juan is Byron's masterpiece because into it he put the whole of his real self and nothing of the false self which he had manufactured for his earlier poems. And just because it is true to experience, the technique is entirely adequate and cannot be blamed for carelessness. In it Byron speaks not in a slack version of the grand manner, but with the rich ebullience of his conversation and his incomparable letters. He uses the whole living language as he himself knew it and spoke it. It is wonderfully natural and unaffected, and the tone of the words responds with perfect ease to Byron's wayward moods. If he derived his form from Pulci's *Morgante Maggiore,* he showed excellent judgement in doing so. For Pulci has something of Byron's careless gaiety and of his ability to temper seriousness with mockery. The *ottava rima* with its easy progress is well adapted to story-telling, and the clinching couplet in each stanza gives excellent opportunities for epigram such as were denied by the Spenserian stanzas of *Childe Harold.* The easy flowing stanzas suit Byron's different effects, and though they lack polished art, they are a perfect vehicle for what he has to say. They are so flexible that in them Byron's carelessness does not matter and indeed becomes a virtue, since it is part of his conversational manner. All kinds of elements pass easily into this style. It is equally suited to lyrical description and scurrilous satire, to sustained narrative and personal outbursts, to stately declamation and slapdash slang. The brilliantly ingenious rhymes keep it fresh and lively, and the sprightly, uninhibited movement of the stanzas is in perfect accord with the darts and flashes of Byron's mind.

In *Don Juan* Byron speaks as freely and as candidly about himself as Wordsworth does in *The Prelude.* Of course, *Don Juan* is cast in the form of objective narrative and deals with imaginary incidents, but what holds it together and provides its amazing vitality is Byron's personality, and the contrast with Wordsworth's self-portrait shows how far apart the two men were. Their differences of taste and of temperament are matched by their differences of outlook on the nature of poetry. When Wordsworth conceived the idea of *The Prelude,* he was entirely absorbed in his Romantic creed and believed that his was a dedicated task which must be fulfilled through communion with nature. In his earlier work Byron had assumed some of the airs appropriate to such a creed without feeling its mystical appeal. But when he wrote *Don Juan,* he wished to do something different. He decided that he must tell the truth in the hope of making men better. He was not surprised that *Don Juan* shocked a large number of people, but he held that he himself was not to blame. As he wrote to Murray:

I maintain that it is the most moral of poems; but if people won't discover the moral, that is their fault, not mine.[11]

His purpose was to expose the hypocrisy and the corruption of the high society which he knew so well, and in his hero to depict

a vicious and unprincipled character, and lead him through those ranks of society, whose high external accomplishments cover and cloak internal and secret vices.[12]

Byron knew his subject from the inside, and, though his moral earnestness may sound impertinent to those who think that they are better men than he, there is no doubt of his sincerity. He wished to expose a disgraceful sham by telling the full truth about it.

In other words, Byron turned from his own kind of Romantic escape to satirical realism. At the outset nothing could be more alien to the serious Romantic spirit, the essence of which was to concentrate on some mysterious corner of existence and to extract the utmost possible from it. In writing *Don Juan,* Byron was no doubt moved by more than one reason. In the first place, he seems to have seen that his early art was not worthy of his real capacity, and he wished to replace it by something which satisfied the artist in him. In the second place, he was outraged by the behaviour of English society, which had first petted and idolized him and then turned malignantly on him. He felt that

such behaviour deserved punishment, and he knew how to in-
flict it. In the third place, he was compounded of so many elements that he had, sooner or later, to find a poetry which should
contain them all. His earlier work reflected something in himself,
especially his discontent and his longing for some dramatic splendour of circumstance and character. But in him the dreamer and
the solitary were countered by the wit and the man of the world,
and these could not be kept permanently out of his work. His
creative spirit moved not on a single, straight line like that of
Wordsworth or Shelley, but by devious and circuitous paths.
But when he wrote *Don Juan,* he had found his direction. He
wished to tell the truth as he saw it with all the paradoxes and
contradictions of his nature. The result is an extremely personal
document in which the whole of Byron is contained. The exag-
gerations and the fantasy of the story only serve to bring into
prominence and set in a clear perspective his individual views
of existence and his conflicting feelings about it.

Byron differs from the authentic Romantics not merely in his
low estimate of the imagination but in the peculiar quality and
power of his wit. Indeed, his wit rises largely from his loss of
belief in the imagination. Once he ceased to believe in the reality
or the relevance of his wilder inventions, he turned on himself
and laughed. All these fine ideas, he seems to say, are rather
ridiculous: we have only to look at them in practice to see what
they mean and how unlike the reality is to the dream. Of course,
such a point of view was a natural product of the high society in
which Byron had lived. The world of the Regency pursued its
pleasures in an atmosphere of malice and mockery, and Byron
had his fair share of both. But there was something else deep in
his nature. His emotions and his intelligence were at war, and
through wit he found some sort of reconciliation between them.
If one side of him was given to wild dreams, another side saw
that these could not be realized, and he resolved the discord with
mockery. Indeed, the conflict was deeper than this. Even his emotions were at war with one another, and he would pass by sudden

leaps from love to hatred and from admiration to contempt. He was a true child of his age in the uncertainty of his temperament and its wayward responses to experience. But since he was extremely intelligent and observant, he did not deceive himself into thinking that all his responses were right. He marked their inconsistencies and treated them with ironical disdain as part of our human imperfection. At the outset *Don Juan* is a criticism of the Romantic outlook because it says that human beings may have beautiful dreams but fail to live up to them.

In embarking on this realistic and satirical task, Byron was careful not to exaggerate on certain matters which concerned him. He saw that though he had largely outlived his wilder notions or seen their limitations in actual life, they still counted for something and could not altogether be rejected. His aim was to put them in a true setting, to show both their strength and their weakness, to assess them at their right worth. So his poem moves, as it were, on two lines. On the one hand he gives an abundance of delightful poetry to some subjects which the Romantics would approve and which still appealed to him. On the other hand he stresses with wit and irony the defects and contradictions and pretences which belong to these subjects. His acid temper works on his material and destroys anything false or pretentious in it, with the result that his Romantic longings are countered by a searching irony and are not allowed to claim too much for themselves. If the special successes of Wordsworth and Shelley were possible because humour never raised its head in the sacred places of their imagination, Byron's success comes from the opposite cause, that through humour he gave a new dimension and a greater truth to his creations. His poetry comes closer to the common man because it is more mixed and more complex than was allowed by his great contemporaries in their austere devotion to ideal worlds.

Byron's dual approach to his subject is reflected in a mannerism which is extremely common in *Don Juan*. He will begin to discourse seriously of a subject and speak nobly and finely about it, only to end with some calculated anticlimax, which makes us

think that after all he does not care very much about what he has
said. We almost feel that he has tricked us by making us respond
to a serious topic, only to say that there is nothing in it. But this
is not a correct analysis of what Byron does. When he treats of
love or nature or liberty in this way, it is not because he has seen
through them or wishes us to think that he has. The moods of
admiration and of mockery exist concurrently in him and are
merged in his outlook. As a poet he feels the one strongly and
writes about it with all his powers, but as a man of the world he
sees that other men may ridicule him, and he forestalls them by
getting in the first laugh. His mockery is partly protective, partly
the expression of a sincere conviction that few things in life are
what they appear to be and that most things, however noble in
some aspects, are ridiculous in others. Byron makes no attempt to
harmonize the two points of view, but is content that life should
be like this. Nor can we say that he is wrong. Laughter is entitled to have its way where it will, and nothing is ultimately the
less serious because in some moods and in some times we make
fun of it.

Byron differed from his Romantic contemporaries in the complex character of his response to experience. In his earlier poetry
he had tried to look at things from almost a single point of view,
but in *Don Juan* he abandoned this and exploited the whole
range of his feelings. Whereas the other Romantics tended to
follow a single principle in their approach to life, Byron followed
his own wayward, changing moods. Just as the Romantics were in
their own way perfectly true to themselves, so was Byron in his,
but his nature was more complicated than theirs and could not
be confined to a single channel. If he lacks their simplicity and
the special power which comes with it, he makes up for this by
the range of his tastes and the wonderful variety of his responses.
Of course, the result is that he misses the peculiar intensity of the
great Romantics, but he makes much of many themes which are
beyond their reach, and gives in *Don Juan* a panorama of contemporary life which is much richer than anything they could

have produced. Those who saw in *Don Juan* the epic of the age were not entirely wrong. It touches many facets of actual life and gives an appropriate poetry to each. Byron had an omnivorous taste for experience and tried most things that came his way. The result is that his great poem provides a vivid and searching commentary on the contemporary scene.

Though Byron abandoned the Romantic view of the imagination and practised a new realistic art, he did not altogether abandon some themes and ideas which meant much to the Romantics. He seems rather to have applied his critical mind to their favourite topics and to have kept only what he thought to be real and true. If he had no sense of a transcendental order behind reality, he did not forsake all the subjects in which his contemporaries looked for it. Rather, he felt that matters like nature and love were sufficient in themselves to inspire poetry, and that he need not look beyond them for something else. Though he had little interest in the work of Wordsworth, Coleridge, and Keats, and had a genuine admiration for Dryden and Pope, he was in fact a child of his time, and his poetical powers were brought into action not by the refined sentiment and economical fancy of the Augustans, but by wild and vaulting ideas which came from the French Revolution. If in some ways he looks like a counter-revolutionary who tried to confine poetry in its old discipline, he is actually closer to Rousseau and Chateaubriand than to Pope and Johnson. The new age had formed in him tastes which he could not abandon and which dictated the course of his life. He was more typical of his time than either Wordsworth or Shelley; for while their outlooks were limited by their private philosophies, Byron absorbed the life around him and expressed what thousands of his contemporaries felt. Indeed, so wide was his understanding that he is a poet not merely of England but of all Europe.

Byron's position with regard to the other Romantics can be seen in his attitude towards nature. He loved it beyond question, and was perhaps happiest when he was alone with it. But his conception of nature lacked the mystery which Wordsworth,

Coleridge, and Keats found in it. Or rather, he found a different mystery, more immediate and more homely, which absorbed his being and engaged his powers without opening doors into some unknown world. In his own way perhaps he had a religion of nature, and we need not disbelieve him when he says:

> My altars are the mountains and the Ocean,
> Earth — air — stars, — all that springs from the great Whole,
> Who hath produced, and will receive the Soul.   (III, CIV, 6–8)

But though Byron might hold such a belief, it was not what inspired his poetry of nature. His genius was set to work not by a sense of immanent divinity but simply by what he saw and by the appeal which it had for him. He marked the appearances of nature with an observing eye, and he was delightfully free of conventional prepossessions about what he ought to look for and like in it. He had been brought up in the English country, and in early manhood he had travelled in Greece. His knowledge of nature was different from Wordsworth's, and in some ways wider. He certainly responded to it in a different way. While Wordsworth sought vision or moral inspiration, Byron took nature as he found it and appreciated much that Wordsworth missed. His poetry of nature is instinctive and immediate, free from theory or ulterior intention. He liked it, and that was enough for him. But because he liked it as much as he did, he differed from his predecessors of the eighteenth century who saw it through a haze of literary associations and preferred it in its sentimental aspects. Byron knew it as it is and wrote abundantly about it.

Byron of course often speaks of nature's more attractive aspects, and it is characteristic of *Don Juan* that some of its best passages of description are taken from Greece and the Aegean, from the land and the sea which Byron loved because in them he had escaped from ties and responsibilities which harassed him. If he wrote some of his finest cantos at Ravenna when he was under the spell of La Guiccioli, his memory turned back to his first voyage in Greece and to the days when, alone with a few friends and the simple Suliotes, whose natural nobility won his admiration, he had not yet tasted of success and failure. Now Greece was again in his mind because of the revolt against the Turks, and before long he was to obey her irresistible summons. In the interval he put into *Don Juan* scenes which come from his first delight in Greek lands, sunlit and solitary and washed by an azure sea. The island to which Juan swims as a castaway is authentically Greek in its roughness and its wildness no less than in its moments of magical calm:

> It was a wild and breaker-beaten coast,
>   With cliffs above, and a broad sandy shore,
> Guarded by shoals and rocks as by an host,
>   With here and there a creek, whose aspect wore
> A better welcome to the tempest-tost;
>   And rarely ceased the haughty billow's roar,
> Save on the dead long summer days, which make
> The outstretched Ocean glitter like a lake.   (II, CLXXVII)

The description is truthful and accurate. This is just what many Greek islands look to the visitor, and Byron shows his sterling sense when he sketches the scene as he himself has known it. There was no need to make more of it, and the straightforward description has its own full poetry. Each detail is given with a sure eye to its significance, and the scene lives not merely for the sight but for the imagination.

Byron of course had more enchanting memories of Greece than this. In no country does the evening come with more unexpected splendours, when the whole landscape changes from colour to colour and the light reflected from the sea gives a limpid purity to the outlines of the mountains and to the inlets of water which pierce them. It is this incomparable beauty which Byron uses as an appropriate setting for his young lovers:

> It was the cooling hour, just when the rounded
>   Red sun sinks down behind the azure hill,
> Which then seems as if the whole earth it bounded,
>   Circling all Nature, hushed, and dim, and still,
> With the far mountain-crescent half surrounded
>   On one side, and the deep sea calm and chill
> Upon the other, and the rosy sky
> With one star sparkling through it like an eye.   (II, CLXXXIII)

The ancient Greek poets were not concerned to praise the beauties of their country with words so precise as these, but Byron, bred in a northern clime where colours are dimmer and outlines less clear, catches the brilliant hues of the Greek evening, when the red sun, the azure hills, and the rosy sky unite to form a perfect harmony. The scene, as he paints it, has a peculiar charm because he writes from loving memory and recalls what this miraculous land once meant to him. He does not look for a soul in nature, but in its company he is entirely absorbed and happy. It is the setting for moments in which his spirit has been at peace and all his attention caught in the delight of visible things. He pays nature more notice than the Greek poets ever did, but he owes something to them in his feeling for it as a background to human life—even more than a background, for nature provides the frame in which we live and shapes our feelings to suit it.

If Byron's greatest love was for Greece, his love for the English landscape was hardly less powerful, and in this too he went his own way and found his own kind of poetry. In Canto XIII he describes a Norman abbey, which is of course Newstead, where he spent his childhood. When he wrote these lines, he had not seen Newstead for eight years, and he was never to see it again. But time and separation have not dimmed his memory; they have rather sharpened and refined it. Byron, exiled in Italy, recalls this characteristically English scene in its tranquil beauty and gracious ease. He catches the charm of an old English country-house in surroundings where nature has been tamed but only to become more truly itself. He, who knew the sunlit splendour of the Aegean, felt also the appeal of quiet waters and liked to recall the lake near his own home:

> Before the mansion lay a lucid Lake,
>   Broad as transparent, deep, and freshly fed
> By a river, which its softened way did take
>   In currents through the calmer water spread
> Around: the wildfowl nestled in the brake
>   And sedges, brooding in their liquid bed:
> The woods sloped downwards to its brink, and stood
> With their green faces fixed upon the flood.   (XIII, LVII)

This is perhaps nature as a country gentleman of the Regency might admire it in his own domain, but it has its own charm and beauty, and Byron's account reflects his typically English pleasure in nature as it works for the comfort of man.

Because he had no gospel of nature and did not seek any special revelation through it, Byron was able to face its cruel and inhuman aspects as most of the Romantics could not. It is true that in "Ruth" Wordsworth suggests that a childhood spent in the violent climate of Georgia may not be entirely beneficent to the character, but he shied away from the painful topic and found in the quiet hills of Cumberland and Westmorland a nature which suited his theories. It is also true that in his last years Keats began to be troubled by the savage side of nature and the system by which life exists by preying on other life, but he did not survive long enough to develop his doubts. With Byron it is different. He sees nature as it is and is not afraid of dwelling on its sinister side. He does so without comment and without complaint, but he knows what he is talking about. For instance, the storm in *Don Juan* stands in marked contrast to the storm in "The Ancient Mariner." While Coleridge catches the alluring magic of a wild moon and dancing stars, Byron dwells on the sullen, brooding atmosphere before the storm comes:

'T was twilight, and the sunless day went down
　　Over the waste of waters; like a veil,
Which, if withdrawn, would but disclose the frown
　　Of one whose hate is masked but to assail.
Thus to their hopeless eyes the night was shown,
　　And grimly darkled o'er the faces pale,
And the dim desolate deep: twelve days had Fear
Been their familiar, and now Death was here.　　(II, XLIX)

The helplessness of man before nature was a subject from which
the Romantics shrank, but Byron saw it and spoke sincerely about
it; and his words come with a sudden fresh breath at a time when
nature was too often seen only in its gentler moods.

Byron's keen eye for the world about him took him beyond
nature to human dwellings and great towns, and he was one of
the first poets to feel the magic of modern London. It had been
the scene of his glittering triumph, and he was well acquainted
with the haunts where society took its pleasures, but it meant
more than that to him. He liked its bustle and its crowds, its lights
and noise and stupendous air of life, its dirt and its magnificence.
His view of London may be contrasted with Wordsworth's.
Wordsworth had his moment of vision, when from Westminster
Bridge he saw the Thames and the giant city in the calm of the
early morning:

　　　　　　　silent, bare,
Ships, towers, domes, theatres, and temples lie
Open unto the fields, and to the sky;
All bright and glittering in the smokeless air.

That shows how even in a great city Wordsworth's genius could
be inspired to its finest rapture, but none the less what inspires
him is not the bustle of the city but its temporary quiet. For a
moment in London he feels as if he were among the silence of his
lonely hills. Byron looks at a similar sight and finds something
quite different:

A mighty mass of brick, and smoke, and shipping,
  Dirty and dusky, but as wide as eye
Could reach, with here and there a sail just skipping
  In sight, then lost amidst the forestry
Of masts; a wilderness of steeples peeping
  On tiptoe through their sea-coal canopy;
A huge, dun Cupola, like a foolscap crown
On a fool's head — and there is London Town!   (X, LXXXII)

Byron sees in London what most men see in it, but with a more
observant and more malicious eye. His is a realistic art of topo-
graphical poetry. Instead of looking for some manifestation of the
ideal in the actual, he is quite content with the actual and says
what he thinks about it.

Byron created what was in effect a new poetry of the visible
world, both in country and in towns, by the variety of his responses to it. Where he began, other poets have continued, until
we are now familiar with a poetry of cities and suburbs as well as
of all kinds of countryside. His triumph was to pass beyond his
early love of pathless woods and lonely shores to more common
and familiar scenes, and to prove that they too have their fascination. His conception of the world in which we live grew from his
delighted observation of it, but this observation was itself shaped
by the new outlook which belonged to his generation and lay
behind all its poetry. Byron differs from the other Romantics in
his interpretation of nature and his lack of interest in any ulterior
significance to be found in it, but he agrees with them in thinking that it is a primary subject of poetry and plays a large part in
human life.

A second Romantic subject to which Byron gave great attention is love. In this he was far more adventurous than Wordsworth and more experienced than Keats. If he had an equal in
the importance which he attached to love, it was Shelley, but
Shelley's view of it was quite different. For Shelley love is a
union of souls, foreordained in some celestial scheme of predesti-
nation, and guided by the powers which move the universe. Byron

saw nothing in such speculations. He lacked Shelley's gift of thinking that every woman with whom he fell in love was an incarnation of heavenly virtues. Nor is it clear that Byron ever fell completely in love with anyone. He needed the support and the society of women; he liked to be admired and petted and comforted by them; he found that with them he could unburden his troubles. But of the several women whom he is thought to have loved, there is hardly one for whom he felt an absorbing and dominating passion. Perhaps the strongest affection which he knew was for his half-sister, Augusta, and for that he had to pay in scandal and calumny, with the result that he came to believe that the noblest devotions are doomed to come to a violent or an ignoble end. His other chief devotion was for La Guiccioli. She awoke his political ambitions and made him a man of action, and there is no doubt of his affection for her. But even in the happy years which he spent with her, he yearned for something else, complete and innocent. He seems indeed to have been haunted by two dreams. One was of some woman older than himself who would give to him the affectionate care of which his stern, strong-minded mother was incapable; the other was of an ideal first love, tender and natural, and not at all like what he had felt for Lady Caroline Lamb. When he dealt with love in *Don Juan*, Byron, despite his realism, could not but describe something which he had never actually known, an ideal condition which he was always seeking but never found.

The love of an older woman for a young man is sketched in Julia's love for Juan. Despite the elements of mockery and farce which enliven the episode, Byron puts into Julia's passion his ideal of what such a thing should be. Her husband means nothing to her, and she pines both to give and to receive affection. In her own way she fights against a passion which she thinks wrong, but Juan is eager for her, and his proposals are more than she can resist. So Byron, in his most engaging manner, sums up her surrender:

A little still she strove, and much repented,
And whispering "I will ne'er consent" — consented.

(I, CXVII, 7–8)

For Juan it is perhaps no more than an exciting experience, the first adventure in an amorous career, but for Julia it is different. She has staked everything on an act which she feels to be wrong and yet desires with all her being, and in the end she fails. What most concerns Byron and draws out his best poetry is the pathos of her failure, the tragic dilemma of a woman who gives her whole nature to something which is not really for her. It is his imaginative sympathy which gives such power to the letter which Julia writes to Juan, and especially to those words in it which record her defeat and her unwilling and imperfect acceptance of it:

> You will proceed in pleasure, and in pride,
>   Beloved and loving many; all is o'er
> For me on earth, except some years to hide
>   My shame and sorrow deep in my heart's core:
> These I could bear, but cannot cast aside
>   The passion which still rages as before, —
> And so farewell — forgive me, love me — No,
> That word is idle now — but let it go.   (I, CXCV)

This is of course a poetry of sentiment, but of genuine and noble sentiment which is none the less fine because it rises not from actual experience but from longing for an ideal. It is not surprising that when, a few years later, Pushkin wrote *Evgeny Onegin* and made his heroine, Tatyana, write a declaration of love to a vain and insensitive man, he should have learned something from Byron's tenderness and understanding.

Byron's other haunting obsession, of an ideal, first love, is presented in the love of Juan and Haidée on a Greek island. Haidée is a child of nature in the sense that she has not been corrupted by society but follows her instincts without questioning their worth or their consequences. She has a noble heart and a noble style, as befit one who is in her own small world an important person. She presents an implicit contrast to the young aristocratic English women who pursued Byron when he was in fashion. She begins by saving Juan from death, and, because she has nursed him, falls in love with him. Such a love comes suddenly and naturally and needs no explanation. Nor has the moralist in Byron anything to say against it, since it is entirely sincere and single-minded. He is content to contrast Haidée's trustful surrender with the false protests of constancy made by more sophisticated young women. This love finds and fulfils itself in natural surroundings which show how natural it too is:

> They were alone, but not alone as they
>   Who shut in chambers think it loneliness;
> The silent Ocean, and the starlight bay,
>   The twilight glow, which momently grew less,
> The voiceless sands, and dropping caves, that lay
>   Around them, made them to each other press,
> As if there were no life beneath the sky
> Save theirs, and that their life could never die.
>
> (II, CLXXXVIII)

This may be a dream, but it is a dream enhanced by authentic emotions and an ideal of what first love ought to be. It may be closer to actual life than Shelley's Platonic visions, but it is more truly Romantic than any love-poetry written by Wordsworth or Keats.

In these two love-affairs, with all their ideal quality, Byron does not forget his critical self. He, who felt the claim of such passions and wrote his finest poetry about them, was well aware that there was another side to the question, and he shows this in more than one way. In the first place, each love leads to disaster. Julia goes to a convent, and Haidée dies of grief. Byron may dream of ideal love and show what a woman may feel for a man, but he knows that the woman will pay for it and that the world will not be indulgent to her. Society, whether in the form of Julia's husband or of Haidée's father, will exact its punishment. Under his cynical exterior, Byron was tender-hearted and chivalrous, and his two ideal love-affairs reveal how well he understood the woman's point of view. In the second place, Byron takes a lower view of men than of women, and seems to think that men are incapable of real constancy and devotion. Juan is certainly much attracted by Julia, and he is truly in love with Haidée. But in both cases, when the end comes, he takes it lightly. After Julia he goes away on his voyage without much thought of her, and after Haidée he uses his natural charms to improve his worldly position. As his career proceeds, he learns to exploit more fully his physical advantages, and Byron describes with a sharp insight his motives when he yields to the demands of the Empress Catherine of Russia:

> He, on the other hand, if not in love,
>   Fell into that no less imperious passion,
> Self-love — which, when some sort of thing above
>   Ourselves, a singer, dancer, much in fashion,
> Or Duchess — Princess — Empress, "deigns to prove"
>   ('T is Pope's phrase) a great longing, though a rash one,
> For one especial person out of many,
> Makes us believe ourselves as good as any.   (IX, LXVIII)

Though Byron felt the claims of ideal love and longed for it, he believed that it is inevitably frustrated by society and spoiled by the corrupt instincts of men. He shows how life blunts a man's finer feelings and obliterates even his memories of the purest love. He tempers his Romantic ideal with realistic considerations, but the result is that the ideal remains as alluring as before.

In his treatment of nature and of love, Byron shows what he gained from the common outlook of his age and what affinities he had with his Romantic contemporaries. But deeper perhaps than his interest in these two subjects was something else which lay at the centre of his being and determined much that was best in him. Byron was representative of his generation in his belief in individual liberty and his hatred of tyranny and constraint, whether exercised by individuals or by societies. He wished at all costs to realize his powers, to be truly and fully himself, not to compromise with convention or to hide behind cant. While Blake wished for an unimpeded freedom in the activity of the imagination, Byron wished for something similar in the familiar world. For him, as for some of his contemporaries, the failure of the French Revolution was a challenge to put its ideals into action, and chief of these was the belief in personal liberty and in the importance of the individual man. More fortunate than Pushkin or Lermontov, who felt the same urgent need but were prevented by circumstances from realizing it, Byron found a way to say what he pleased and to do what he liked. If he sometimes followed mere whims and impulses, if some of his ambitions were no more than affectations, he was not without guiding principles, and his death at Missolonghi shows that he was not an actor but a soldier, a man of affairs, and a master of men. Despite all his self-mockery, he knew that he had a star and that he must follow it, that there was something in himself which must be translated into fact and that he must be true to it. No doubt his conception of liberty was more instinctive than intellectual, and he did not see what difficulties and contradictions it contained. It was an ideal, a driving power, a summons to make the best of certain possibilities in himself. Much more than Wordsworth and Coleridge, who after their first enthusiasm for the French Revolution surrendered to caution and scepticism, more even than Keats, whose love of liberty was hardly developed to its full range, Byron wished to be free and insisted that other men must be free too.

This ideal Byron shared with Shelley, but though he shared Shelley's passion, he did not share his vision of an ideal future; he was content to do his best for the moment by attacking tyrants wherever they existed and pleading the cause of oppressed humanity. Not that he was pessimistic about the future. He could not believe that men would for long tolerate the senseless restrictions to which they were subjected. He wished to stir them to revolt, to make them get rid of their monarchs, and he says frankly:

> For I will teach, if possible, the stones
> To rise against Earth's tyrants. Never let it
>   Be said that we still truckle unto thrones; —
> But ye — our children's children! think how we
> Showed *what things were* before the World was free!
>
> (VIII, cxxxv, 4–8)

Byron was on the side of liberty against the Holy Alliance and the government of George IV. He was not afraid to attack so popular a hero as the Duke of Wellington as the "best of cut-throats"; he covered Brougham with abuse; his treatment of the European monarchs is delightfully contemptuous:

> Shut up the bald-coot bully Alexander!
>   Ship off the Holy Three to Senegal;
> Teach them that "sauce for goose is sauce for gander,"
>   And ask them how *they* like to be in thrall?
>
> (XIV, lxxxiii, 1–4)

At a time when his countrymen were proclaiming their championship and love of liberty, Byron accused them of being its most violent enemies. England, on whom such great hopes were once placed, has now betrayed them:

> How all the nations deem her their worst foe,
>   That worst than *worst of foes,* the once adored
> False friend, who held out Freedom to Mankind,
>   But now would chain them — to the very *mind.*
>
> (X, lxvii, 5–8)

In Byron the ideals of 1789 were still a living force. He saw that the free fulfilment of the human self would be possible only when the powerful obstacles of thrones and courts were removed, and that the cruelest of tyrannies is that which seeks to enslave the mind.

In the great appeals for liberty which ring through *Don Juan,* and in the attacks which Byron makes on its enemies, we can see the fundamental purpose of the poem. Byron set out to tell the truth, but his views were determined by a powerful and positive belief in the worth of individual man. He resembled Blake in his condemnation of senseless cruelty and of the hypocrisy which it breeds for its support. He was appalled by the habits of high society which claimed to do one thing and did another, and hid its vices under good manners and high-sounding principles. It evoked his sharpest irony:

> Oh for a *forty-parson power* to chant
>   Thy praise, Hypocrisy! Oh for a hymn
> Loud as the virtues thou dost loudly vaunt,
>   Not practise! Oh for trump of Cherubim!   (X, xxxiv, 1–4)

He hoped that by telling the truth he would awake the world to the evils which blighted its happiness, and expose its respected social system as a corrupt and corrupting sham. On the positive side, what he liked was the free play of the affections as he depicted it in his ideal love-scenes and in the care-free happiness of his Greek island. Much more than any other poet of the time, he had a keen appreciation of the natural man and thought his ordinary pleasures right and worthy of protection. He might not agree with the moral code of his age and his country, but he had his own values. Above all, he thought that truthfulness is a paramount duty, and that only through it can mankind be liberated from many ugly and degrading bonds.

Though *Don Juan* stands almost alone among poems of the Romantic age, it belongs to it and is in its own way a true product of it. Though Byron rejected the Romantic belief in the imagination, he was true to the Romantic outlook in his devotion to an ideal of man which may have been no more than a dream, but none the less kept his devotion despite the ordeal of facts and his own corroding scepticism. He knew how difficult this ideal was to realize and what powerful obstacles it met in the corruption of society and the contradictions of human nature. He made many discoveries, seldom creditable, about himself and other men, and that is why at times he seems cynical and disillusioned. Disillusioned perhaps he was, in the sense that he had few hopes that all his dreams would come true; but cynical he was not, at least about the matters which lay nearest to his heart. It was not their worth which he questioned, but the possibility of translating them into fact. Of course, he rejected any suggestion that he treated his task seriously, and no one could accuse him of being solemn. But serious he is, not merely when he speaks directly about his convictions, but when he presents them with irony and mockery. He made a bold attempt to put the whole of himself into *Don Juan,* and the result is something quite outside the range of his great contemporaries. The alternations of his moods are matched by the extraordinary range of his subjects. There seems to be almost no topic on which he has not got something interesting or witty or penetrating to say. The story is only half the poem; the other half is a racy commentary on life and manners. *Don Juan* is the record of a remarkable personality, a poet and a man of action, a dreamer and a wit, a great lover and a great hater, a man with many airs of the eighteenth century and yet wholly of the nineteenth, a Whig noble and a revolutionary democrat. The paradoxes of his nature are fully reflected in *Don Juan,* which is itself both a romantic epic and a realistic satire, and it owes the wide range and abundant wealth of its poetry to the fact that Byron had in himself many Romantic longings, but tested them by truth and reality and remained faithful only to those which meant so much to him that he could not live without them.

VIII

EDGAR ALLAN POE

EDGAR ALLAN POE died nearly a hundred years ago,[1] and when we honour his centenary, we shall pay the tribute due to a writer whose work has sufficiently survived the corrosion of time to have a place in the literature of the world. But Poe's centenary has a more special significance than this. For perhaps the most extraordinary thing about him is what has happened to him in the hundred years since his death, the myth which has been created about him, the influence which he has had in many countries of both the Old and the New World, his transfiguration into a symbol of that kind of genius which after a life of misery and frustration wins imperishable fame. With Poe we have to deal less with a man than with a legend, less with an actual performance than with a theory, less with the poetry which he actually wrote than with what he wished to write or might have written. As a writer of prose he has an assured place. What he did for the short story, whether in horror or adventure or detection, is **complete**, and his own, and needs no defence. But with his poetry it is different. It has been judged more variously than that of any other poet whose reputation has survived equally long. At one extreme Poe has been regarded as the most creative and most original writer of the nineteenth century; at the other extreme as a minor figure who may have had interesting ideas but failed to realize them and left no achievement of unquestionable worth. The paradoxical nature of Poe's reputation is an appropriate comment on his work. He deserves both praise and blame, and since he liked to mystify, he cannot, from whatever afterworld he inhabits, complain of what has happened to him.

Of his enormous fame there is no doubt. The history of

French poetry in the nineteenth century bears full witness to it. It is true that Baudelaire, who discovered and in some ways invented Poe, paid more attention to the tales than to the poetry, but for the poetry he had an almost unqualified reverence. It was for him "quelque chose de profond et miroitant comme le rêve, de mystérieux et parfait comme le cristal." [2] To it he paid a homage, by imitating it, which he paid to very few poets. There are echoes of Poe, which Baudelaire gladly admitted, in *Le Flambeau vivant*[3] and *Héautontimorumenos*,[4] and there are others hardly less striking elsewhere. Where Baudelaire led the way, Mallarmé followed, when he translated the poems into his own inimitable prose. For him Poe was "the spiritual prince of the age," the master whose example was an inspiration and whose every poem was a flawless diamond.[5] Mallarmé's sonnet, *Le Tombeau d'Edgar Poe*, written for the unveiling of Poe's monument at Baltimore in 1876, is one of the most magnificent tributes ever paid by one poet to another, and shows the reverence which Mallarmé had for Poe's achievement:

> Tel qu'en lui-même enfin l'éternité le change,
> Le poète suscite avec un glaive nu
> Un siècle épouvanté de n'avoir pas connu
> Que la mort triomphait dans cette voix étrange.

Once Mallarmé had spoken in these terms, his authority carried such weight that Poe's worth was settled beyond question for most French poets. They accepted him as the forerunner and master of most that was best in contemporary poetry.

The cult of Poe which began in France spread far and wide. On one side of the world, it has had a special prominence in Latin America, where its influence can be seen equally in the Uruguayan Julio Herrera y Reissig,[6] the Colombian José Asunción Silva,[7] and the Nicaraguan Rubén Darío.[8] Nor are these minor figures in an unimportant world; they have added something permanent to poetry, and their influence has passed far beyond their own countries. On the other side of the world, Poe has played a part in Russia. When Russian poetry revived so brilliantly at the beginning of this century, the distinguished Symbolist, Konstantin Balmont, translated Poe's complete works and founded for him a reputation which has survived the Revolution and the rejection of the West. Even in 1940 the Soviet poet, Semen Kirsanov, in a volume mainly concerned with such social themes as the new Constitution and the Moscow subway, included a translation of "Annabel Lee." [9] Whatever Anglo-Saxons may say, Poe's reputation is securely founded in countries where English is not spoken.

It is easy to dismiss Poe's European and Latin American fame as an error due to an inability to appreciate English poetry at its proper worth. It is of course true that no foreigners can understand a poet so well as his own countrymen can, and the parallel of Byron may be adduced to show how wrongly English poets may be judged by those who are not fully acquainted with the English language. But few Englishmen will deny that Byron is a considerable poet, who had much of interest to say. But can the same be claimed for Poe? Did he do anything that had not already been done better by Coleridge or Keats? Has he really added to creative experience, except in a small, not very important section of it? Others, again, argue that Poe's reputation is due not to his poetry but to his life, because Baudelaire and Mallarmé believed that a poet must be at war with his age, and found in Poe a supreme example of this. In Poe's struggle with his contemporaries, Mallarmé saw a heroic story and held it much to Poe's credit:

Eux, comme un vil sursaut d'hydre oyant jadis l'ange
Donner un sens plus pur aux mots de la tribu
Proclamèrent très haut le sortilège bu
Dans le flot sans honneur de quelque noir mélange.

There is no doubt that for Baudelaire and Mallarmé Poe's life had a peculiar appeal and confirmed their belief that he was a great poet. But this was no more than an additional assurance for something which they already believed, a confirmatory testimony to his indubitable greatness. Nor is it his life which has made Poe's reputation in Latin America and Russia. Beyond it and any appeal which it may make there is the poetry, and that is what is admired and imitated.

Poe's astonishing reputation is founded both on his theory of poetry and on his practice of it. While the theory excites poets to new ventures, the practice is an encouragement to them, and in any consideration of Poe the two must be taken together. The theory is not difficult, and most of its tenets can be found in *The Poetic Principle,* which Poe delivered as a lecture at Lowell and at Providence in December 1848. It may be supplemented by essays, such as *The Rationale of Verse* and *The Philosophy of Composition,* and by various remarks in reviews and articles. Poe's theories are simple and lucid. However much he liked mystery in poetry and fiction, he did not like it in that kind of prose which is meant to expound and explain.[10] He liked to set out a theory as a self-evident proposition and to draw far-reaching conclusions in what looks like a chain of indisputable arguments. Indeed, his whole manner of argument has a much more French than English air, and it is not surprising that French writers have been impressed by it. If at times he is almost too logical to be entirely persuasive, that is because he is himself so convinced of his theories that he fails to see what difficulties others may find in them.

Poe's theory of poetry is based on a simple proposition. He sees the human self as divided neatly into intellect, conscience, and soul. The first is concerned with truth, the second with duty, and the third with beauty. In poetry the third alone is in question. From this important consequences follow. Since poetry is the product of the soul and a means to the discovery of beauty, it has nothing to do with either truth or morals. In an age when poets liked to instruct and improve, Poe spoke up for beauty. It was this in the first place that won the admiration of Baudelaire and Mallarmé. Appalled by the way in which poets like Victor

Hugo expended their talents on didactic and ethical themes, they longed to create a poetry which should be poetry and nothing else. They defined their goal as the Beautiful and assumed that it excluded anything which merely imparted information or sought to make men better. They may have exaggerated the degree in which didactic and ethical elements should be kept out of poetry, but they were inspired by a passionate desire to make their work do its proper task. Poe indeed was less severe than they, since he admitted that truth and morals "may serve incidentally, in various ways, the general purposes of the work." [11] Nor was Poe so unique a pioneer as the French poets thought. When he stated that poetry is primarily concerned with beauty, Keats had already said something of the kind, and Rossetti was soon to pick up his doctrine and give it a new application. But because Poe said it so emphatically and gave it so unequivocal a form, he deserves the credit which he got from Baudelaire and Mallarmé.

Poe does not stop at this. Since in his scheme poetry is inspired by beauty, and the love of beauty is an activity of the soul, it is important to mark what he means by the soul as distinct from the intellect and the conscience. On this point Poe is no less emphatic. For him the soul is the immortal part of man which survives beyond the present into life after death. In his doctrine the thirst for beauty

belongs to the immortality of Man . . . It is no mere appreciation of the Beauty before us — but a wild effort to reach the Beauty above. Inspired by an ecstatic prescience of the glories beyond the grave, we struggle, by multiform combinations among the things and thoughts of Time, to attain a portion of that Loveliness whose very elements, perhaps, appertain to eternity alone.[12]

Now this is a thorough-going doctrine. On the one hand it has affinities with certain beliefs of the English Romantics. Just as Wordsworth believed that poetry is partly inspired by memories of a celestial existence before birth, or Shelley that it is dictated

by powers from an ideal world, so Poe assumes that it is necessarily connected with what he calls supernal loveliness. But,
though his theory is based on assumptions similar to those of
Wordsworth and Shelley, it leads to different results. For them
the poet is still concerned with the phenomenal world, though he
may see it in the light of an everlasting morning or as a visible
image of eternity; but for Poe the phenomenal world hardly
counts, since the only reality is the supernal, and poetry's task is
to catch glimpses of it. Poe's theory of poetry takes it further from
the earth than either Wordsworth's or Shelley's, and illustrates
how rigid he is in pursuing his views to their full conclusions.

This outlook, as much as his concentration on beauty, drew
the French poets to Poe. Equally for Baudelaire and for Mallarmé
it was some other world that really mattered. This was the home
of Baudelaire's Ideal Beauty, and was symbolized by Mallarmé
in the image of the azure sky. Both believed that their task was to
catch glimpses of this eternal absolute and to express them in a
way which men could understand. They would agree with Poe
that beauty is recognized through "an elevating excitement of the
Soul" [13] and that, when this happens, we ask for nothing more.
Because, like Poe, they believed in supernal beauty, Baudelaire
and Mallarmé were, like him, haunted by it, even to their own
distress and anguish. Baudelaire contrasted his moments of vision
with the impotent and irritated state of "spleen" which was nor-
mal to him, and Mallarmé complained that, because he was unable to express the absolute, he lived in sterility. When they discovered Poe, these poets were right in claiming that he clarified
ideas which already existed in their own minds.[14] He offered a
simple answer to their questions and comforted them in their
assurance that their own troubled search for beauty was rightly
directed to an unseen world.

Poe's theory of poetry agrees with his practice of it and may
be treated as a truthful account of what he thought himself to be
doing. Indeed, since he composed *The Poetic Principle* in the

last year of his life, the theories advanced in it may be taken as his mature views on his own task. He certainly owes much to Coleridge, and indeed most of his ideas are not ultimately his own. What is his own is his selection of ideas and his combination of them into a new and rigorous theory. His *ars poetica* is in its own way the last word on the Romantic outlook. What others had left inchoate and tentative, Poe organized into a consistent dogma. The Romantics sought for another world, but left its outlines and its characters vague; Poe knew what it was and identified it with the world beyond the grave. The Romantics had agreed that poetry was in some sense concerned with beauty; Poe asserted that it was concerned with nothing else, and that this beauty was to be found through the search for supernal reality. The Romantics used the given world as a means of entry into another order of things; Poe thought nothing of this world and tried to concentrate entirely on another known only in hints and suggestions. In Poe the Romantic theory of poetry reached a climax. By reducing it to his own kind of order, he limited the scope of poetry and made it conform to his own narrow ideas.

What his beliefs meant to Poe is clear from his early poetry. Even in youth he was haunted by the idea of another, more splendid world, the thought of which enthralled and exalted him. This idea permeates "Israfel," where Poe has chosen for his symbol an angel from the Koran "whose heart-strings are a lute and who has the sweetest voice of all God's creations." For Poe, Israfel is the ideal singer whom he himself would like to resemble. He contrasts the ecstasy of songs in heaven with the broken and imperfect songs of earth, and surmises that if he were in heaven he could do no more than repeat mere echoes of celestial music:

> Yes, Heaven is thine; but this
>   Is a world of sweets and sours;
>   Our flowers are merely — flowers,
> And the shadow of thy perfect bliss
>   Is the sunshine of ours.

If I could dwell
Where Israfel
  Hath dwelt, and he where I,
He might not sing so wildly well
  A mortal melody,
While a bolder note than this might swell
  From my lyre within the sky.

Poe symbolized his ideal of song in the figure of Israfel. In essence, perhaps, he was not very different from Shelley and Keats, who found their ideals of song in the skylark and the nightingale. But Poe gave a more restricted and more literal meaning to his symbol. For him real song actually exists in heaven, and only in heaven can it be found.

From his notion of ideal song, Poe advances to his view that poetry is necessarily sad. He knows that poetry and music melt into tears, and he argues that on such occasions we weep

through a certain, petulant, impatient sorrow at our inability to grasp *now* wholly, here on earth, at once and forever, those divine and rapturous joys, of which *through* the poem, or *through* the music, we attain to but brief and indeterminate glimpses.[15]

Now this is a new view of poetry, and not everyone will accept it. Poe assumes in the first place that the tears which poetry evokes are a sign of real sadness, and in the second place that this sadness is to be explained by the broken character of human experience and by our longing for a supernal world. Both assumptions are highly questionable, and it is interesting to note that on this point neither Baudelaire nor Mallarmé goes the whole way with Poe. For Baudelaire the principle of beauty is beyond the emotions:

Et jamais je ne pleure et jamais je ne ris,[16]

while for Mallarmé the ideal mocks his efforts by its remoteness and its impersonal character:

De l'éternel azur la sereine ironie.[17]

On this point Poe speaks from his own special experience. The powers which break down a poet's inner barriers and release his creative powers are many and various, but among them grief is certainly one. Like Tasso and Leopardi, Poe found that grief set them to work, and, since it arose from a profound dissatisfaction and a longing for another existence, he assumed that other poets resembled him and that all poetry is written in this way.

Through melancholy Poe found his entrance into another kind of existence and believed that he was close to that other world for which he longed. When he set out to describe the conditions in which his poetical powers began to work, he saw it as a sort of anguish, a troubled state between dreaming and waking, a haunted, dark frame of mind, whose only inhabitants were creatures of fear and dread. When he knew this inner anarchy, Poe found that his powers were liberated and that his desire for another world became more vivid and more insistent. In "Dreamland" he depicts this strange condition and gives his impression of the disorder which prevails in it:

> Bottomless vales and boundless floods,
> And chasms, and caves, and Titan woods,
> With forms that no man can discover
> For the dews that drip all over;
> Mountains toppling evermore
> Into seas without a shore;
> Seas that restlessly aspire,
> Surging, unto skies of fire;
> Lakes that endlessly outspread
> Their lone waters — lone and dead, —
> Their still waters — still and chilly
> With the snows of the lolling lily.

This world lies

> Out of SPACE — out of TIME,

and it is possible that Poe owes his idea of it to Coleridge's Limbo, which is

> not a Place
> Yet name it so; — where Time and weary Space
> Fettered from flight, with night-mare sense of fleeing,
> Strive for their last crepuscular half-being.[18]

But, though both Poe and Coleridge seem to have passed through a similar condition and known the chaos of a state which is neither fact nor vision but something ambiguous and intermediate, Poe differs from Coleridge in the conclusions which he draws from it. For Coleridge, Limbo is a symbol for that wasting inertia in which he spent so much of his life, but for Poe it is the very condition which sets his creative powers to work. To pass from his ordinary life to the vision of a supernal world, he has to traverse this state of destruction; for it alone breaks down the wall of his habits and sets his faculties free.

This condition is dominated by the thought of death. Poe desired death as a release from his troubles and as an entry to another world where all imperfections would be mended. But his hope of it was not confident or joyous, but dark and melancholy. It had for him the dread fascination of the incalculable and the unknown. The mere thought of it excited the melancholy which meant so much to him, and it is not surprising that he viewed it with awe and fear. In "The City in the Sea" he presents the myth of his feelings. He imagines a world of death in which there is no living thing, but a weird, sepulchral magnificence. This is the appeal which death has for him, and he feels to the full the awful enchantment of this absolute not-being:

> Resignedly beneath the sky
> The melancholy waters lie.
> So blend the turrets and shadows there
> That all seem pendulous in air,
> While from a proud tower in the town
> Death looks gigantically down.

This is the reflection of Poe's enthralling anguish, of his conviction that to gain his desires he must be annihilated through grief and suffering. But beyond this anguish is something else, and Poe imagines that this enormous waste will be transformed through a vast catastrophe:

> But lo, a stir is in the air!
> The wave — there is a movement there!
> As if the towers had thrust aside,
> In slightly sinking, the dull tide —
> As if their tops had feebly given
> A void within the filmy Heaven.
> The waves have now a redder glow —
> The hours are breathing faint and low —
> And when, amid no earthly moans,
> Down, down that town shall settle hence,
> Hell, rising from a thousand thrones,
> Shall do it reverence.

From his present misery Poe sought for a deliverance which was no less than a complete destruction of himself and his circumstances, to be followed by a new existence in another world. He assumed that this would come and that life had no meaning except in the anticipation of it. He enlarged the melancholy in which he could best write into a scheme of existence, and gave to it a concrete form in which some universal catastrophe would destroy life as a prelude to its rebirth.

If "Dream-land" and "The City in the Sea" are myths for the state of mind in which Poe composed poetry, such a state needed a direction and a determining impulse towards that supernal world which was the goal of his longing. This he found in love. In his theory, the aspiration for "supernal beauty" is largely manifested in love, and he says:

Love — the true, the divine Eros — the Uranian, as distinguished from the Dionæan Venus — is unquestionably the purest and truest of all poetical themes.[19]

Why Poe thought this is clear enough. He believed that love like that of which he speaks is ultimately for a soul, and that souls exist in a pure state only in heaven. Love on earth is a foretaste of this divine love, but no more. That is why Poe's strange marriage was what it was. When he married Virginia Clemm in 1836, she was only a child, and a child she seems to have remained until her death in 1847. Little is known of her, and she plays a much smaller part in Poe's biography than her eccentric and charming mother. It is wrong to assume that Poe had no real love for her: why else did he marry her, and why was he so broken when she died? Nor is much gained by applying to Poe's marriage the methods of the new psychology and assuming that he married her because he and she were physically and psychologically under-developed. What matters are his conscious thoughts about her, his actual feelings and motives. In fact, Poe seems to have married Virginia just because he held unusual beliefs about love and saw in her not so much a mortal woman as an immortal soul whose full existence would be realized in Paradise, and who in this life gave hints and forecasts of her celestial being. When she died, Poe was, as a man, deeply grieved, but, as a poet, he was fulfilling his destiny. In the depths of his nature he desired not so much a union with a living wife as a union of souls in anticipation of what would come in the celestial world which fascinated and haunted him. When Virginia died, she did what Poe must have foreseen and even in some sense desired; for in it his central beliefs were realized.

That something of this kind is true receives support from the fact that Poe wrote no love-poetry in the ordinary sense of the word, that is, poetry addressed to a living person as a living person. His nearest approach to it is the famous poem "To Helen," which he wrote when he was still a boy, and even this speaks to an ideal rather than a real woman, to a goddess from another world who impresses him with her holiness:

Lo! in yon brilliant window-niche
How statue-like I see thee stand!
The agate lamp within thy hand,
Ah! Psyche, from the regions which
Are Holy Land!

In later years Poe said that this was addressed to his "first purely
ideal love," Helen Scullard, though here she seems to be less a
real being than an ideal. But there is no doubt that Poe attached
importance to the poem and took pains to make his intention
clear. He rewrote his first version, and when he substituted "brilliant window-niche" for "little window-niche," and "The agate
lamp within thy hand" for "The folded scroll within thy hand,"
he stressed the divine radiance which he found in his beloved,
whom he associates with Greece and the Greek word for "soul."
Even in youth Poe's devotion was given to celestial love and was
concerned with another world.

This other world took a clearer and more remarkable shape
as Poe's strange logic drove him to conclude that only through
death can love be fully realized. If poetry rises from our frustrated longing for another world, so love-poetry above all must be
concerned not with living women as we know them here, but
with the spirits of those whom we have known and lost or with
whom we have only a partial and fleeting acquaintance in
dreams. In this Poe indulged the fascination which he felt for
death and his belief that grief is a positive and creative power.
He was no doubt quite sincere when he said that "the death of a
beautiful woman is unquestionably the most poetical topic in the
world." [20] He could imagine no sadder event, and for this reason
it allured him. Through such a topic his powers were set to work,
and in dealing with it he sometimes attained to his own kind of
pathos. In "To One in Paradise" he tells of a woman whom he
has loved and lost and with whose death his life has ceased to
have any meaning; but for this he finds consolations in the
glimpses which he has of her spirit and in the sense that she is
still somehow with him:

For, alas! alas! with me
   The light of Life is o'er!
"No more — no more — no more —"
(Such language holds the solemn sea
   To the sands upon the shore)
"Shall bloom the thunder-blasted tree,
   Or the stricken eagle soar!"

And all my days are trances,
   And all my nightly dreams
Are where thy dark eye glances,
   And where thy footstep gleams —
In what ethereal dances,
   By what eternal streams!

Though Poe has not yet reached his final conclusions about love and death, grief already unveils something of the unknown to him and allows him to look with broken glimpses into it.

"To One in Paradise" is based on dreams, not on fact, but Poe's dreams were soon enough translated into fact when his wife died, and it is difficult not to connect her death with the composition of "Annabel Lee." Poe wrote this at the end of his life, and it surely reflects, however indirectly, his own feelings. The individual events have been transformed into something more in accord with Poe's views of an ideal reality. The dead child-wife is now someone whom he has known from childhood in some mysterious realm which is certainly not Baltimore; and this love, even in this world, was complete and perfect with the completeness and the perfection of childhood's affections. Poe places it in a distant, almost legendary past, and this gives to it a mysterious and supernatural air:

It was many and many a year ago,
   In a kingdom by the sea,
That a maiden there lived whom you may know
   By the name of Annabel Lee;
And this maiden she lived with no other thought
   Than to love and be loved by me.

The story unfolds, and it has little immediate relation to common life. Annabel Lee dies because the seraphs in heaven covet her and send a chilling wind to kill her. The love, which is severed by death, can never be broken, and the poet's soul will always be close to hers, not merely in the memory of her, but in her presence:

> For the moon never beams, without bringing me dreams
>   Of the beautiful Annabel Lee;
> And the stars never rise, but I see the bright eyes
>   Of the beautiful Annabel Lee;
> And so, all the night-tide, I lie down by the side
> Of my darling — my darling — my life and my bride,
>   In the sepulchre there by the sea,
>   In her tomb by the sounding sea.

This poem is far from being a record of fact, but it is a record of day-dream and inspired longing. Poe may well have had such thoughts when his wife died, and this was the way in which he dramatized them, making them more real through the relations which he establishes between her death and the world of his dreams and desires.

In "For Annie" Poe takes his subject another step forward. He may indeed be addressing his dear friend, Annie Richmond, but the experience which he imagines surely owes something to Virginia's death. The subject is nothing less than the awakening after a last illness into the peace of Paradise, where the poet finds at last what love really is. He begins by telling of the sense of infinite relief and deliverance which is his on being rid of life's troubles:

> Thank Heaven! the crisis —
>   The danger is past,
> And the lingering illness
>   Is over at last —
> And the fever called "Living"
>   Is conquered at last.

This illness, which is Poe's name for life, is portrayed in forcible imagery, with a keen eye for illuminating parallels. Poe describes in turn the terrible throbbing, the sickness and pain and nausea, the burning fever, and above all the terrible thirst. Now at last this thirst is assuaged as he drinks

> Of a water that flows,
>   With a lullaby sound,
> From a spring but a very few
>   Feet under ground —
> From a cavern not very far
>   Down under ground.

The soul has found peace, and Poe imagines what this means, as he enjoys the sweet fragrance of flowers and knows that all his struggles are ended and that his heart is bright with his beloved's love for him. In this poem Poe tried to give clearer expression to the vision which sustained him, to his special ideal of a love which is fulfilled only after death. He succeeds at least in conveying both his horror of life as a tormenting disease and the wonderful relief which he feels when it is over.

The experience which Poe put into verse was determined by the harassing circumstances of his life, which turned him away from its depressing squalor to a world of dream. Unlike Coleridge, to whom he owed much, he did not create independent worlds of the imagination, but wrote obliquely about himself and his own destiny. In his devotion to a supernal world, he carried the Romantic desire for a "Beyond" to a new limit. No other Romantic was so thorough as he in the rejection of the phenomenal world, or so literal about the goal of his desires. For him the other world exists only after death, and his poetry is largely directed to it. However much Keats may sigh for "easeful death" or Shelley wish that death may steal on him like sleep, neither of them forgot or hated the visible world or regarded death as a final consummation of their powers. With Poe it is different. His inability to control his life made him long to escape from it, and he imagined a region where all his powers would be free and his love satisfied. For him the ideal which makes sense of the fragmentary and painful actual was not to be found in this life, and he was forced to look for it beyond the grave. In him the man and artist were one. The artist needed harmony and perfection and sought them through art, while the man needed them no less and sought to create a system in which all failures and imperfections would be transcended at the last.

Poe saw that the special character of his outlook demanded a special technique to translate it into poetry. With his usual appearance of logic, he decided that since the subject was mysterious, so must the treatment of it be. He expresses his views in some words which he wrote on Tennyson:

> The *indefinite* is an element in the true ποίησις . . . I *know* that indefinitiveness is an element of the true music — I mean the true musical expression. Give to it any undue decision — imbue it with any determinate tone — and you deprive it, at once, of its ethereal, its ideal, its intrinsic and essential character. You dispel its luxury of dream. You dissolve the atmosphere of the mystic upon which it floats.[21]

What Poe admired in Tennyson, he sought to practise on a larger scale himself. This was his doctrine, and it comes from Coleridge, who says that the soul ought to reserve deep feelings "for objects which their very sublimity renders indefinite no less than their indefiniteness renders them sublime." But Poe again goes beyond his master. The objects which Coleridge classes as "indefinite" and "sublime" are great philosophical ideas such as "form, life, the reason, and the law of conscience, freedom, immortality, God." Coleridge follows Kant in thinking that such issues are beyond the reach of reason, but he assumes that they are not beyond the reach of the imagination. Poe was not interested in such subjects, and his idea of the indefinite and the need for it differs from Coleridge's. He assumes that since his knowledge of the supernal world is indefinite, his presentation of it must be equally so. This is a dangerous assumption, and it led Poe to some curious results.

The method which Poe adopts to secure this end is his own, though others have taken it from him. He sometimes tries to make words appeal entirely or almost entirely through their sound, and in so doing anticipates modern attempts to invent a language of "trans-sense." On the whole, he limits this process to proper names which create an unearthly atmosphere and suggest that we are no longer in the familiar world. A striking example of this is in "Ulalume." Poe sets the scene in a landscape of his own invention to which he gives names appropriate simply because of their sound. It would be useless to ask more about them, and we accept at their sound-value the "dim tarn of Auber," the "misty mid region of Weir," and the volcano "Mount Yaanek." So too we must accept the more adventurous word which is inscribed on a tomb:

> And I said: "What is written, sweet sister,
>   On the door of this legended tomb?"
>   She replied: "Ulalume — Ulalume —
>   'Tis the vault of thy lost Ulalume!"

Ulalume is the name of some dead person, and that is about all we can say. The name is presumably intended to reflect Poe's sense of loss, and it is possible that he meant it to suggest some connection with the Latin word *ululare*. It creates an effect, and perhaps we should ask no more from it.

At times Poe also uses a familiar, intelligible word in a way which almost defies understanding. In "Ulalume" he begins by saying:

> The skies they were ashen and sober;
>   The leaves they were crisped and sere —
>   The leaves they were withering and sere;
>   It was night in the lonesome October
>   Of my most immemorial year.

The setting is clear enough and, for Poe, almost precise; but what does he mean by "most immemorial year"? The meaning of "immemorial" is "old beyond memory," and since this is purely negative, it does not admit degrees of comparison. Of course, it is possible that, in defiance of linguistic usage, Poe is trying to suggest an infinitely remote past. But is it not also possible that he is trying to do something else, to give to "immemorial" a new meaning, which, according to his precepts, is indefinite and amounts to some such significance as "deep in the memory"? [22] Again, we may take the first verse of "To Helen":

> Helen, thy beauty is to me
>   Like those Nicean barks of yore,
> That gently, o'er a perfumed sea,
>   The weary, way-worn wanderer bore
>   To his own native shore.

Here the word in question is "Nicean." What does Poe intend to suggest by it? He is almost certainly speaking of the return of Ulysses to Ithaca, and for some obscure reason says that he was borne not by Phaeacian barks but by Nicean. The ancient world had several places called Nicaea, and, though it is possible by some stretch of scholarship to connect one or the other of them with Ulysses, the results are not convincing. Nor does it seem likely that Poe had some wanderer other than Ulysses in mind; for no known wanderer is connected with Nicaea, nor is the most important place called Nicaea near the sea. Poe seems to have preferred "Nicean" to "Phaeacian" for its sound and the vague echoes which the sound wakes. Perhaps in it he intended a hint of the Greek word νίκη, meaning "victory," and meant to indicate the triumphal character of the hero's return. Or perhaps he simply liked the word, and there is no more to be said about it.

Poe's belief that vagueness is essential to poetry gave to his work its most characteristic quality. No doubt through it he hoped to hypnotize his readers into a trance, and for this reason

he uses words as an incantation. In most poetry there is an element of incantation, and in Romantic poetry there is plenty of it.
But Poe uses it in a special way. For him the associative and
evocative qualities of words are more important than their meaning and act almost independently of it. His words have a meaning, but it is much less emphatic than the echoes which they start
through their sound. Indeed, his words seem sometimes to act
apart from their meaning or to leave it behind. This is true not
merely of some of his proper names but of some passages which
are perfectly intelligible and yet reach beyond statement to a
purely emotional result. Take, for instance, the end of "The
Bells":

> Keeping time, time, time,
> In a sort of Runic rhyme,
>   To the throbbing of the bells —
> Of the bells, bells, bells —
>   To the sobbing of the bells;
> Keeping time, time, time,
>   As he knells, knells, knells,
> In a happy Runic rhyme,
>   To the rolling of the bells —
> Of the bells, bells, bells —
>   To the tolling of the bells,
> Of the bells, bells, bells, bells,
>   Bells, bells, bells —
> To the moaning and the groaning of the bells.

In this there is a single, violent, repeated effect, which obliterates
anything else that the intervening words may say. It is a monotonous clang which so overwhelms us that we cease even to think
of bells ringing. Perhaps Poe intended this and wished to pass
beyond bells to something more mysterious. But even so he hardly
succeeds, since in the end he creates not mystery but stupefaction.

Poe's kind of incantation is different from what, for instance,
Coleridge does at the end of "Kubla Khan." Coleridge is not in-

deed too worried about the intelligible meaning of what he says, but he creates a state of ecstasy in which sight and hearing and consciousness are alike enchanted. This is not what Poe does. Take, for example, "The Raven." Whether we believe or disbelieve Poe's statement that he composed it with "the precision and rigid consequence of a mathematical problem," [23] it is clear that he intended it to be an incantation which conjures up some mysterious dread. In a way it does this, but never in the highest degree. It has moments which, despite their strangeness, leave us perplexed and uncertain how to respond to them. It does not force the intellect to take a full part in the appreciation of it, and for this reason we are in two minds about it. The actual, intelligible story appeals in one way, the musical effect in another. It is quite possible that Poe was aware of this and justified it by his theory that poetry is an activity not of the intellect but of the soul. Yet though this may explain his practice, it fails to take account of the ordinary workings of the consciousness which mingles its feelings with thought and expects to exercise both when it is confronted with a poem.

In his search for mystery, Poe undervalued sense and failed to see that meaning and effect must be united in a single, complete impression. He may indeed have set himself a task which was beyond his powers and perhaps beyond the powers of any man. To catch only the mystery, to speak only of fitful gleams of another world, is indeed a difficult task. Nor, to be fair to Poe, did he think that he had been successful. In his Preface to the Collection of 1845, he says:

Events not to be controlled have prevented me from making, at any time, any serious effort in what, under happier circumstances, would have been the field of my choice.

The story of Poe's life is too familiar to need recapitulation. He was always dogged by poverty and forced by it to tasks which drained his creative energy. Poverty drove him to drink, and drink to poverty, and it is not surprising that he could not give to poetry the concentration which it needs. Indeed, considering what he did in prose, it is remarkable that he wrote as much good poetry as he did. But it is dangerous to explain the failure of a poet's art by his failure in life. Other poets more poverty-stricken and more dissolute than Poe have surpassed him in actual achievement, and we must look elsewhere when we ask why so little of his poetry really succeeds in conveying the mystery which he claimed to find in existence.

Of course, it may simply be the case that Poe lacked a truly creative gift, that his actual ability to write poetry was not equal to the ideal which he set himself. There is certainly some truth in this. Poe has his excellent moments, but he seldom sustains them through a whole poem. But a more powerful cause of his relative failure seems to be that his theory of poetry accentuated certain weaknesses in his natural equipment for it. He lived in dreams and desires and wished to write of them; yet not only was he himself content to keep them vague, but his theory justified him in doing so. The result is that instead of using images which display his themes vividly and concretely, he remains misty and indefinite. Too often his main mood is of an indeterminate, melancholy longing, which may have a transitory charm but is not the stuff from which great poetry is made. Moreover, just as Poe sought an escape from life in drink and deceptions, so in his poetry he pays a heavy price for his lack of grip on reality. His poetry has not enough authentically mature experience to make it really powerful and persuasive. It exploits something which is certainly human and worthy of exploitation, but by some trick of character or fortune Poe seems never to have extracted all that he might have even from his own special field.

Still, Poe is none the less an important figure in the history of the Romantic movement, because he carried to an extreme conclusion certain ideas and aspirations which others pressed less rigorously. The "Beyond," which he sought so eagerly, was undeniably a "Beyond," not something hidden in the known world.

Both in his successes and his failures, in the unquestionable insight of his theories and the ambiguity of some of his practice, he was a thorough Romantic, always in search of another world. The nearest parallel to him is Gérard de Nerval, whose life had a similarly tragic character and who also loved a woman more in dreams than in life. Nerval's great sonnets, it must be admitted, are finer than anything that Poe ever wrote, but they are only a small part of his work, and he never equalled them elsewhere. Romanticism nursed in itself a dangerous disease. By setting its strongest hopes on some supernal order of things, in the end it broke the bonds which kept the poet to earth, and by doing this made poetry itself unnecessary. If all that matters is the final vision, and if this world is an ugly sham, there is no need for the poet to put his experience into words. He can more happily live among dreams and neglect his art. Perhaps Poe did something of the kind. Perhaps he knew some moments which so far transcended words that he kept silent about them. Or perhaps, after all, though he desired such moments with all his being, he never knew them, and his life in the spirit was as frustrated as his life in the flesh. And with that uncertainty we must leave him.

IX

THE HOUSE OF LIFE

WITH THE death of Keats in 1821 and of Shelley in 1822 the main movement of English Romanticism came to an end. It is true that Coleridge had another twelve years to live and Wordsworth another twenty-eight, but, so far as Romantic poetry was concerned, their work was done. Both were still to write good poems, but neither was any longer inspired by the visions which had once made him great. The Romantic genius seemed to have been buried beside the Pyramid of Caius Cestius in the Protestant Cemetery in Rome. The new poetry turned from vast mysteries and intoxicating ideas to delicate sentiment and careful description. A greater sense of security grew as the shocks of the French Revolution and the Napoleonic Wars receded into the past, and the emergence of a new moneyed class, conscious of its worth and its destiny, hushed the eager, searching questions which had troubled rebellious aristocrats like Shelley and Byron. Poetry contracted its ambitions and was content to combine mild instruction with grace and charm. At its worst it produced the pompous platitudes of Martin Tupper, at its best the noble and serious art of Tennyson. Though Tennyson learned much from the Romantics, he was not of their number. The familiar world was good enough for him, and, even when he sought to pierce behind the veil, he did so in a practical way as a man who is puzzled by something which he does not understand, not as an explorer who advances into the unknown because of the mysterious lure which it has for him. If sentiment was the dominant note of early Victorian poetry, it was soon countered to some degree by a realism which made a disturbing appearance in 1840, when Browning published *Sor-*

dello and said farewell to his youthful admiration for Shelley.
Tennyson and Browning became the protagonists of English poetry, and the Romantic generation passed into history.

Such indeed was the general picture, but the Romantic spirit
was not dead and was before long to make a new appearance in
the Pre-Raphaelites. In different ways the two Rossettis, Swinburne, and Morris had drunk deep from the Romantic well and
felt more sympathy for Keats and Coleridge than for the generation which immediately preceded their own. They were not hostile to Tennyson and Browning, but their spiritual needs were
satisfied neither by the grave sentiment of the one nor by the
realism and the didacticism of the other. Unlike these two poets,
they were in revolt against their age and needed a special gospel.
They sought a life richer than contemporary conditions seemed
able to give, and they found it in the construction of imaginary
worlds. If they owed much to a vision of an ideal past, whether in
Italy or Greece or the Middle Ages, their special debt was to great
literature and great painting. They found a selection from human
experience at an exalted level and tried to live up to it. They
believed that by absorbing the spirit of great art they would find
an intenser vision and a less confused approach to the present.
Like Keats, they rebelled against the scientific spirit, and, like
Coleridge, they savoured the lure of the remote and the unfamiliar. In their search for an ideal which should be an extension of experience and at the same time throw light on many
neglected aspects of actual life, they continued in reduced circumstances the work of the great Romantics.

The Pre-Raphaelites were the conscious inheritors of the Romantic outlook, but they adapted it to new needs and, in so doing,
narrowed it. When we turn to them, we feel that we are in a
more circumscribed world and that poetry, to save itself, has had
to make considerable sacrifices. Nor is this due merely to an in-
feriority of talent. It may well be true that none of the Pre-
Raphaelites has the sweep of the great Romantics, but their work
was limited by other factors. First, though they were poets of

revolt, they revolted not against a scheme of society in the hope of replacing it by something better, but against the whole spirit of an urban and industrial world. They were poets of escape not into a bright future but into happy day-dream and exalted fancy. At the very start they admitted defeat, and even Morris, most delightful and most courageous of reformers, was in his poetry an advocate of flight into a world which never existed on earth and was the more attractive for that reason. The Pre-Raphaelites lacked the adventurous curiosity of the Romantics, and the result is a contraction of confidence and energy. Secondly, the different imaginary worlds which they fashioned for their consolation were on the whole built less from an immediate experience of life than from art and literature. They thus lacked the vigour which comes from direct contact with the living scene. They gave their attention to the masterpieces of the past, and this made their work in some degree derivative. They transcended this by the intensity of their devotion and the strength of their personal vision, but their work is none the less narrower than the best work of the Romantics. Thirdly, whereas the Romantics, in their belief in a world beyond the senses, made little attempt to define it exactly or to know precisely its nature, the Pre-Raphaelites tried to find out what it was, to see within what limits its manifestations appeared, and to relate it to some coherent plan. The result was a lack of that cloudy magnificence which permeates the work of the Romantics, and its replacement by something which is perhaps easier and more intelligible but is also less magical and less alluring. Though the Pre-Raphaelites revolted against realism, they were touched by it to the extent that they wished even their wildest longings to be directed to some definable goal.

The most imposing figure of the Pre-Raphaelites was Dante Gabriel Rossetti. In his own circle his position was paramount. He was the master, whose work was an inspiration to others and whose criticisms were gratefully and dutifully accepted. Alike to his sister, Christina, and to his friend, Swinburne, he was the most eminent poet of the time, and he left indelible marks on their work. He meant little to Tennyson or Browning or Arnold, and, though his poetry found admirers from the start, he did not enter into his full renown until after his death. The reasons for this are not far to seek. Rossetti differed from the other great Victorians not merely in his foreign origin but in his uncompromising doctrine of what poetry ought to be. For them the poet had duties to society and must not only delight but instruct and improve; but as William Michael Rossetti said, "in all poetic literature anything of a didactic, hortatory, or expressly ethical quality was alien from my brother's liking." [1] Rossetti was as unusual a figure in England as Baudelaire was in France. Just as Baudelaire set his cult of Ideal Beauty against such eminent figures as Victor Hugo, who too often treated poetry as an instrument of propaganda, so Rossetti concentrated on the beautiful and gave himself to its service. In this he was undoubtedly strengthened by the example of Keats, for whom he had an almost unqualified admiration. He accepted Keats not with reservations as Tennyson and Swinburne did, but with his whole heart as a man who sought beauty and nothing else. This was an imperfect view of Keats, but it was what Rossetti believed, and he justified his own practice by it. Such an ideal was not to the usual Victorian taste, and Rossetti went his own way in pursuit of it. In an age of uncertain technique, he was a rigorous technician and an exacting critic both of his own and of others' work: religious passions left him cold, and such religion as he had was instinctive and intermittent; though he was brought up in an electrically political atmosphere, he never took any interest in politics; and, though he lived through years in which science assumed an ever increasing importance, he followed Blake and Keats in wishing "Confusion to the memory of Newton." [2]

Though Rossetti was inspired by Keats in his devotion to poetry, his actual field of creation lay elsewhere. His ballads owe something to Coleridge, and his more realistic poems to Browning, but the essential quality of his work must be understood in relation to his Italian origins and especially to his love for that poetry which preceded Dante and found its culmination in him. Though modern European poetry came into existence when the love-songs of Provence moved to Sicily in the time of Frederick II, and though what poets then wrote set the lines on which poetry was to move until almost our own time, at its beginning this poetry had a special and indeed startling character. It was inspired and shaped by the ideal of courtly love. In the language of feudal homage, poets sang of their mistresses in an allusive manner which suggested the union of physical love to some divine devotion. This was preëminently a poetry of love, and of a special kind of love, in which a human passion both keeps its earthly strength and is transcended by its attachment to a celestial order. The service of a living lady passes into the service of God and of an ideal world. Rossetti learned of this poetry from his father. He studied it with a scholar's care and translated it with an extraordinary accomplishment. His literary art might owe something to Keats, but its roots were in mediaeval Italy. He was in some sense a troubadour born out of due time, a child of that early Italian world which found in the cult of ideal love a satisfying field for its energies and was not afraid to speak freely about the flesh because somehow it was the visible image of the soul.

Rossetti's cult of beauty may be traced to this Italian poetry. He assumed the existence of an ideal world and sought to find it through beautiful things. He was a kind of Platonist both by nature and by education. In the Italian Middle Ages he found a way of life which he recognized as his own because it answered his innermost needs. And in this sense he was a Romantic, different indeed from his English predecessors in the special concentration of his genius on a limited goal, but like them in his assumption that the ideal world makes sense of the actual and is to be sought through it. Rossetti's pursuit of the ideal was his metaphysics, his gospel, his scheme of life, and his hope of salvation. To it he gave his powerful intellect and his no less powerful senses. He never wavered in his devotion to it, and it was the purity of this devotion, no less than his own commanding gifts, which gave him a predominant place in his own circle. In his life he paid a heavy price for it. His tragic marriage, his troubling and troubled passions, his last years of broken health and haunting hallucinations, all arose directly from his inflexible outlook. For him anything that contributed to the creation of beauty was right, and to this he sacrificed his health, his happiness, and something of what lesser men might call his honour.

In such a career any document which throws light on its determining principles has a special interest, and such Rossetti has left in the hundred and three sonnets of *The House of Life*. The title, drawn from astrology, suggests that these were intended to reveal Rossetti's complete view of life, and, though this is to claim too much, they occupy a special place in his work and provide a centre to which his other poems can be related. *The House of Life* occupied Rossetti at intervals through almost his whole career. The earliest sonnet in it, "Retro me, Sathana," was written in 1847, when he was nineteen years old, and the latest, "True Woman," in 1881, a year before his death. In *The House of Life* Rossetti presented his innermost convictions on almost all matters which really concerned him. The range of themes is not large, but in his devoted cult of beauty Rossetti restricted himself to a comparatively narrow field, and his strength lay less in range than in intensity. What matters is that these sonnets reveal a highly unusual personality in those moments when he abandoned narrative-poetry for communion with himself and spoke of what lay nearest his heart. More even than in his lyrical poems, Rossetti gives in the sonnets his most considered and most intimate conclusions about his life and his life-work.

The House of Life is not, strictly speaking, what Rossetti calls it, a sonnet sequence. It differs not merely from those Elizabethan series of sonnets, by Shakespeare or Drayton or Daniel, in which a kind of story, whether real or fictitious, is presented, but also from the sonnet sequences in which some Victorian poets recorded a crisis in their lives, as did Elizabeth Barrett in *Sonnets*

from the Portuguese, Christina Rossetti in *Later Life,* and Wil-
frid Blunt in *Esther.* Rossetti's sonnets reflect not a crisis but a
lifetime, and through them he tells what his most enthralling
discoveries have been. Although they are based on actual experience, and it may in some cases be possible to trace them to their
source, there is no need to do this, and it is almost an irrelevant
task, since Rossetti transmutes particular occasions into moments
of universal interest and is concerned only with their lasting and
essential appeal. The sonnets are arranged not according to some
chronology, whether real or imaginary, but according to subject;
and the subjects are divided into two main parts, which Rossetti
calls "Youth and Change" and "Change and Fate." The first is
almost entirely concerned with love, the second with a variety of
matters which rise from Rossetti's outlook and the issues which
it forces upon him. *The House of Life* is a unity because it reflects a consistent and closely knit personality and shows its progress along a clearly marked path. It needs no story to hold it
together, and, because it has no story, it is all the more impressive
as a personal record.

Rossetti had clear views on the nature and the function of a
sonnet. For him it is an independent unit which presents as fully
as possible a single exalting experience:

A Sonnet is a moment's monument, —
Memorial from the Soul's eternity
To one dead deathless hour.

So, when he arranges his sonnets in a series, it is not with the
intention of making them mere parts of a whole. Each sonnet is
complete and fulfils its own task. Nor is it concerned with common or trivial subjects. It is reserved for moments of crisis,
whether to celebrate some rapturous moment or to lament some
dark catastrophe. And more than this, inside its unity it has a
twofold function. It concerns the soul, but it must also place the
soul in relation to whatever powers govern it:

A Sonnet is a coin: its face reveals
  The soul, — its converse, to what Power 'tis due: —
Whether for tribute to the august appeals
  Of Life, or dower in Love's high retinue,
It serve; or, 'mid the dark wharf's cavernous breath,
In Charon's palm it pay the toll to Death.

Rossetti believed that a sonnet must do more than unlock the heart: it must treat of those moments when through some intense experience he sees himself in relation to supernal powers and realizes that, before the mysteries of love or life or death, he can best express himself in this special kind of poetry which concentrates on some distilled thought or passion and pours all its strength into a narrow vessel.

Having decided to put his most intimate thoughts into sonnets, Rossetti proceeded to apply with rigour some of his most considered convictions about the composition of poetry. He gave much thought to technique and formulated clear views of it. In the first place, he said that poetry must be "intense." The word, which he may have got from Keats, passed into common currency and provided excellent jokes against the votaries of the Aesthetic Movement in the eighties and nineties, but for Rossetti it had a real meaning. It meant a full concentration on every theme, and implied that a rigorous discrimination must govern the composition of a poem. He developed his thesis when he said:

It seems to me that all poetry, to be really enduring, is bound to be amusing . . . as any other class of literature; and I do not think that enough amusement to keep it alive can ever be got out of incidents not amounting to events.[3]

By "amusing" Rossetti means "lively" — the positive quality which redeems from dullness and triviality. In his view a poet should choose not minor, unimportant incidents, but events which are in themselves attractive or exciting. Rossetti applied this doctrine in *The House of Life*. Its subjects are the perennial subjects of poetry, the high moments when a man feels that his whole being is engaged by some enthralling occurrence. Such matters must be treated "intensely," that is, with a full awareness of their worth and a desire to make every word contribute fully to the total result. Such an ambition rules out on the one side the spacious ease of Tennyson, with its tendency to make much of incidents which are in themselves trivial, and on the other side the crowded, tumultuous sweep of Browning, with his lack of care for individual words and his many lapses from a truly poetical mood. But Rossetti gained other advantages than these. In his concern with ideal beauty, he acted in almost a religious spirit, to which his special kind of intensity was well suited. It reflected the special quality and strength of his feelings as he looked at visible things and saw in them a manifestation of the ideal.

This conception of poetry explains some marked characteristics of Rossetti's style in *The House of Life*. He was a slow worker, who envied Swinburne's gift of rapid composition and said of himself:

I lie on the couch, the racked and tortured medium, never permitted an instant's surcease of agony until the thing on hand is finished.[4]

Even when "the thing on hand" was finished, Rossetti did not leave it alone, but was continually turning back to it and changing it. This method of writing emphasized what Rossetti believed: that a poem must be charged with as much meaning as possible. He would use dictionaries of rhymes and of synonyms to get the words which he wanted, and of course the result is elaborate and self-conscious. At first sight his sonnets may seem rather too burdened with meaning, too stiff, and too slow in their movement. Part of this effect comes from their vocabulary, to which Rossetti's taste for resounding words of Latin origin gives a more than Miltonic weight. Yet these words are necessary for the majesty at which he aims and are part of his protest against the artificial simplicity of some Victorian poetry. Nor are his Latin words usually pompous or alien. He combines them with short words of Anglo-Saxon breed in such lines as

Blazed the momentous memorable fire

or

As the cloud-foaming firmamental blue,

and the result is both English and his own. Rossetti needed an unusual vocabulary because his subject itself was highly unusual. In approaching matters remote from the common world, he had to stress their almost hieratic character. No doubt this manner was largely natural to him, but he enhanced it through his deliberate, slow art and emphasized its strangeness. He had something uncommon to say, and for him this was the right way to say it.

The same elaboration can be seen in the way in which Rossetti fashions a sentence. His space is limited to the fourteen lines of a sonnet, and into this he puts as much as he can. To keep his architectural structure, he will combine several themes into a single sentence. The result is that he is often difficult to understand at a first reading, and that, even when we understand him, he seems to be trying to do too much. This manner has a marmoreal, Latin quality, reminiscent in some ways of Horace's Odes. It might well be argued that a language which has so few inflexions as English should not be modelled on an inflected language like Latin, and perhaps in the last resort Rossetti tried to do too much with his sentences. Yet we can see why he composed as he did. Since a sonnet is "a moment's monument," it must present as much as possible of such a moment, and present it in a monumental form. The various elements of an experience must be fused into a single whole, and, if this demands some excess of syntax, it cannot be helped. The result at its best is certainly grave and serious and rich in sound and meaning, and this is what Rossetti thought poetry ought to be.

In the second place, Rossetti thought that poetry must be pictorial and explained what he meant:

Picture and poem must bear the same relation to each other as beauty in man and woman; the point of meeting where the two are most identical is the supreme perfection.[5]

If for painting this means that the subject of a picture must have a literary or poetical appeal, for poetry it means that a poem must have an appeal to the eye as well as to the ear and the understanding. For Rossetti poetical experience is complete only when it is presented through images which convey pictorially what is beyond the power of abstract words to convey in its full nature. No doubt he thought this because he was a painter and because his imaginative vision passed readily into concrete, pictorial shapes. He wished to do in poetry what he did in painting, to achieve through the medium of words an effect comparable to what he achieved through line and colour. This is of course quite different from making poetry imitate painting by an objective description of visible objects. Rossetti was no Parnassian. He sought in poetry the same end as in painting, but he knew that the two arts have different methods and materials. In both he hinted at concealed beauties, and in poetry he used visual effects to make them more vivid. Through images he transforms thoughts and feelings into solid shapes. For instance, in "The Hill Summit" he tells how towards evening he climbs a hill, and this careful account of what looks like an actual occasion has a symbolical purpose. The arrival at the hill-top is his own arrival at middle age. He keeps his symbols clear and consistent and creates by visual means the atmosphere of such a situation with its imaginative appeal to him:

And now that I have climbed and won this height,
    I must tread downward through the sloping shade
And travel the bewildered tracks till night.

> Yet for this hour I still may here be stayed
> And see the gold air and the silver fade
> And the last bird fly into the last light.

This is how Rossetti, at a turning-point of his life, pauses while he looks back to the past and forward to the future. The situation needs no comment from him, since it is complete in itself and belongs to common experience.

Unlike much of Rossetti's work, the sonnets of *The House of Life* deal with events which take place largely in the mind. He might of course have conveyed their character by describing their external symptoms, and at times he does so. But to limit himself to such a method would be to leave unsaid much that means a good deal to him. Indeed, though Rossetti introduces natural scenes, it is usually as a prelude to something else. He sets his figures in their visible surroundings, and then advances from the sight of them to their significance. Thus he begins "Youth's Spring-Tribute":

> On this sweet bank your head thrice sweet and dear
>   I lay, and spread your hair on either side,
>   And see the newborn woodflowers bashful-eyed
> Look through the golden tresses here and there.

This is more than a background; it prepares the way for a situation in which the poet feels the spring both in nature and in himself and hears a summons to love. The physical setting is transcended as it becomes the symbol for a spiritual condition. So too in "Silent Noon" Rossetti begins by describing himself and his beloved at noon in the silence of the king-cups and the cow-parsley. But this external situation is the visible image of the flawless peace which he and his beloved feel:

> Deep in the sun-searched growths the dragon-fly
> Hangs like a blue thread loosened from the sky: —
>   So this winged hour is dropt to us from above.

> Oh! clasp we to our hearts, for deathless dower,
> This close-companioned inarticulate hour
>   When twofold silence was the song of love.

In the visible scene Rossetti sees hints of the spiritual state which is born from it and is so much a part of it that, when he seems to do no more than describe, he is also speaking in symbols.

Rossetti used this technique for his cult of the beautiful. Like the great Romantics, he was glad to lose himself in some ulterior scheme of things, to penetrate beyond the familiar world to secrets and mysteries, to find that even the most casual phenomena hold the key to unknown places of the spirit. Some sight might so captivate his senses and his intelligence, so excite and exalt him, that he was forced out of his habitual ways of thought into flights of imagination and moments of clairvoyant vision. When he defined the twofold task of the poet, he knew that his creative duty was to present both the immediate experience which engaged him and the remoter mystery which lurked in it. In responding to such calls his whole being was transformed. This was the most enthralling thing that he knew, and in "Soul's Beauty" he spoke of it with religious reverence:

> Under the arch of Life, where love and death,
>   Terror and mystery, guard her shrine, I saw
>   Beauty enthroned; and though her gaze struck awe,
> I drew it in as simply as a breath.

He believed that he was chosen by nature to absorb the influences of beautiful things, but he found them in the actual world. He did not share Baudelaire's conception of a remote ideal with its hatred of movement and its detachment both from laughter and from tears. But like Baudelaire, he knew how wayward and unpredictable the appearances of beauty are. It may be a single law which binds sea and sky and woman, but it is unaccountable in its comings and goings, as it lures men after it and exacts a life-long service from them:

This is that Lady Beauty, in whose praise
　Thy voice and hand shake still, — long known to thee
　By flying hair and fluttering hem, — the beat
　Following her daily of thy heart and feet,
How passionately and irretrievably,
In what fond flight, how many ways and days!

Though Rossetti moves from one beautiful sight to another and is enslaved by each in turn, he believes that behind them all is the same celestial power, which irresistibly draws him and gives a direction and a pattern to his existence.

The pursuit of beauty was Rossetti's predominant passion and provides the main theme of *The House of Life*. The subject develops and expands and opens new prospects, but it remains his constant concern. It is inevitably connected with love. Rossetti's Southern blood freed him from most Victorian and English restraints, and his inevitable response to beautiful sights made him a ready victim to the beauty of women. In his first poem, "Love Enthroned," he speaks of the appeal which hope, fame, youth, and life make to him, but he goes on to say that love is more important than any of them:

Love's throne was not with these; but far above
　All passionate wind of welcome and farewell
He sat in breathless bowers they dream not of;
　Though Truth foreknow Love's heart, and Hope foretell,
　And Fame be for Love's sake desirable,
And Youth be dear, and Life be sweet to Love.

For Rossetti love has a paramount position because it brings him into contact with beauty in the most direct and most absorbing way. In his outlook we naturally expect to find the influence of Dante, and there are certainly traces of it. Just as Dante in the *Vita Nuova* makes love a principle of life and goodness, so does Rossetti, though of course his conception of goodness is not at all like Dante's. But here the resemblance ends. While Dante sees in love a divine power which brings man nearer to God, Rossetti is content that it should bring him nearer to beauty. He may be religious in his devotion to an ideal and in his sense of another, superior order of being, but he is not Christian like Dante. Perhaps he has more in common with Dante's predecessors, who were franker about the bodily claims of love and denied that it could or should be merely ideal. Rossetti is a Platonist in so far as he believes that love wakes the soul to enchanting visions and stirring enterprises, but he has nothing of the true Platonist's contempt for the flesh. Behind him lay centuries of Mediterranean life in which love, exalted to a very special cult, had been victorious over attempts to reduce it to an ethical discipline or to confine it to sanctified wedlock. To Rossetti love was a necessity both of the body and of the soul, and it satisfied the soul largely because it satisfied the body. Through it all his faculties were set to work, and he lived in that exalted awareness of the beautiful which was the spring of his creative being.

Many English poets have sung of love and have had new things to say of it. At one extreme are those, like Donne, who are not shy of speaking of its physical aspects, and find in it something alluring and fierce and exciting. Such poets do not attempt to glorify it or to claim that it belongs to anything but the body. At the other extreme are those like Shelley for whom love is the quintessence of ethereal flame, a union of souls in some unearthly sphere of harmony. But few have resembled Rossetti in his fusion of both elements and in his ability to make the best of both worlds, of the flesh and the spirit. If he was denounced by George Buchanan for his fleshliness, others have found him deplorably idealistic and remote from actuality. Both counts are unfair. Though Rossetti often describes physical beauty and its effect on him, though he is sometimes startlingly candid, he is never coarse. He redeems and transforms bodily passions by his sense of a spiritual world to which he penetrates through them, and by the exalted mood which is always his even when he is enraptured by his mistress's hair or eyes or body. Conversely, he never loses himself, as Shelley does, in an atmosphere so rarefied that it seems to have no relation to any familiar world. Rossetti knew that there is one beauty of the flesh and another beauty of the spirit, but he believed that in the end both are united in a single harmony and that each fulfils and glorifies the other. If he sought for the unseen beauty which lies in visible things, he knew that such glimpses of it as are permitted to men are to be found in this earth through the flesh which is the garment of the soul.

Rossetti's outlook gives a special quality to his poetry of love. It is never wild or ecstatic, and though it beats with powerful emotions, it keeps them in control and does not allow them to upset the prevailing balance. In his approach to love Rossetti is as grave as any of his early Italians, and his gravity is uniformly sustained. In his poetry there are always evidences of that "fundamental brainwork" which he claimed to be necessary for poetry.[6] His is a highly premeditated art, because he was able to exploit creative impulses only after a considerable struggle with himself and his emotions. He had first to extract all that he could from them, put them in order and see them in their right perspective, then relate them to his ideal of beauty and interpret their particular manifestations through some wider idea or more comprehensive vision. With him even physical passion is disciplined to this end, and Rossetti's poetry of it, outspoken as it often is, is always redeemed by the conviction that passion in itself is not enough but must be treated as a means to discover something beyond it.

The result is that even in those poems which most shocked Rossetti's contemporaries, the poetry passes beyond physical appetite to something exalting. As Rossetti meditated on his experience and related it to his own kind of metaphysics, he gave to it a new character and new depths. Take, for instance, "Nuptial Sleep," which Rossetti omitted from certain editions of *The House of Life* because some readers found in it "an unpleasant excess of realism."[7] The octet presents the actual situation with Rossetti's usual truthfulness, but what counts is the prevailing mood, and this is certainly much more than physical satiety. Even so, it is only an introduction to what follows, and should not be treated as if it contained the whole substance of the poem. In the sestet Rossetti passes to something else, to the sense of wonder and restored life which the situation brings, and in the magnificent image in which he portrays this, he conveys its essential mystery, its hints of a half-revealed world beyond the present occasion:

> Sleep sank them lower than the tide of dreams,
>   And their dreams watched them sink, and slid away.
> Slowly their souls swam up again, through gleams
>   Of watered light and dull drowned waifs of day;
> Till from some wonder of new woods and streams
>   He woke, and wondered more: for there she lay.

The search for beauty, which began in physical sensations, has passed to something else which illuminates them and gives them a new character.

The truth is that, when Rossetti fell in love, he felt himself in the presence of something so wonderful that he could not understand it or feel anything but awe before it. For him the women whom he loved were not so much human beings as visible manifestations of eternal beauty, embodiments of spiritual perfection, starry creatures of grace and tenderness. He found it almost impossible to believe that he, who was none of these things, could be so inexplicably privileged. It was as if the secrets of the universe were suddenly revealed to him in a flashing splendour and he was allowed to consort with beings from a celestial world. Before such a revelation he felt his inability to grasp all that was shown to him, and he saw how much more it meant than he could say:

> Not I myself know all my love for thee:
>   How should I reach so far, who cannot weigh
>   To-morrow's dower by gage of yesterday?

Shall birth and death, and all dark names that be
As doors and windows bared to some loud sea,
  Lash deaf mine ears and blind my face with spray;
  And shall my sense pierce love, — the last relay
And ultimate outpost of eternity?

With an idealism entirely natural and sincere, Rossetti saw in his beloved not merely her visible self but great impersonal powers which move the world. He believed that his particular love was an individual manifestation of something sublime and eternal and universal. This vision he saw not as a philosopher but as a poet, and he gave his powers to showing what enchantment it put on him:

Sometimes thou seem'st not as thyself alone,
  But as the meaning of all things that are;
  A breathless wonder, shadowing forth afar
Some heavenly solstice hushed and halcyon;
Whose unstirred lips are music's visible tone;
  Whose eyes the sun-gate of the soul unbar,
  Being of its furthest fires oracular; —
The evident heart of all life sown and mown.

In moments like this Rossetti felt that he had pierced beyond the visible to the invisible and had begun to fathom its secrets.

Through love Rossetti found the ideal beauty which gave direction to his life's work. The story of his actual career has its painful and humiliating chapters, but it has little relevance to the interpretation of his poetry. In this we see him at his best, and most truly himself; for it presents all that he took most seriously. His poetry moves in a world not of fact but of imagination. Through the chequered events of his life he found something permanent and satisfying. But absorbing and exalting as his scheme was, it could not always be maintained at its highest level, and even in his most glorious moments Rossetti felt its insecurity and feared for its collapse. He was fully aware of the gulf be-

tween the ideal and the actual, between the high rapture when
he found beauty and the black, bleak moments when he was
alone with himself and empty and afraid:

> What of the heart without her? Nay, poor heart,
>   Of thee what word remains ere speech be still?
>   A wayfarer by barren ways and chill,
> Steep ways and weary, without her thou art,
> Where the long cloud, the long wood's counterpart,
>   Sheds double darkness up the labouring hill.

Even when he was most in love, Rossetti might fear that it could
not last and that he would before long be robbed of everything
that mattered most to him. For him the loss of love was much
more than a personal sorrow; it meant that he was cut off from
the main aim of his existence and from the vision which sustained him. It is not surprising that, when he thought of this,
he was assailed by something close to despair and turned his
thoughts to death:

> O love, my love! if I no more should see
> Thyself, nor on the earth the shadow of thee,
>   Nor image of thine eyes in any spring, —
> How then should sound upon Life's darkening slope,
> The ground-whirl of the perished leaves of Hope,
>   The wind of Death's imperishable wing?

Rossetti's ideal beauty was a fugitive and inconstant power, and
he knew that at times it would abandon him and leave him alone
with his fears.

This uncertainty was the flaw in Rossetti's scheme of things.
Beauty was his goal, and love the means by which he found it,
but he had no assurance that love would always be his and that
he would not suffer from defeat or frustration or some failure in
himself to give all that he could or should. He might of course
still find solace and inspiration in beautiful things and be moved

by them to write poetry. But this was a second-best course. Physical nature and dramatic events meant much to him and provided him with excellent material for his art, but they touched only the fringes of his creative self and not its centre. His most characteristic and most authentic art was inspired by love, and he could not be sure that it would always be his. Of course, all poets are in a high degree dependent on the whims of inspiration, but with Rossetti the problem was more serious. Love gave him not only inspiration but his whole philosophy, since through it he found beauty. It was only natural that at times he should question his system of life and doubt if he had chosen the right way. At the outset of his career he saw the problem and shaped it into the three sonnets of "The Choice." With impartial justice he speaks in turn with the voices of the voluptuary, the religious ascetic, and the enquiring thinker. He comes to no explicit conclusion and makes no declared choice between the three lives. Each case is treated with an imaginative insight into its claims. The first catches the glamour of love and wine, the second the appeal of a life dedicated to self-denial in the hope of celestial reward, the third the driving optimism of thought which is never satisfied but always looks for more horizons beyond the known. There was something of each element in Rossetti. He knew the absorbing lure of women and wine; he had his moments of dark humiliation, when the world and its glories seemed to be nothing; he knew the restless ambitions of the creative mind. Ideally, perhaps, all three might be included and transcended in the cult of the beautiful, but in practice this was not possible, and it is not surprising that Rossetti wondered which course he ought to pursue. In effect he rejects the first and the second and gives his approval to the third. He puts it last, and with it alone he ends on a note of confident effort:

> Nay, come up hither. From this wave-washed mound
>   Unto the furthest flood-brim look with me;
> Then reach on with thy thought till it be drown'd.

Miles and miles distant though the last line be,
And though thy soul sail leagues and leagues beyond, —
   Still, leagues beyond those leagues, there is more sea.

No doubt a courageous hope of this kind sustained Rossetti through many hours of defeat, but he did not always hold to it, and there were times when it was of little help to him.

In shaping his life so deliberately to an end which suited many elements in his nature, Rossetti did not take full account of other elements which were discordant and intractable. For all his neglect of conventions, he was not able to rid himself of a very human sense of guilt. Artist and aesthete as he was, he was not beyond considerations of good and evil. Of course, he never seriously doubted that the pursuit of beauty was good, but he did doubt whether he had always been as eager and as energetic in it as he might have been. He, who knew so well the glory and the glitter of life, knew also at times its other side and was deeply distressed by his own shortcomings. In "The Sun's Shame" he speaks of the discords and shams and failures of the world, of power and success given to the corrupt or the feeble, of love unrequited and lives ruined by poverty, but, though he is indignant against these flaws and faults, he knows that he himself is in no way superior to those whom he condemns, and ends with a confession of his own inadequacy:

   Beholding these things, I behold no less
   The blushing morn and blushing eve confess
   The shame that loads the intolerable day.

Rossetti was perfectly honest with himself and saw that in an imperfect world he too had his share of imperfections.

The most persistent and most painful remorse which assailed Rossetti was that he had not given all that he might have to his chosen work. He was so purely an artist that in the last resort devotion to art was his standard of behaviour, and he judged himself by it. Lost opportunities and failures due to sloth or cowardice haunted him as they haunt other men and brought sharp pangs of regret and repentance:

> Look in my face; my name is Might-have-been;
>   I am also called No-More, Too-Late, Farewell.

He knew that there is no final protection against such feelings and that, though he might for the moment find peace, it would be only for the moment, and the cruel presences would again harry him. He brooded over them and asked what they meant. The religious faith of his childhood came back to him and intensified his sense of guilt, as he wondered how his failures would be judged in the afterworld when they would be seen in their naked reality. He felt that he, who had possessed remarkable gifts, had so neglected and squandered them that he had ruined himself and would rightly be denounced by all his murdered selves:

> I do not see them here; but after death
>   God knows I know the faces I shall see,
> Each one a murdered self, with low last breath.
>   "I am thyself, — what hast thou done to me?"
> "And I — and I — thyself," (lo! each one saith,)
>   "And thou thyself to all eternity!"

Just as Baudelaire found that, in his devotion to an ideal beauty, he himself fell woefully below his standards, so too did Rossetti. Though he indulged himself in many ways and had no great respect for established morality, he had his own moral system, which was part of his whole system of life, and it was no less exacting than other more traditional codes.

This was the price which Rossetti had to pay for his convictions. No doubt, as his powers began to fail, such moments became more frequent and more harassing. But he would not have been himself without them, and they give a special depth to his poetry. They provide a contrast to his ecstatic flights and enable us to see against what difficulties he contended in his struggle to find an ideal world. They make him appreciate the ideal all the more keenly when he has glimpses of it and knows that his efforts have not been in vain, that he has in part lived up to his standards. They introduce a note of anguish into what might otherwise be rather remote and impersonal. Nor in the end did Rossetti allow himself to be defeated by them. Like all men of strong emotions and exacting ambitions, he had his dark hours of depression and defeat, and they were all the darker because he felt that he himself was to blame for them. But his outlook was not pessimistic. After all, he had his sublime rewards and knew that they more than compensated for anything that he might suffer. He was fully justified when he closed *The House of Life* with a sonnet which is indeed far from jubilant, but which displays his courageous persistence in his task. To this he had given everything, and in the end he might well ask if it had been worth while:

> When vain desire at last and vain regret
>   Go hand in hand to death, and all is vain,
>   What shall assuage the unforgotten pain
> And teach the unforgetful to forget?

He looks forward to another world and asks if he will find peace in it or perhaps even joy. Beyond the present he hopes for a consolation, a chance that something will survive and reward him, and in this he puts his final trust:

> Ah! let none other alien spell soe'er
> But only the one Hope's one name be there, —
>   Not less nor more, but even that word alone.

Though Rossetti does not explicitly say so, it is legitimate to infer that the hope which sustains him is that after death his longing for love, and for beauty through love, will be realized, and that at last he will know in perfection what he has hitherto known uncertainly and fragmentarily.

The House of Life presents what was most powerful in Rossetti's creative being. These sonnets stand apart in his work because they reflect something which is not common at any time and which Rossetti possessed in a high degree. He pursued the beautiful more vigorously and more consistently than Ruskin or Pater, and his aestheticism was a much sterner discipline than Wilde could have endured. There is something noble and impressive in this dedication of a life to an ideal end, and in this determination to follow an exacting gospel without fear of consequence. Though Rossetti lacks the sweep and the scope of the great Romantics, though at times he seems remote or exotic, too enclosed in his special outlook and too careless of the world about him, he stands in the true Romantic tradition because of his belief in the mystery of life. His place is secure because in his pursuit of the beautiful he gave all his powers to an ideal which he valued beyond everything else and felt in his inner being to be sacred. If at times he thought that he had failed, he mastered his doubts through his command of his art and his unfailing sincerity with himself, and his confessions of weaknesses give to his poetry another dimension which adds greatly to its strength and brings him closer to us.

X

ATALANTA IN CALYDON

IT IS undeniably strange that at least three eminent English poets should have tried to reproduce in their own language the form of Greek tragedy. At first sight no literary form is more remote than this stiff, archaic art with its interchanges of long speeches or single complete lines, its choral songs breaking across the dramatic action, its stylized narratives spoken by anonymous messengers, its abundance of homely maxims, its attachment to the unities of time and place. But such is the power of Greek poetry that men so different as Milton, Arnold, and Swinburne each wished to pay to it the affectionate tribute of noble rivalry. For Milton the three Attic tragedians were "unequall'd yet by any, and the best rule to all who endeavour to write Tragedy." Arnold is less dogmatic, but his motives are not dissimilar when he writes in the Preface to *Merope*:

I have long had the strongest desire . . . to try to obtain through the medium of a living, familiar language, a fuller and more intense feeling of that beauty which, even when apprehended through the medium of a dead language, so powerfully affected me.

This natural desire is strengthened by the challenge which the strict form of Greek tragedy makes to a poet. He has to secure his individual effects through means established already with a high degree of convention, to adapt his tone to a majestic and austere outlook, and to show his mastery both of dramatic and of lyrical utterance. Even the oddities of the form have their own appeal and stir the poet to see how far the exuberant English spirit can be submitted to Hellenic discipline and restraint.

In Swinburne's case these reasons for imitating Greek tragedy were strengthened by something else. Like the other Pre-Raphaelites, he found much of his inspiration in works of art from the past. In them he admired a liveliness and a dignity which were less common in contemporary life, and through his remarkable gift for absorbing the poetry of many climes and times, he found an extension of his experience and indeed of his personality. Just as Rossetti owed much to the early Italian poets, so Swinburne owed even more to Elizabethan England and to classical Greece. In these worlds of noble gestures and princely words he felt at home, and from them he derived much that was best in his poetry. If his love of the past was partly an escape from life, it was also an enrichment of it. For through the past Swinburne built up his own outlook, and in it he found the models of beauty and conduct which were the centre of his system. Above all he sought an essential poetry, an indefinable essence, which he knew when he read the works of the great masters and which he sought to reproduce in his own books. Beyond the shapes into which past poets had cast their imaginative thoughts, Swinburne saw something more important and more real, the living spirit which works in words and makes poetry what it is. He found this in many places and tried to reproduce it in many forms, but of all his sources of inspiration perhaps the strongest was ancient Greece. His love for it was early and lasting, and from it he wrote at least one undisputed masterpiece.

Swinburne published *Atalanta in Calydon* in 1865. He was not yet thirty years old, and he was in the full flood of his creative powers. Living as he did by devoted loyalties, and able as he was to absorb the manners of the masters whom he adored, he could not but wish to reproduce in English something of what he had gained in his passionate love of Greek poetry. He had an unbounded admiration for Aeschylus, knew most of his plays by heart, and thought the *Oresteia* "on the whole the greatest spiritual work of man." His admiration for Sophocles was hardly less great, and though all through his life he despised Euripides for his sophistry and his scepticism and claimed that he had Jowett's authority for doing so,[1] he knew his plays well and liked parts of them more than he admitted. Just as his love for Elizabethan tragedy moved Swinburne to write *The Queen Mother* and *Rosamond* in 1860, so his love for Greek tragedy irresistibly drove him to write *Atalanta in Calydon*. It was his tribute to Aeschylus and Sophocles, his attempt to reproduce the poetical spirit which he found in them. He was not discouraged by the example of Arnold's *Merope*, published in 1858. Though he admired the characterization of Polyphontes, he felt, as he wrote to Lady Trevelyan, that "the clothes are well enough, but where has the body gone?"[2] Moreover, it was at this time that he met Walter Savage Landor, and Landor's love of the ancient world and cult of a classical style won Swinburne's enthusiasm. He read passages of *Atalanta* to Landor and dedicated it to his memory after his death. In such circumstances he turned away from his Elizabethan and French models and looked back to the Greeks.

The story of the Calydonian boar-hunt and the doom of Meleager was a splendid choice. It was a favourite with the Greeks both in their poetry and in their visual arts. Aeschylus wrote an *Atalanta*; Sophocles and Euripides each wrote a *Meleager*. Almost nothing survives from the first, a few lines from the second, and some sixty lines from the third. So far as the ancient tragedians were concerned, they left the field clear for Swinburne. He knew that they approved the subject, but he was not hampered by their treatment of it. Nor had the sands of Egypt yet given up the fifth poem of Bacchylides, which tells the story with unfailing grace and moments of magical beauty. Swinburne used more than one source. He certainly knew the prose abstract of the story in the *Bibliotheca* of Apollodorus, but, as we might expect, it was the poets who inspired and guided him. He derived his ideas from a few lines in the *Libation-Bearers* of Aeschylus, from the speech of Phoenix in Book IX of the *Iliad*, and, more surprisingly, since he hardly ever spoke in praise of Ovid, from some three hundred lines in Book VIII of the *Metamorphoses*. To Aeschylus Swinburne probably owed his first interest in the story of the fatal brand which marks the limits of Meleager's life and brings his death when his mother burns it; in Homer he may have found a sketch for his Althaea, the mother who kills her son because he has killed her brothers.

But the main outline and the chief episodes of *Atalanta in Calydon* come from Ovid. Swinburne expands and adds and alters, and his whole approach and spirit are different, but the plan is Ovid's. From him come the heroes who take part in the boar-hunt, the account of the boar's lair which Swinburne elaborates into a glittering speech by a Messenger, the details of the slaying, and the fight which follows it. From Ovid comes above all the conception of the virgin huntress, Atalanta, and of Meleager's love for her with its tragic consequences. Ovid tells his tale with much dash and spirit and courtly brilliance, but with little tragic emotion or apprehension of great issues at stake. Yet in this version of the old story, Swinburne found what he needed. Behind Ovid's wit and elegance he saw a stern Greek story, and in re-creating this in English he passed beyond the Roman adaptation to something like a Greek original. His creative insight enabled him to see what the story really was and to present it again. In this task scholarship has justified him. For the story which Ovid tells, with its emphasis on Meleager's tragic love for Atalanta, probably comes from Euripides, whom Swinburne despised but who was at least a Greek.

Swinburne did not adhere to the form of Greek tragedy with any servile pedantry. *Atalanta in Calydon* is half as long again as the longest Greek play. Swinburne's exuberance needed a wider scope than an ancient tragedian was allowed, and he rightly took it. Though in some ways, notably in the stichomythia or conversations in single complete lines and in his Messengers' speeches, he adheres to the old form, in other ways he breaks away from it. His choral songs have not the formality of their Greek prototypes, and are not usually composed in regular strophes and antistrophes. The result is that they soar with a wilder flight than the more correct choral songs of Arnold. Moreover, they are rhymed, a liberty which Arnold did not dare to take; but Swinburne was not a man lightly to forsake rhyme, and it might be argued that through it he conveys some of the variety and sprightliness which are possible in Greek quantitative verse but impossible in English unless rhyme comes to the rescue. Finally, the great lamentations which come towards the close of the poem, when four characters and the Chorus are on the stage together, are outside the Greek canon which allowed no more than three characters to appear together, for the good reason that the playwright had only three actors at his disposal. Yet the spirit and the purpose of these lamentations are undeniably Greek. They create a musical effect like that at the end of the *Persians* or the *Eumenides*. What Aeschylus did with actual song, Swinburne does with the music of words. Though he sometimes deserted the strict form of Greek tragedy, he had good reasons for doing so.

Though the form of *Atalanta* is not always or strictly Greek, its subject and spirit are. Swinburne had so absorbed the Greek outlook that he was able to create a tragedy which in almost all essential points would be acceptable to Aeschylus and Sophocles. The tragic outlook which he displays is profoundly and inescapably Greek. Swinburne owes nothing even to Shakespeare in his approach to his subject and his handling of it. His plot is tragic in the most exacting, the most Sophoclean, sense. The harmonious order of life has been disturbed. Artemis, insulted by Oeneus' neglect of her, sends the Calydonian boar to ravage his lands; and to hunt the boar comes Atalanta, with whom Meleager falls in love. So the tragic situation rises with its elements of conflict and infatuation. Meleager kills his uncles when they affront Atalanta, and from this comes the tragic choice. Meleager's mother, Althaea, has to choose between her love for her son and her love for her brothers. In such a choice any decision brings disaster: if she forgives her son, she dishonours her brothers; if she honours her brothers, she must kill her son whom she admires and loves. She decides to kill her son, and this means not only his death but her own, since after his death she cannot endure to live. Swinburne has chosen a plot which contains the most fundamental and most essential elements of Greek tragedy. The choice which Althaea makes resembles that which confronts Deianira in *The Women of Trachis*, when she has to choose between accepting a rival in her home and using illicit magic to win back her husband. She chooses the second and kills both him and herself. The plot of *Atalanta* is equally final, equally tragic. The only consolation for the catastrophe is that the gods' will is done and men are taught a lesson in humility.

In making Althaea come to her decision, Swinburne shows how well he understood the deeper currents of the Greek soul. She is torn between intolerable alternatives, and she decides that loyalty to her brothers is more important than love for her son. In presenting her anguish and her decision, Swinburne makes use of a famous and disputed passage in Sophocles' *Antigone*, where Antigone says that she would not have broken the law for anyone but a brother, not for a son or a husband. Behind this apparently inhuman and sophistical argument lies a deep Greek conviction that identity of blood through common parents is a closer and more binding tie than marriage or motherhood. Althaea carries Antigone's argument to its fatal conclusion. She feels that she is less near to her son than to her brothers, that he is half of another's flesh, while they are wholly blood of her blood and have the first claim on her. There are places in the world where this is still believed, and Swinburne, with his imaginative insight into the ways of Greek thought and his own profound sense of family ties, was entirely justified in using it. Althaea's decision may be primitive and irrational, but it is real and it is Greek. She is driven to it by her instinctive sense of loyalty and acts in frenzied haste. She rises to the height of a truly tragic heroine when she feels fierce forces working in her and sees the Fates in the gateway of the palace spinning her own doom and her son's.

Fire in the roofs, and on the lintels fire.
Lo ye, who stand and weave, between the doors,
There; and blood drips from hand and thread, and stains
Threshold and raiment and me passing in
Flecked with the sudden sanguine drops of death.

Once Althaea begins to kindle the fatal brand and so to bring
death to her son, she sees the full horror of her action. But she
does not relent. She is the victim of doom. The Fates have worked
their will on her, and she never speaks again.

Althaea's tragic decision rises from a situation in which harmony and order have been broken by what the Greeks would
regard as dangerous and improper assertions of the human spirit.
Meleager dies because he has insulted his mother's brothers by
giving the body of the slain boar to Atalanta, and he does this
because he loves her. Into this Swinburne has woven two Greek
conceptions. The first is that love is an extremely dangerous
power. The Greek poets often dwell on this, and Swinburne
agrees with them. In his play the incalculable, reckless, pitiless
power of love is at work. Althaea is quick to speak of it to the
Chorus and warns Meleager of its consequences, contrasting its
wild spirit with the modesty which befits men. The Chorus sings
of the ambiguous character of love:

Thou art swift and subtle and blind as a flame of fire;
Before thee the laughter, behind thee the tears of desire;
And twain go forth beside thee, a man with a maid;
Her eyes are the eyes of a bride whom delight makes afraid;
As the breath in the buds that stir is her bridal breath:
And Fate is the name of her; and his name is Death.

It is because he is infatuated by love that Meleager gives the
boar's body to Atalanta. Just as in the *Women of Trachis* Heracles' love for Iole leads to hideous disaster, so in *Atalanta* Meleager's love for Atalanta breaks the harmony of life and leads to his

doom. Love creates the tragic situation and produces the crisis when Althaea, following her primeval instincts, decides that her son must die.

With this Greek notion Swinburne combines another. His Atalanta is by Greek standards an unwomanly woman. Her cult of virginity, her lack of common ties and affections, her avoidance of wedlock and of motherhood, and her participation in activities properly reserved to men, put her outside the ordinary ranks of women and suggest that she is consumed by a reckless pride. It is not for women to break the rules of their sex in this way. Just as the virginal Hippolytus refuses honours to Aphrodite and creates a situation which leads to Phaedra's death and his own, so Atalanta, by not accepting her proper lot, brings disorder and disaster. Althaea speaks as an ordinary Greek woman when she tells Meleager:

> A woman armed makes war upon herself,
> Unwomanlike, and treads down use and wont
> And the sweet common honour that she hath.

She already distrusts and condemns Atalanta, and her feelings are the more bitter because she is jealous of her son's affection for this foreign woman. So, when Althaea is faced with the choice of dishonouring her brothers or killing her son, the thought of Atalanta is vivid in her mind and hardens her heart. She cannot endure to think that, when Meleager killed her brothers, Atalanta rejoiced:

> She the strange woman, she the flower, the sword,
> Red from spilt blood, a mortal flower to men,
> Adorable, detestable — even she
> Saw with strange eyes and with strange lips rejoiced,
> Seeing these mine own slain of mine own, and me
> Made miserable above all miseries made.

In Swinburne's tragic scheme, Atalanta is the instrument of doom because she pursues her own will against the rules of men.

Though Swinburne follows his Greek models in building his tragedy on a theological or ethical scheme, this does not in any way interfere with the free play of his poetry any more than it would in Aeschylus or Sophocles. The gods may act as they do, but that places no obligation on the poet to make less attractive those characters who fight against the divine will. Just as Sophocles throws his full imaginative power into the creation of Ajax who defies Athene, so Swinburne does his best to make his characters enjoy all the poetry which he can give them. If Althaea goes too far in preferring her brothers to her son, the deep call of her blood is presented in noble, human words. If Meleager is blinded by his love for Atalanta, there is nothing ignoble in this love, and Swinburne is well within his rights when he makes Meleager address his last words to Atalanta and win our final sympathy before he dies. If Atalanta is condemned by Althaea and spreads doom around her, yet she has her own beauty and appeal, the charm of her woodland innocence and strength:

> She is holier than all holy days or things,
> The sprinkled water or fume of perfect fire;
> Chaste, dedicated to pure prayers, and filled
> With higher thoughts than heaven; a maiden clean,
> Pure iron, fashioned for a sword; and man
> She loves not; what should one such do with love?

The poetry clothes the theological scheme and gives it truth and life. The characters may not be human beings in the short space allotted to them, but they have the reality which belongs to any true creation of the poetic mind.

Greek tragedy demands more than a situation and a crisis. Sooner or later it raises questions about man's relations with the gods and gives to the gods, directly or indirectly, some part in its action. Swinburne was not likely to shirk this obligation. Indeed, it held dangerous attractions for him. His hatred of priests and of organized religion had been strengthened by his recent association with Landor and was one of the most abiding elements in his system of beliefs. The *Atalanta* presented him with a difficult choice. He could either present the Olympian gods and goddesses as creatures of light and beauty as he had presented them in his "Hymn to Proserpine" to the detriment of their Christian successors, or he could use them as targets for his own anti-religious ideas. Each alternative must have had its attractions and its disadvantages for him, but on the whole the second prevailed. There are, it is true, moments in *Atalanta* when the vision of Olympian gods infuses the poetry with light and happiness, but they are rare. Individually the gods may appear in attractive guise, but collectively they are harsh and sinister, and we cannot but feel that at times Swinburne's feelings towards them are determined by a theology later than that of Olympus. Vague, anonymous divinities cast their shadows on the action, and their presence is never quite withdrawn. We may well ask what Swinburne meant by this treatment of the gods, and what he secured by it.

There are moments in Greek tragedy, even in the devout Sophocles, when in the stress of anguish or despair characters break into denunciations of divine indifference or cruelty. So when Swinburne's characters do the same, he may claim august precedent. We cannot complain when Althaea, after proclaiming the need of obedience to the gods, shows no very high opinion of their morality:

> But the gods love not justice more than fate,
> And smite the righteous and the violent mouth,
> And mix with insolent blood the reverent man's,
> And bruise the holier as the lying lips.

This is certainly no more than some characters of Euripides say, and not much more than Sophocles' Jocasta and Philoctetes say in the agony of fear or doubt. But more difficult to justify is the way in which Swinburne uses the Chorus to state views which are beyond dispute his own and not justified by Greek example. It is not surprising that the third song of the Chorus shocked

many of Swinburne's contemporaries, and that both Christina
Rossetti as a Christian and Bishop Thirlwall as a scholar took
exception to the Chorus which denounces

The supreme evil, God,

and proclaims

All we are against thee, against thee, O God most high.

Greek poetry provides no justification for such outbursts. Perhaps
Euripides would have liked to say something of the kind, but he
would hardly have been allowed to give such words to a chorus in
the theatre of Dionysus. Though Sophocles may say that all the
sufferings of Heracles and Deianira come from Zeus, that is not
denunciation but acceptance. Swinburne goes much further than
a Greek dramatist would have dared, when he extends the license
allowed to a single character to the impersonal Chorus which
speaks almost with his own lips. His emotions ran away with him,
and it is not surprising that he has been criticized.

None the less, these outbursts occur only in one place, and
the Chorus itself denies them before the end of the song. Nor
have they any real relation to the plan of the poem. Indeed, in
planning the action, Swinburne follows a more respectable and
more Hellenic theology. Althaea lays down the rules when she
tells Meleager that if man obeys the laws of the gods, all will be
as well as can be expected in this life:

Be man at one with equal-minded gods,
So shall he prosper; not through laws torn up,
Violated rule and a new face of things.

But this observance of the law is violated first by Atalanta's unwomanly behaviour, then by Meleager's reckless devotion to her.
The law is not so much moral law as embodied use and wont,
established habit and respected rules, the harmonious frame in

which man can best live. It is this harmony which is broken, and, being broken, produces the tragic situation and the tragic crisis. That is why Swinburne's great antiphonies of lament towards the close of the play end with emphatic words from the Chorus, which speaks here with a special authority:

> The gods guard over us
>   With sword and with rod;
> Weaving shadow to cover us,
>   Heaping the sod,
> That law may fulfil herself wholly, to darken man's face before God.

This is a perfectly Greek idea. It lies behind much work of Sophocles, and at times even Euripides pays his tribute to it.

The skill with which Swinburne reproduces Greek ideas would not in itself be enough to create a poem. Indeed, the more faithful a modern poet is to an ancient outlook when he copies its form, the greater is the danger that his work will be no more than a *pastiche*. But *Atalanta* is no *pastiche*. It is poetry which catches even those who know no Greek and are not much interested in Greek ideas. And much of this success comes from the fact that Swinburne was able to put into it some things which he enjoyed in his own experience and not through his admiration for other poets. Most characteristic is the delight which he takes in sky and sea, in wide landscapes and natural forces like sun and wind and rain. In the presence of these Swinburne felt his blood tingle and his senses awaken. It was therefore right that he should introduce them into his poem. When the Chorus sings its first song, it praises the coming of spring and gives voice to the most delightful and most powerful emotions of which Swinburne was capable, his delight in the renewal of life and in the enlarged consciousness which comes with it:

> And time remembered is grief forgotten,
> And frosts are slain and flowers begotten,
> And in green underwood and cover
>   Blossom by blossom the spring begins.

The same love of the open air inspires the marvellous line with which Meleager makes his first appearance:

O sweet new heaven and air without a star,

and Swinburne again makes Meleager reflect his own healthiest tastes when he tells of the voyage of the Argo:

when the sail
First caught between stretched ropes the roaring west,
And all our oars smote eastward, and the wind
First flung round faces of seafaring men
White splendid snow-flakes of the sundering foam.

The same love of adventure in lonely places among the powers of nature gives reality to Atalanta's account of her life:

Me the utmost pine and footless frost of woods
That talk with many winds and gods, the hours
Re-risen, and white divisions of the dawn,
Springs thousand-tongued with the intermitting reed
And streams that murmur of the mother snow —
Me these allure, and know me.

This is the essential voice of Swinburne, lover of wild places, the wind, and the cold.

No less characteristic are those passages where Swinburne writes from the heart about human, especially domestic, affections. His range is not very wide, but within his limits he has a special charm and tenderness. Though in later life he became sentimental when he wrote about children, in *Atalanta* he more than once touches with truth and insight on what childhood means between mother and son or between sister and brother. This is of course necessary to his plot, which turns on the conflict between Althaea's love for her son and love for her brothers, but Swinburne rises to it with noble ease. There is a special beauty in the way in which Althaea still thinks of her son, the great hero Meleager, as a child, and remembers not his present prowess but his childhood:

> But always also a flower of three suns old,
> The small one thing that lying drew down my life
> To lie with thee and feed thee; a child and weak,
> Mine, a delight to no man, sweet to me.

Hardly less true is the way in which Althaea, torn between conflicting affections, decides for her brothers because she has such vivid memories of what they did for her when she was a child:

> For this man dead walked with me, child by child,
> And made a weak staff for my feebler feet
> With his own tender wrist and hand, and held
> And led me softly and shewed me gold and steel
> And shining shapes of mirror and bright crown
> And all things fair; and threw light spears, and brought
> Young hounds to huddle at my feet and thrust
> Tame heads against my little maiden breasts
> And please me with great eyes.

There is no imitation, nothing second-hand, in this, but a real force of experience and personal feeling. Swinburne gives life to his old story by making it the vehicle for emotions which mean a great deal to him and are entirely authentic.

The great qualities of *Atalanta* are characteristic of Swinburne at his best, in his love of brave actions and his tender attachment to the sanctities of home. These inspire his best poetry and provide the core of his drama. In choosing his myth he showed a sure insight; for it was well suited to his personal tastes. In Althaea he had a theme which appealed to his understanding of deep affections and primitive loyalties. In the Calydonian boar-hunt, in the heroic Meleager, in

> Arcadian Atalanta snowy-souled,

he had subjects very near his heart. They gave him an opportunity to show his love of physical prowess and adventurous spirits. His hero and heroine, Meleager and Atalanta, the warrior lover and the virgin huntress, stand apart in their unlikeness to other men and women. In their truth to themselves they belong to that class of simple, direct people whom Swinburne liked both in literature and in life. The poetry of *Atalanta* is as good as it is because the story appealed to something deeper in Swinburne than his admiration for the Greek tragedians. That is why *Atalanta* is not an imitation but stands in its own right as a true work of art.

In other words, it is the poetry that counts, and the poetry is of a very unusual kind. When we first read *Atalanta,* we may hardly notice the plot or the thought behind it, so overwhelming is the effect of the words, so strange the impression which they make. Whatever we may think of Swinburne's use of language, there is no doubt of its power. We may resist it, as Browning did when he called *Atalanta* "a fuzz of words," but even such a comment is a kind of tribute to the poet's originality. Here Swinburne found an entirely original and individual style. What had been foreshadowed in *Chastelard* and in the earlier pieces of *Poems and Ballads* appeared now in ripe abundance. This is the Swinburnian style which was to affect many writers and not least Swinburne himself when he retired to Putney and pursued into old age the style which he had formed in his first manhood. Though the germs of his later mannerisms are present in *Atalanta,* they are not troublesome. His style is emphatically a manner, but a high, adventurous, and exciting manner which combines the confidence of youth with the judgement of maturity.

On closer inspection this language reveals many unsuspected qualities. It bears no relation to that of Keats, whom Swinburne imitated in his early "Hyperion." It shows no affinities to Morris or Rossetti such as we find in *Poems and Ballads*. It is common form to say that it is based on the Old Testament, and there are certainly moments in the third choral ode when the Chorus denounces God in language reminiscent of Isaiah or Ezekiel. But these are only a part of the whole. Swinburne's receptive and imitative capacity shows itself in other debts. There are times when he harks back to his Elizabethan manner, as when Althaea says:

> Lo, I talk wild and windy words, and fall
> From my clear wits, and seem of mine own self
> Dethroned, dispraised, disseated.

There are other times when Swinburne breaks into sonorous Latin words in the manner of Milton and speaks of a child who

> moaned
> With inarticulate mouth inseparate words,

or of the boar breaking out of its lair,

> fiery with evasive eyes
> And bristling with intolerable hair.

There are many translations of Greek idioms which sound strange in English, and there are adaptations of them which go beyond mere translation, as when Oeneus addresses Atalanta with a more than Sophoclean decorum:

> O flower of Tegea, maiden, fleetest foot
> And holiest head of women.

There is a Greek simplicity in the use of certain images like

> Night, a black hound, follows the white fawn day,

or

> Love, a thwart sea-wind full of rain and foam.

Many different elements may be found in *Atalanta*, but they are only elements. The language presents a singular unity of tone and character, and the marks of a strong, selective, personal taste. It is indeed so individual and in some ways so unprecedented that we cannot but ask why Swinburne fashioned it as he did.

Swinburne needed a striking manner to give life to his antique theme. Just as Milton evolved his most advanced effects of language and metre for *Samson Agonistes*, so Swinburne felt the need of a great effort to give life to *Atalanta*. Not only was he dealing with a remote world: he was restricted to a narrow scope in which every word must tell. And more than this: to give a full poetry to the stiff conventions of Greek drama, he had to keep his language unusually lively and exhilarating. Otherwise the form would stifle the words, as it tends to do in Arnold's *Merope*. So the first effect at which Swinburne aims, consciously or unconsciously, is surprise. His language provokes unexpected shocks. He brings together things which are not usually associated and yet are rightly associated by him. So when his Huntsman addresses the dawn,

> O fair-faced sun, killing the stars and dews
> And dreams and desolation of the night,

stars, dews, dreams, and desolation do not belong to a single order of things, and their combination is startling; but Swinburne means to startle, to make us look with fresh eyes at the sunrise and see what it means to him and his Huntsman. Again, in the second choral song, he writes:

> Before the beginning of years
>   There came to the making of man
> Time, with a gift of tears;
>   Grief, with a glass that ran.

The critics have complained that he would have been wiser to write:

> Grief, with a gift of tears,
>   Time, with a glass that ran.

But Swinburne did not do this. It is too obvious. He wishes to surprise, to say something unexpected, and he is justified because it is perfectly true that time brings tears and that grief devours our days. He rises beyond the commonplace to something else, and his way of doing it is to use words and ideas in unexpected combinations, so that we keep awake and move from shock to delighted shock.

To make his surprises tell, Swinburne has his own kinds of emphasis. Chief among these is a tendency to repeat words or ideas or sounds within a short space. By so doing he stresses the significance of what his characters say and gives an additional force to it. At times he picks up a single word and repeats it, as when Althaea says:

> for all
> There comes one sun and one wind blows till night,
> But when night comes the wind sinks and the sun.

The words "sun" and "night" are repeated with solemn emphasis, and the result is that the imagery, which might otherwise not be very distinguished, has an impressive gravity. So, too, an idea may be prolonged, even though different words are used to do it, as in

> Light sharper than the frequent flames of day
> That daily fill it with the fiery dawn.

The impression of piercing light is sustained through the six different words which refer to it and stress it. Sometimes, the repetition is merely of sound, as in

> She bore the goodliest sword in all the world,

and then the emphasis is less on meaning than on emotional and evocative effects. The sound common to "bore" and "sword" and "world" gives weight to the line and dignifies the occasion of which it speaks.

Sound plays an extremely important part in Swinburne's poetry. He had a special taste for certain sounds like "i," and it is no accident that among his favourite words are "fire," "light," "bright," "shine," "desire," "high," "sky." He had an equal taste for the uncorrupted long "e" as in "dream" and "sleep." This was his way of combating the tendency of English vowels to degenerate into a dead monotony. But it was also more fundamental to his art. Sound counted with him more than sight. His visual imagery is not abundant and not very distinguished. He does not resemble his Pre-Raphaelite friends in their love of minute details. Even when a landscape clearly delights him, he sketches it in broad vague lines, as when his Chorus imagines the wild place where the boar is killed:

> O that I now, I too were
> By deep wells and water-floods,
> Streams of ancient hills, and where
> All the wan green places bear
> Blossoms cleaving to the sod.

Natural sights moved Swinburne not to make a picture of them but to stress mental associations which they awoke in him. Thus he has no dearer word of praise than "bright." He applies it not only to eyes and faces but, more strangely, to "the brown bright nightingale." The nightingale may be brown to the eye, but to the heart and the imagination she is "bright" because of the echoes which the mere idea of her evokes. Swinburne strains past the visible world to a world of poetry which lives by its own right and has its own brilliance, and in his desire to catch its radiance he uses words which are necessarily inexact but create the special effect which he values.

A style so formed has a peculiar quality. In some ways it reads like a translation from a foreign tongue, though it is no tongue known to man. And this strangeness is essential to it. It gives that distance between the poet and his subject which Swinburne needs. He had to avoid the domestic elegance which was becoming the current speech of Victorian verse and had recently made a popular appearance in *Enoch Arden*. The origins of Swinburne's language may be traced in his reading of foreign tongues, but his use of it was something special. It helps him to keep his readers continually startled and delighted by each new combination of words. It succeeds because Swinburne's genius for words enabled him to keep them fresh and lively. This was his way of creating a grand style, and though his language is very different from Milton's, it has at least this in common: it is a highly artificial creation, with its own rules and manners, its own character and resonance. The words are real words, drawn from the rich accumulations of English poetry, but they are so used that they have an air of remoteness, even of unreality. Swinburne's style is both strange and extremely personal. In some ways it is limited. There are many sounds which he never exploited, many habits of speech which meant nothing to him. With the passing of years these limitations were to become more obvious, but in *Atalanta* they are an advantage. They suit the Greek story and its distance from modern experience. The story is perfectly alive, but it lives among words which have the dignity and the unfamiliarity of an ancient tongue.

There is something stranger than this grand manner in Swinburne's use of words. He did not in the least think that the meaning of words does not matter. Every sentence that he writes has a perfectly intelligible meaning. The *Atalanta* can even be translated into Greek verse, not indeed easily, but without any great loss to the sense. But we cannot read it without feeling that the auditory value of the words is somehow separate from their intellectual value. We enjoy the sounds without always troubling too much about what they mean, without perhaps following the structure of a sentence or seeing its relevance to the dramatic action. Though the plot of *Atalanta* is thrilling and tragic, it is so somehow in spite of the words, which suggest a different kind of excitement from that which the mere story evokes. It does not awake emotions in the way that a play of Sophocles does: it gives quite a different kind of pleasure, in which we respond not to a variety of human feelings but to a single, overmastering magic. It is therefore natural to compare Swinburne's effects with those of music, especially in his choral odes, where the words sing so sweetly and so boldly that we are lulled into enchantment and forget to look for their intelligible meaning. The result is peculiar. The meaning is there in abundance. The play is constructed with hard thought, but it touches us at two levels, the one almost purely musical, the other largely intellectual. The music and the meaning are not merged into a single impression. When we have responded to the sound and to the evocative quality of the words, we look for the meaning, but the two activities seldom coincide. Take, for instance, the lines spoken by the dying Meleager to his mother:

> But thou, O mother,
>   The dreamer of dreams,
> Wilt thou bring forth another
>   To feel the sun's beams
> When I move among shadows a shadow, and wail by impassable
>   streams?

The words are straight to the point: Althaea is indeed a dreamer of dreams. And the sentiment is undeniably Greek in its sense of the shadowy life which belongs to the dead. The lines are no less undeniably poetry of a high order. They haunt the memory, and long familiarity with them does not dim their splendour. But are they tragic or even human? Does the emotion in them have any close connection with the emotions of a dying man? I doubt it. I feel rather that they are poetry of a special kind, in which the actual experience is left behind and replaced by something distilled from it, by the special sweetness which lurks in all truly tragic poetry and is here separated from the fuller emotions which create it. It is too sweet to be distressing, and yet it is none the less poetry.

Writing in 1877, twelve years after the publication of *Atalanta*, Walter Pater made his famous pronouncement that "All art aspires constantly to the condition of music." There is no reason to think that he had Swinburne in mind, but his words are curiously apposite to the language of *Atalanta*. Pater approached poetry from an unusual standpoint and judged it partly by the qualities which he found in common between it and the other arts. The exalted, aesthetic state which he regarded as the proper end of the arts was, in his view, most purely exemplified in music. In poetry he valued the final effect which it creates, and he found that, when he had this, the intellectual and even the emotional content were of secondary importance. What mattered was the strictly poetical result in which both meaning and emotion are transcended in delight. Pater was the forerunner of the Aesthetic Movement, its prophet and·its master. His views had something in common with those of the French Symbolists, especially Mallarmé, who used the analogy of music to justify the reduction of poetry to an art of echoes and hints and suggestions. It is perhaps not fanciful to think that in his own way Swinburne believed something of the same kind. He had a most uncommon sensibility to poetry, and his instinctive flair taught him to look for those indefinable effects which lie beyond meaning and beyond emotion in the essential and authentic delight which comes from inspired words. In his own poetry he provided this delight at the cost of much else which we usually seek in poetry. *Atalanta* is the fruit of this belief. The evocative quality of its words is much more powerful than either their intellectual significance or the emotional condition which they imply but somehow leave behind.

We may perhaps explain this peculiar quality of Swinburne's work by saying that in him the Romantic search for an ideal

world was directed towards an ultimate poetry which is indeed
realized in words, but can almost be conceived as existing independently of them. In his attachment to Greece and Elizabethan
England and mediaeval France, he loved not so much a way of
life or a way of thought as some evanescent and elusive fragrance
which he found in their poetry. In his own mind he was able to
separate this from the forms in which it is contained, and he saw
that, however different these forms might be from each other, the
essential quality was somehow the same. It was this which enabled him in his criticism to enjoy the poetry of those whose opinions he repudiated with scorn. Though for instance Christina
Rossetti's religion was abhorrent to him, and though he thought
Keats flabby and unmanly, in neither case did he fail to admire
the poetry which they wrote. He sought poetry and nothing else,
and he could not but separate its essence from the intellectual and
emotional associations in which it usually appears. In his own
work he followed this conviction, and that is why *Atalanta* is
what it is. Dante Gabriel Rossetti sought an Ideal Beauty through
love; Swinburne sought the essence of poetry. It was perhaps a
dangerous thing to do, and it may not only have limited his scope
but have caused the contraction of his powers in later years. But
in his time it was natural that he should do this. Like others of
his generation, he had a Romantic yearning for a "beyond," but
for him the "beyond" was the essential experience of poetry and
nothing else.

This attitude does not create the highest kind of poetry. In
Sophocles or Dante or Shakespeare the meaning of words and
their emotional power are perfectly blended with their evocative
magic, and the result is a single impression in which each element
gains from the others. But what Swinburne gives is undeniably
poetry and nothing else, and it was the right kind of poetry for
him to write. He trained himself less on life than on books, and
he lacked that kind of creative temperament which lives on its
own resources and has a peculiarly individual vision of existence.
His human range was limited, and though it inspired his best

work, he could not but supplement it with what he gained from poetry not his own. In his love of poetry he knew that what pleased him most, what seemed essential and indispensable, lay in certain musical effects of sound which give those mysterious, magical hints that are poetry's central function. Swinburne was not a Symbolist, but he resembled the Symbolists in his concentration on this special aspect of his art. The events which he depicts in his drama make a special kind of appeal, not intellectual nor even emotional, but purely poetical. They belong to a world of the imagination in which experience is refined and distilled and passes into a "condition of music."

XI

CHRISTINA ROSSETTI

ONE OF the paradoxes of the Romantic spirit is that though nearly all its chief exponents were deeply concerned with an ideal and spiritual world, none of them found it in the Christian conception of God. It is true that Coleridge and Wordsworth became orthodox members of the Church of England, but their poetry owed little to it and gained nothing by it. Nor is this hard to understand. They were concerned with a peculiarly private and individual search for a reality beyond the senses. They followed their own intuitions as far as they possibly could, and inevitably they found not the common goal of Christian faith, but orders of being which answered their own unusual needs and were related to their unprecedented speculations. What is true of the Romantics is on the whole true of their Pre-Raphaelite successors. Though Swinburne might write poems which seem to breathe an impeccable faith, they are no more than exercises in an archaic manner, and he maintained into old age his hostility to priests and creeds. Though William Morris hungered for the Middle Ages, it was for their craftsmanship and their chivalry, not for their theology or their mysticism. Though Dante Gabriel Rossetti had his intermittent moments of instinctive belief, they arose too often from some crisis in his health or his fortunes and were not habitual to him. Even his beautiful "Ave" is exceptional in his work, and he had qualms about including it in his collected poems. The Pre-Raphaelite poets left Christianity alone and pursued their own schemes of salvation. Yet among these powerful and turbulent personalities there moved with shy assurance and self-effacing modesty a woman who was at least their equal in the art of words and whose outlook was very different from theirs. Christina Rossetti has a place not far from the highest among English religious poets. She learned her art from the Pre-Raphaelites and has many affinities with them, but she turned her genius to a different end and won her own special triumphs.

Christina Rossetti formed her beliefs in childhood and clung tenaciously to them until her death. Her leanings were not towards Keble and Pusey but towards the old-fashioned High Church, which still kept some of the grace and the gentleness of the seventeenth century. Though neither of her brothers shared her faith, she remained on terms of unbroken affection with them, and was well rewarded by the identity of her convictions with those of her mother and her sister Maria. When Maria died, Christina entered the Anglican Sisterhood of All Saints, and a large part of her last years was passed in devotional duties and exercises. Her beliefs shaped the course of her life and gave her a curious position in her own circle. She was in her own way a notable member of the Pre-Raphaelite company. The fame of her poetry preceded that of her brother's, and there is no reason to think that she was displeased when Swinburne, with less than his usual felicity in compliment, saluted her as "the Jael who led their host to victory." She seems not to have passed adverse judgement on any act or word of her brother Gabriel, nor did she commit to paper any anxiety or misgiving which she may have felt about him. In her devoted austerity and saintly detachment she went her own way and followed her own ideals, but she was none the less a true child of her generation and her circumstances. In her we see a truly Romantic temperament, trained to look for beauty in mysterious realms of experience, and able to find it without any strain or forcing of herself. She might have been a purely secular poet, so great were her gifts for the interpretation of strange corners of life and fancy. But her taste for this world was countered by a belief in God, and this broke into her life and gave to her work a new direction and a special distinction.

Christina's poetry reveals an almost dual personality. One side of her was Pre-Raphaelite, fond of pictorial effects and unusual images, capable of telling a story with a proper sense of its dramatic possibilities, and, what was rarer in her circle, with a certain whimsical humour and playful fancy. She was often enough content to withdraw into fancies and dreams and to find a full satisfaction in the world of her imagination. The publication of *Goblin Market, and Other Poems* in 1862 shows how naturally and how well she practised a Pre-Raphaelite art without surrendering any of her originality. The charming poem which gives its title to the book is an authentic feat of the creative imagination, an extension of experience into an unknown world which she has invented and made real. It shows perhaps some traces of influence from Coleridge and Hood and Allingham, but they are few and unimportant. Christina speaks in her own voice and in her own way. Her command of a rippling metre and the fresh conversational simplicity of her language, so unlike her brother's elaborate majesty, reveal a talent which has fully found itself and translated into its own idiom the vague ideals of her friends. She advances at one step into her own special sphere and finds her way with confident ease. "Goblin Market" lives of its own right in its own world as an ingenious and brilliant creation. It is less a criticism of life than an addition to it. No doubt things do not happen like this, but it would be exciting if they did, and we are almost persuaded by the coherence of Christina's invention that in some conditions they do.

"Goblin Market" is Pre-Raphaelite in the predominance which it gives to a charming pictorial element. Though Christina spent much of her time in London and still more in contemplation of an unseen world, she had a keen eye for physical things and shared her brother's belief that poetry must to a large degree be pictorial. She differs from him in not making her word-pictures symbols of something else, being content to exploit them for their own sake. They reflect her love for the humbler and less exciting denizens of the animal world, for mice and wombats and other small furry creatures. The curious little beings whom the girls,

Laura and Lizzie, meet in the market-place, have an impish oddity. They are not elves or gnomes, but goblins, as much animal as human in shape and more animal than human in character:

> One had a cat's face,
> One whisked a tail,
> One tramped at a rat's pace,
> One crawled like a snail,
> One like a wombat prowled obtuse and furry,
> One like a ratel tumbled hurry skurry.

Despite their undoubtedly alluring ways, the goblins are rather sinister beings, strange, wild little creatures, who move with a ferocious energy and make uncouth, bestial noises:

> Laughed every goblin
> When they spied her peeping:
> Came towards her hobbling,
> Flying, running, leaping,
> Puffing and blowing,
> Chuckling, clapping, crowing,
> Clucking and gobbling,
> Mopping and mowing,
> Full of airs and graces,
> Pulling wry faces,
> Demure grimaces.

No doubt the goblins come ultimately from fairy-tales which Christina heard in childhood. They have certainly some of the heartless independence and irresponsibility which belong by right to gnomes and elves and their kind. But Christina has imposed her own rules on them. They are more alive than the figures of fairy-tale and seem to have an appropriate place in the common world. Christina's creative vision makes them live their own lives in accordance with their unusual character.

"Goblin Market" represents one side of Christina's character, the side which fitted easily into the Pre-Raphaelite circle and was honoured by it. But she had another side, grave and serious and intimately bound with her inner life. Even in "Goblin Market" there is an undercurrent of this seriousness, and though she herself said that she did not "mean anything profound by this fairytale," it has its little moral: that it is dangerous to play with the unknown and that human beings who so do pay for it. Behind and beyond her charming fancies, dominating and correcting and at last subduing them, was her religious faith which looked for a divine consummation in another world and demanded a self-denying devotion in this. Christina was not a mystic nor a visionary. She was a devout member of the Church of England who recited its creeds and carried out its duties. When others explained or equivocated or criticized, she obeyed and conformed and believed. For her the Scriptures were the Word of God, and she accepted them without qualm or question. In an orthodox age she practised religion as countless others did, and never sought to be unusual even in the smallest respect. In her unquestioning faith she needed no metaphysics to explain what was to her self-evident truth, nor was the Bible to her a book to be read with a searching eye for inner meanings. She was completely orthodox. But she was also a poet of genius, and she brought to her religion a concentration and an intensity which only a poet could bring. Her faith was the centre of her life, and to it she gave her passionate allegiance, her ruthless self-examination, and her unremitting candour.

The two sides of Christina's nature account for the twofold character of her poetry. On the one side is her poetry of imagination and fancy, whether in long pieces like "Goblin Market" and "The Prince's Progress," or in short pieces in which, with an uncommon charm and delicacy, she sketches some situation which has touched her heart or appealed to her love of the living scene. On the other side are her many devotional pieces, not indeed always of equal merit, and sometimes rather perfunctory, but at their best unsurpassed for their sureness of touch and their passionate sincerity. Nor were the two sides always kept separate. Indeed, some of her most characteristic poems are those in which she allows her conscientious attachment to the sacred texts to be enlivened by her love of decorative details. Though she drew her idea of the invisible world from the Song of Songs and Revelation, she was not afraid to make the most of what they provided and to give to it some little turn of her own. She picks up the time-honoured images and uses them again with a new delicacy. She sketches the celestial landscape in broad but vivid lines, as though she were afraid of inventing too much, but could not altogether refrain from allowing some freedom to her imagination in trying to see what the other world is really like. And through her pictorial creation we see her deep longing:

> As I lie dreaming,
>   It rises, that land;
> There rises before me
>   Its green golden strand,
> With the bowing cedars
>   And the shining sand;
> It sparkles and flashes
>   Like a shaken brand.

She sees this land rich with gems and bright with birds golden-winged and silver-winged. She uses the details which the Bible provides, but her fancy takes command and presents them with new lights and a new appeal.

Christina indeed believed so literally in the myths of her religion that she could not at times refrain from presenting them in this way. This was what they meant to her, and so in all devoutness she interpreted them. When she thinks of an angel, she allows herself no wild flights of fancy, but none the less creates something which recalls her brother's picture *Ecce Ancilla Domini* or those early Florentine and Sienese paintings on which he drew for his models:

> She holds a lily in her hand,
> Where long ranks of Angels stand:
> A silver lily for her wand.
>
> All her hair falls sweeping down,
> Her hair that is a golden brown,
> A crown beneath her golden crown.

So too, with a more adventurous and more imaginative spirit, Christina conjures up the scene of the Nativity as if it had happened not in Palestine but in her own Northern clime and had possessed the legendary characteristics of an English Christmas:

> In the bleak mid-winter
>   Frosty wind made moan,
> Earth stood hard as iron,
>   Water like a stone;
> Snow had fallen, snow on snow,
>   Snow on snow,
> In the bleak mid-winter
>   Long ago.

Like Pieter Brueghel, Christina translates the circumstances of the first Christmas to conditions which are familiar to her in many vivid associations, and by this she enriches the significance of her traditional theme.

In such cases Christina found no difficulty in putting both sides of her self into her poetry, in reconciling her religious beliefs with her fanciful, Pre-Raphaelite art. The art enriches the presentation of the beliefs and makes them more actual. Sometimes she took greater risks and gave a greater license to her invention. A preëminent example of this is "Eve," in which Christina tells of the heart-rending moment when Eve sits by Abel's dead body and sees what her original transgression has cost the world. For Christina the Fall of Man was a fearful reality, not to be shirked or explained away, but a permanent source of shame and sorrow. Into Eve she puts her own deep feelings about the Fall; in Eve her own sense of sin is concentrated and magnified. The Mother of Mankind is the prototype of all sinners and carries the burden of the guilt which will belong to all her descendants. So the poem begins with a majestic music in which the dark horror of the Fall is expressed in words which show the full meaning of sin's entry into the world. As Eve watches over Abel's dead body, she laments what has happened and knows that she must bear the blame for it:

> While I sit at the door,
> Sick to gaze within,
> Mine eye weepeth sore
> For sorrow and sin:
> As a tree my sin stands
> To darken all lands;
> Death is the fruit it bore.
>
> How have Eden bowers grown
> Without Adam to bend them?
> How have Eden flowers blown,
> Squandering their sweet breath,
> Without me to tend them?
> The Tree of Life was ours,
> Tree twelvefold-fruited,
> Most lofty tree that flowers,
> Most deeply rooted:
> I chose the Tree of Death.

The story lives again because of the passionate conviction which Christina puts into it, and becomes a symbol of all men and women who understand that the evil of the world is their own fault.

Then, as Christina develops her poem, she introduces another note, sweeter and more fanciful and in full accord with her delicate, human sensibility. She indulges her love of birds and animals, as she makes both forget their joys when they hear Eve's lamentations:

> The mouse paused in his walk
> And dropped his wheaten stalk;
> Grave cattle wagged their heads
> In rumination;
> The eagle gave a cry
> From his cloud station:
> Larks on thyme beds
> Forbore to mount or sing;
> Bees dropped upon the wing;
> The raven perched on high
> Forgot his ration;
> The conies in their rock,
> A feeble nation,
> Quaked sympathetical;
> The mocking-bird left off to mock;
> Huge camels knelt as if
> In deprecation;
> The kind hart's tears were falling;
> Chattered the wistful stork;
> Dove-voices with a dying fall
> Cooed desolation,
> Answering grief by grief.

This comes from the playful, fanciful side of Christina's character, the side which loved living things and made an early appearance when, as a little girl, she surprised a Mrs. Potter by saying, "The cat looks very sedate." In her delighted appreciation of birds and animals she has almost forgotten the graver thoughts with which she began the poem, and has allowed herself to create a scene in the childhood of the world when human beings were still close to animals. Then, with a sudden turn, she resumes her serious note. Among the gentle creatures who are sorry for Eve there is one ugly exception:

Only the serpent in the dust,
Wriggling and crawling,
Grinned an evil grin and thrust
His tongue out with its fork.

We are brought back not quite to the original theme, but to something no less grave, to the principle of malice and cruelty in the world. Christina builds her poem in three parts, and each has its own appropriate tone. The result is a little masterpiece in which the Pre-Raphaelite love of odd and captivating details is blended with something deeply serious and disturbing.

The balance between the two sides of her nature, which Christina maintains in "Eve," was always precarious and apt to be upset when her religion asserted itself against her love of this world. If she had to make a choice between the claims of the world and the claims of God, there was never any doubt what it would be. Of course, such a choice was not always forced upon her, and she was often free to make the best of both worlds without any unquiet of conscience. But twice in her life she had to face a terrible choice. She had her full share of human affections and felt a woman's need to lavish them on someone whom she loved. She twice fell in love and was twice betrothed, but she married neither James Collinson nor Charles Cayley. Ostensibly, she did not marry Collinson because, despite considerable shilly-shallying, he was a Roman Catholic, and Cayley because he was an agnostic. That such differences of belief were for her insuperable obstacles we cannot doubt. She could never have entered into perfect intimacy with a man whose faith she did not share. It is true that she soon ceased to care for Collinson, but her love for Cayley lasted for more than twenty years, and she was with him when he died. Yet surely this refusal to marry, impassable though the differences of belief were to her conscious mind, rose from something very deep in her nature, something which made her shrink from the claims of the flesh. It was more than an unusual fastidiousness, more even than a desire to keep herself unspotted from the world. It was a deep conviction that she was dedicated to God and that any concession to the body would be an act of disloyalty to Him. Her religion imposed duties so imperative that she could not compromise with them, but, more than that, it made even marriage an impossibility. Love she knew and exercised with all the strength of her gentle, devoted nature, but deep in her something turned her away from any call which summoned her to give to a human being what must be kept for God.

The episodes of Collinson and Cayley show how violent a conflict started in Christina when she set the claims of her womanhood against those of her sanctity. Of this conflict she was painfully aware, though she hoped to be able to solve it by self-discipline and self-denial. But beyond her control, in her innermost self, strange forces awoke, which might at first sight seem to have no close relation to the actual issue. These inspired her poetry when she was in love and gave to it an unexpected character. It was as if her unconscious self took command and forced her to present in almost dramatic form her most intimate feelings. What she writes is not a direct account of her conscious thoughts, but dreams and longings which did not normally break into her life but lay locked in unexplored corners of her soul. At such times her art passed far beyond the conscious invention of "Goblin Market" to inventions which for the moment she almost believed to be true, so strongly did they affect her, and so much did they mean to her. Through these creations of her imagination she released forces which stirred in her inmost being, and by releasing them she revealed important truths about herself. Her genius took command of her and made her write poems which her conscious self would have repudiated as false records of her feelings, but which none the less reflected her true self. This was the work of imagination, which at such times took on a truly Romantic character and created worlds which have a special strength from the insight which has gone to their making.

The paradoxical character of Christina's genius when she

was in love can be seen from the poems which she then wrote. None of her poems to Collinson reflects joy or hope. On the contrary, at the height of her love for him she wrote some of her most poignant lines on the imminence and the pathos of death. In her the idea of love turned inexorably to the idea of death, and in this association we can surely see her instinctive shrinking from the surrender which love demands. Two of her most famous poems come from this time, and in each Christina is obsessed by thoughts of death. In "Remember" she asks her beloved to remember her when she is dead, because that is all that he will be able to do for her. Then, with characteristic humility, she assures him that even this is not necessary and that all she asks is that he himself should not be unhappy:

> Yet if you should forget me for a while
>   And afterwards remember, do not grieve:
>   For if the darkness and corruption leave
>   A vestige of the thoughts that once I had,
> Better by far you should forget and smile
>   Than that you should remember and be sad.

In the wonderful "Song" which is a kind of counterpart to this sonnet, Christina foresees what death will mean to her and wonders if perhaps she also will forget the past:

> I shall not see the shadows,
>   I shall not feel the rain;
> I shall not hear the nightingale
>   Sing on as if in pain;
> And dreaming through the twilight
>   That doth not rise nor set,
> Haply I may remember,
>   And haply may forget.

In Christina love released a melancholy desire for death, and for a kind of death not closely connected with her usual ideas of an after-world. It is an intermediate condition between sleeping and

waking, a half-conscious state in which memories are dim and
even the strongest affections fade into faint shadows. Even before
her love for Collinson was at an end, Christina wrote a little poem
to show what it really meant to her:

> Oh roses for the flush of youth,
>   And laurel for the perfect prime;
> But pluck an ivy branch for me
>   Grown old before my time.
>
> Oh violets for the grave of youth,
>   And bay for those dead in their prime;
> Give me the withered leaves I chose
>   Before in the old time.

She felt that the claims of love were not for her, that her way of
life was unsuited to it, and that she must go back to her old denials
and refusals.

Yet though Christina accepted and almost courted defeat in
her love for Collinson, she could not put the thought of it entirely away from her mind. In the years after its close she often
wrote of love, and there can be little doubt that part of her still
longed for love and delighted to imagine what it might be. This
was another side of her Romantic transformation of experience,
her creation of an imaginary world in which some of her desires
would be fulfilled. In 1857 she wrote "A Birthday," with its
rapturous anticipation of her beloved coming to her. It is a true
product of her Pre-Raphaelite circumstances in its choice of
decorative details, but it rises from something deep in her nature,
which she might not acknowledge to be valid but which shows
her secret, hardly conscious hopes:

> My heart is like a singing bird
>   Whose nest is in a watered shoot:
> My heart is like an apple-tree
>   Whose boughs are bent with thickset fruit;

My heart is like a rainbow shell
  That paddles in a halcyon sea;
My heart is gladder than all these
  Because my love is come to me.

For a moment some bright memory or alluring fancy welled up
in her and inspired her to write in this spirit, when to the outer
world she presented a cloistral calm and detachment. She forgot
her celestial calling and strict duties and lost herself in an enchanting dream.

If Christina learned in imagination the joys of love, in life
she felt its wounds, and at times we can see what her sacrifices
cost her. In "Echo," with its longing for something known and
lost until it can be sought only in dreams, we see what a depriva-
tion she suffered in her innermost being and how she sought to
find consolation in summoning her lost love back:

Yet come to me in dreams, that I may live
  My very life again though cold in death:
Come back to me in dreams, that I may give
  Pulse for pulse, breath for breath:
    Speak low, lean low,
  As long ago, my love, how long ago.

Rigorous though Christina's denial of love was, it was not strong
enough to curb all her womanly and human instincts. She fought
against them and kept them in iron control, but, left alone with
her genius, she could not from time to time prevent them from
bursting into an almost heart-rending poetry, which is all the
more powerful because it rises not from controlled thoughts but
from longings which force themselves on her despite all her
efforts to check them. It is not surprising that, being the victim
of such a struggle, she sometimes felt that it was too much for
her and that she could not endure it any longer. At such times
she would long for release and find no magic even in the spring:

I wish I were dead, my foe,
My friend, I wish I were dead,
With a stone at my tired feet
And a stone at my tired head.

In the pleasant April days
Half the world will stir and sing,
But half the world will slug and rot
For all the sap of Spring.

In these words there is more than a passing mood: there is a deep basis of experience, of misery in a defeat which has been hard for Christina to endure.

When she fell in love with Charles Cayley, Christina was a woman of thirty. What it meant to her can be seen from the four-teen sonnets of *Monna Innominata,* and no one can doubt the unselfish purity of her devotion. These are poems of exalted love, but of a love which cannot be fully realized. It has its wonderful moments, but it is bound to end in defeat. And that this repre-sents Christina's feelings in her long love for Cayley is clear from the poems which she wrote when it was at its height. At the very start she seems to have seen that something was wrong and that her deepest desires could not be fulfilled. In this mood she wrote a poem which she characteristically calls "Mirage":

The hope I dreamed of was a dream,
    Was but a dream; and now I wake,
Exceeding comfortless, and worn, and old,
    For a dream's sake.

I hang my harp upon a tree,
    A weeping willow in a lake;
I hang my silenced harp there, wrung and snapt
    For a dream's sake.

> Lie still, lie still, my breaking heart;
>   My silent heart, lie still and break:
> Life, and the world, and mine own self, are changed
>   For a dream's sake.

The love which began in this spirit was not likely to lead to any success in this world, and it is clear that in her heart of hearts Christina shrank from marriage to Cayley as she had shrunk from it to Collinson.

Christina's poems to Cayley are more direct than those to Collinson. Cayley was the most absent-minded and unworldly of men, a scholar sunk in books and incapable of dealing with the most ordinary duties of common life. No doubt Christina longed to look after him and care for him, and in her demure way she liked to play with him and make gentle fun of him. Yet even into this something more serious makes its way. In "A Sketch" she starts with affectionate banter, as if Cayley were some uncouth bird or furry animal with short sight and clumsy habits:

> The blindest buzzard that I know
>   Does not wear wings to spread and stir;
>   Nor does my special mole wear fur,
> And grub among the roots below:
> He sports a tail indeed, but then
> It's to a coat: he's man with men:
>   His quill is cut to a pen.

Then, having begun in this airy spirit, Christina becomes more serious and sees in Cayley's shortness of sight something more than a physical defect. It mirrors his inability to know her as she really is. He cannot see what lies in front of him or read its obvious lessons. So with a deepening tone and with her own special pathos, she chides him gently for his blindness:

> My blindest buzzard that I know,
>   My special mole, when will you see?
>   Oh no, you must not look at me,
> There's nothing hid for me to show.

I might show facts as plain as day:
But, since your eyes are blind, you'd say,
    "Where? What?" and turn away.

Despite her real love for Cayley and her affectionate playfulness
with him, Christina felt that he could not really understand her,
but moved blindly in another world than hers. Once again she
shrank from the final sacrifice of love because she believed that,
if she were to make it, she would lose something inestimably
valuable in herself.

Just as her love for Collinson awoke strange unconscious
springs of poetry in Christina, so did her love for Cayley. In perfect innocence she would write poems which are to all appearance
dramatic lyrics about imaginary situations, but which none the
less show unmistakable traces of her own feelings and sufferings.
In the famous song at the end of "The Prince's Progress," she
once again connects love with death and in the figure of the dead
princess weaves a myth of her own lost chances. More strikingly
in "Twice" she dramatizes her sacrifice in a poem about a woman
whom her lover has treated with callous carelessness. Though
there is not the slightest reason to think that Cayley ever behaved
like this, or that Christina believed him to have done so, this
poem is none the less revealing for the light which it sheds on her
feelings. No woman could write with this terrible directness if
she did not to some degree know the experience which she describes. Speaking with calculated understatement in the first
person, as if she identified herself with the woman of her poem,
Christina tells the story of love betrayed, of a heart taken up and
scanned and told to wait:

    As you set it down it broke —
        Broke, but I did not wince;
    I smiled at the speech you spoke,
        At your judgment that I heard:
        But I have not often smiled
        Since then, nor questioned since,
    Nor cared for corn-flowers wild,
        Nor sung with the singing bird.

Behind the dramatic cover we see the real experience. This is the spirit in which Christina, largely despite herself, took her defeat. She was woman enough to feel that life had done her an injury, and, though she must not complain, she could not refrain from speaking indirectly about it. Then she turns from complaint to submission, and in words which rise sincerely from her own case, she tells how she now gives her heart to God:

> I take my heart in my hand —
>   I shall not die, but live —
> Before Thy face I stand;
>   I, for Thou callest such:
> All that I have I bring,
>   All that I am I give;
> Smile Thou and I shall sing,
>   But shall not question much.

So Christina dramatizes her own story and shows the process which brings her through suffering to God.

The conflict in Christina between the woman and the saint was hers almost till the end, though with the passing of years her religion became more absorbing and more insistent and allowed her only at intervals to indulge her more human feelings. How strong these were can be seen from more than one poem in which she forgets for the moment her divine calling and laments the emptiness and failure of her life. In her religious hours she believed that the world was as nothing, and then suddenly it would assert its claims, and she would regret her lost chances and her vanishing dreams. She would indeed accept her fate, but not altogether willingly and not without regret. Though she knew that the world passes away and that mortal things wither and die, she loved them too well to be insensitive to their destruction. In tones of agonizing sweetness she sings of her anxieties and fears, and in the same moment knows that regret is useless:

To think that this meaningless thing was ever a rose,
    Scentless, colourless, *this!*
Will it ever be thus (who knows?)
    Thus with our bliss,
    If we wait till the close?

Though we care not to wait for the end, there comes the end,
    Sooner, later, at last,
Which nothing can mar, nothing mend:
    An end locked fast,
    Bent we cannot re-bend.

Though Christina steels herself to the truth as she sees it, we cannot but detect an undercurrent of anguished regret at the passing of what she loves.

Against these regrets and these misgivings, Christina's other self set its faith and its intermittent hopes. If love could not be realized in this world, there was still the hope that it might be in another, and this was her consolation. If she could not give herself to a man, she must give herself to God, and in doing this she trusted that in the end her earthly love would be fulfilled in heaven. This trust enabled her to survive the partings made by death and life. When she thought of this, her anguish faded, and with a calm contentment she believed that all would be well, that her sacrifices would be rewarded by something far better than anything in this world:

To meet, worth living for;
Worth dying for, to meet.
To meet, worth parting for;
Bitter forgot in sweet.
To meet, worth parting before,
Never to part more.

But if she was to win this reward, she must give herself all the more fully to her faith. She must face all the trials and sorrows of a dedicated life and not complain, though the road "winds uphill all the way," and though she feels herself "cold alone on the wold." For though she might not ever see the ultimate vision this side of the grave, she never doubted its reality, but believed that it might be granted even to her. The thought of it was so awe-inspiring that she shrank from it, but in her heart it sustained and strengthened her:

> Marvel of marvels, if I myself shall behold
> With mine own eyes my King in His city of gold.

Christina knew the full cost that a life of devotion demands, and she gave herself ungrudgingly to all its tasks and duties.

This poetry of the soul's search for God and its struggles towards perfection is written in a language of remarkable simplicity. The more serious Christina is, the less she adorns her verse. Her images became rarer and more traditional, and the words are the unpretentious words of every day. But each word expresses exactly what she feels, and her sense of rhythm is so subtle that even in her darkest moments she can break into pure song. She varies her effects with consummate skill, and though she often writes in a very quiet key, her touch is so sure that every movement tells, and her constant changes of tone produce endless delightful surprises. Few poets have her gift of beginning a poem with the most homely and humble words or of using phrases which are consciously trite or commonplace, only to rise to some sudden burst and thereby to show that even in the drabbest conditions there are possibilities of dazzling splendour. Her sonnet "In Progress" illustrates this subtle art, and though it claims to be written about another person, it is a true account of Christina herself as those who knew her saw her:

> Ten years ago it seemed impossible
>   That she should ever grow so calm as this,
>   With self-remembrance in her warmest kiss
> And dim dried eyes like an exhausted well.

Slow-speaking when she has some fact to tell,
   Silent with long-unbroken silences,
   Centred in self yet not unpleased to please,
Gravely monotonous like a passing bell.
Mindful of drudging daily common things,
   Patient at pastime, patient at her work,
Wearied perhaps but strenuous certainly.
Sometimes I fancy we may one day see
   Her head shoot forth seven stars from where they lurk
And her eyes lightnings and her shoulders wings.

Each phrase seems to have been reduced to the lowest possible emphasis and to keep rigorously to an unpretentious account of humdrum facts, but in every sentence there is a special charm and strength, until the end comes with an astonishing glory of light and flame.

The same fusion of matter and form can be seen in Christina's use of metre. She was not a great inventor of metres, but she made many variations inside existing forms, and shaped each to some special need of her imaginative moods. She is equally at home with the sonnet and the song, with staid iambics and the more lively anapæsts and dactyls. She has a remarkable gift for varying the speed of a line partly by punctuation, partly by stressing the important words. Her results are so natural that we hardly notice what control of her craft she has: everything seems to fall so easily into its right place and to reflect so exactly what she feels. Take, for instance, "What would I give":

What would I give for a heart of flesh to warm me through,
Instead of this heart of stone ice cold whatever I do!
Hard and cold and small, of all hearts the worst of all.

What would I give for words, if only words would come!
But now in its misery my spirit has fallen dumb.
O merry friends, go your way, I have never a word to say.

What would I give for tears! not smiles but scalding tears,
To wash the black mark clean, and to thaw the frost of years,
To wash the stain ingrain, and to make me clean again.

The tremendous impact of this poem comes from many causes, but not least from the mastery of the metrical scheme. The internal rhyme in the third line of each stanza conveys with appalling force the chilling drop in the poet's spirit, the change from agonized dismay to something frozen and dark and insoluble. The rhythm responds with extraordinary sensitiveness to the movements of Christina's mood, and shows how at the centre of her anguish is a single gnawing grief.

This poetry has a remarkable concentration. Everything seems to be directed towards a central point and related to it. Once a subject has been started, there is not much development in its treatment, and the element of surprise is kept for small effects inside a narrow compass. It is characteristic of Christina that she loves a kind of rondel in which a phrase is repeated several times, and this device gives a great compactness and concentration. So in what was almost her last poem, Christina expresses her conviction that she will soon have the rest for which her broken body and humble spirit yearn:

Sleeping at last, the trouble and tumult over,
    Sleeping at last, the struggle and horror past,
Cold and white, out of sight of friend and of lover,
        Sleeping at last.

No more a tired heart downcast or overcast,
No more pangs that wring or shifting fears that hover,
    Sleeping at last in a dreamless sleep locked fast.

Fast asleep. Singing birds in their leafy cover
    Cannot wake her, nor shake her the gusty blast.
Under the purple thyme and the purple clover
        Sleeping at last.

The beating repetitions and the internal rhymes give an impression of something all-absorbing and final, something which is so single and overwhelming that it is best displayed by this strict economy of words. The other phrases seem to be variations on the insistent, central theme and to elaborate its implications without in any way interfering with its predominance.

Christina's life of devotion had many trials and sorrows. She had moments when she felt that it was too hard for her and that, despite all her efforts, it was almost more than she could bear. She knew as well as anyone the seeming perversity of the Divine Will, which treats too often Its servants with what looks like wilful harshness. Just as Saint Teresa, in her aristocratic independence, would chide her Creator for His treatment of her, so Christina, humbler but not less frank, complains of the weariness of well-doing:

> I would have gone; God bade me stay:
>   I would have worked; God bade me rest.
> He broke my will from day to day;
>   He read my yearnings unexpressed,
>   And said them nay.
>
> Now I would stay; God bids me go:
>   Now I would rest; God bids me work.
> He breaks my heart tost to and fro;
>   My soul is wrung with doubts that lurk
>   And vex it so.

Then Christina would think that she had gone too far and would abase herself, feeling that any reward which might await her would still be too great and that she must not expect it or even pray for it:

> Give me the lowest place: or if for me
>   That lowest place too high, make one more low
> Where I may sit and see
>   My God and love Thee so.

Her way was hard, and she made it harder by the extreme scru-
pulosity of her conscience. No demand was too severe, no standard too high for her.

Yet she had her rewards, fitful perhaps and tantalizing and
certainly rare, but none the less, when they came, wonderfully
assuring and comforting. In her long search for God she had
moments when she felt that she was in His presence and that He
spoke to her soul. Without this she would surely have lapsed into
despair; through this her doubts were dispelled and her fears
turned to hopes. With characteristic humility she believed that
such moments came when she least deserved them, so neglectful
had she been of her first duties. Then in a radiant moment she
would find herself comforted by a divine voice and know that all
was well:

> I have not sought Thee, I have not found Thee,
>   I have not thirsted for Thee:
> And now cold billows of death surround me,
> Buffeting billows of death astound me, —
>   Wilt Thou look upon, wilt Thou see
>   Thy perishing me?
>
> "Yea, I have sought thee, yea, I have found thee,
>   Yea, I have thirsted for thee,
> Yea, long ago with love's bands I bound thee:
> Now the Everlasting Arms surround thee, —
>   Through death's darkness I look and see
>   And clasp thee to Me."

This life, so tried by sacrifice and sickness, by denial of so much
that Christina valued and yet valued not at the highest price, was
after all to be rewarded by the one thing for which she looked.
Her last years, tormented by cancer and darkened by the deaths
of those whom she loved, were also the time of her surest faith
and strongest confidence in the inestimable felicity which awaits
the chosen. She was still a great poet, still a mistress of passionate

and melancholy song. But this song was now given almost to a single end, and her old love of the living world had ceased to count.

Christina Rossetti presents in a remarkable manner the case of a poet whose naturally Romantic tendencies were turned into a different channel by the intensity of her religious faith. But for it she might have continued to write in the spirit of "Goblin Market" and have illustrated many delightful corners of consciousness by her ingenious and sprightly art. But this spirit was in conflict with her devotion to God and her search for salvation. From this conflict and the sacrifices which it entailed, she wrote a different kind of poetry, deeply personal and intimate and often painful, in which she dramatized her secret feelings in passionate song. This too was a kind of Romantic art, an escape from her actual troubles and at the same time a comment on them, by which she was able to penetrate many hidden corners of her consciousness and to present them in compelling, concrete forms. Indeed, it was this conflict between her human self and her divine calling which created her most characteristic poetry. But her purely religious work owed little to it. In this she might sometimes allow herself a small flight of decorative fancy, but as a whole the subject was too serious for her to stray far from what orthodoxy told her to be true. Her achievement suggests that though the Romantic spirit is concerned with another world, this other world is not that of common faith. It is what the poet finds and fashions for himself, not what has been sought and sanctified by millions of men and women. So when she spoke of it, though she might indeed feel an anguished longing for it, Christina did not try to create it for herself but conformed to traditional ideas of it. In the end she passed beyond the Romantic spirit by the intensity of her faith, and in so doing showed a weakness in that spirit which seems to have no peace for this kind of vision.

Painful though her conflict often was, Christina solved it to her own satisfaction. When she passed beyond her early fancies and beyond even her poems of unsatisfied love, she found something else more absorbing and more inspiring. Nor did her poetry lose by this. The eternity for which she hungered brought all her emotions into play and enabled her to give a final, irresistible power to her words. Because she disciplined herself so sternly to the tasks of religion, she kept a singularly direct approach to many kinds of experience and assessed their worth with uncompromising candour. She had her own peculiar insight into the mystery of things, and it was all the keener because it was supported by the full resources of her rich nature. Her faith, with its passionate honesty and its extremely personal emotions, was the fulfilment of her devoted and tender soul. In the end she is a great religious poet, because religion called out in her all that was essentially and most truly herself. Only in God could she find a finally satisfying object for the abounding love which was the mainspring of her life and character.

XII

THE ROMANTIC ACHIEVEMENT

THE WORD "Romantic" has been used so often and for so
many purposes that it is impossible to confine it to any
single meaning, still less to attempt a new definition of it.
Let it suffice that it is applied to a phase of English poetry which
began in 1789 with Blake's *Songs of Innocence* and ended with
the deaths of Keats and Shelley. This at least fixes a historical
period, and there is no great quarrel about calling it the "Romantic age." In it five major poets, Blake, Coleridge, Wordsworth,
Shelley, and Keats, despite many differences, agreed on one vital
point: that the creative imagination is closely connected with a
peculiar insight into an unseen order behind visible things. This
belief gave a special character to their work and determined their
main contributions to the theory and practice of poetry. But both
within this period and afterwards there were other poets whose
conception of the imagination was not quite this, and who,
though they may have much in common with the great Five, are
not in agreement with them on this essential point. On the one
side, Byron, while sharing many of their subjects and tastes,
denied the importance of the imagination and did not believe in
any transcendental order. On the other side, Poe, erring as it were
by excess, thought that the imagination is so concerned with a
Beyond that it has little connection with the actual world. Between these extremes other poets, notably the Pre-Raphaelites,
sought to find a mean, but none of them accepted the full Romantic view. Dante Gabriel Rossetti certainly looked for another
world, but, since he defined it as beauty and sought it through
love, he narrowed its scope and limited his own achievement.
Swinburne hardly believed in any Beyond, except what he found

in the essence of poetry, and made no attempt to define what this meant to him. Christina Rossetti, despite certain affinities with Coleridge and Keats, passed beyond them when she gave her devotion to the celestial world of Christian faith and showed that the indefinite notions of a Beyond, which meant so much to the great Five, were incompatible with her precise and literal beliefs.

The history of Romantic poetry in England falls into two sections. In one, a bold original outlook is developed and practised; in the other, it is criticized or exaggerated or limited or, in the last resort, abandoned. On the one hand, there is a straight line of development; on the other hand, there are variations and divagations and secessions. But both sections belong to a single movement which rises from a prevailing mood of longing for something more complete and more satisfying than the familiar world. Such a mood, of course, is not in the least new or uncommon, but in the Romantic period and afterwards it dominated many creative minds and had an enormous influence on poetry. This was a truly European phenomenon. France, Germany, Russia, and Spain all show it, but almost alone in England is the poetry which rises from it connected with a visionary insight into a superior order of being. There is hardly a trace of this in Hugo or Heine or Lermontov or Espronceda. They have their full share of Romantic longing, but almost nothing of Romantic vision. Indeed, almost the only Continental poets who resemble the great Five are the German, Friedrich Hölderlin, and the Russian, Fëdor Tyutchev. Hölderlin sought to find through a living Germany the lost vision of the Greek gods, and Tyutchev, who had something like Wordsworth's capacity for responding to the unregarded appeal of natural things, saw behind them another world of powers and dangers and conflicts. But these are exceptions, and, apart from them, the five English poets did something to which there is no parallel in their age. Their work was indeed of a peculiar kind, and it is a remarkable chance that they should have agreed on so original a doctrine. But just because they were so original and so devoted to their special aims, they provoked modifications of their views, and what other poets did to adapt or alter them is an interesting comment on their work.

An outlook so intense and in some ways so exacting as that of the great Five could not fail to be fraught with dangers. Like all creeds which insist on some central article of belief, the belief in the imagination ran the risk that its adherents would pervert the intentions of the founders. It was poised on a perilous compromise. It insisted passionately on the imagination, but demanded that it should be related to truth and reality. This was an admirable ambition, but it was all too easily frustrated, for the good reason that it might run counter to the mood of dissatisfaction and longing on which the whole position was based. Not all poets were as fortunate as Wordsworth and Keats in finding that their discontents could be cured by contact with the nature which lay at their doors, or that, by following their instinctive love of visible things, they could find themselves in the presence of what they called "eternity." Others were content to dream dreams on the chance that they might some day prove to be true, but they did not really care very much whether this happened or not. Of this number, Poe is a notable example. In him the impulse to escape was so powerful that he surrendered to it and did not care what relations his dreams might have to the common world. The result is that his poetry touches actuality at too few points and even then in a tentative, shrinking way. His work has still the attraction which belongs to youthful desires, but, despite its varied accomplishment, it never quite moves us as a record of mature experience and is a criticism of life only in the sense that it is a rejection of it. Poe's ultimate failure is a comment on the Romantic position, which makes it possible for a man to be so absorbed in the Beyond that he pays little attention to the here and now. In contrast to Poe are those other poets who spoiled their work in an opposite way, by assuming the airs of visionaries although they had no visions. It was all too easy to enjoy irresponsible fancies for their own sake and to persuade oneself that it did not matter what was said, provided that it was new and exciting. This is almost what happened to Byron in his earlier years, when his poetry was built not on recognition of truth about himself, but on what he would like the world to think about him. What was bad enough in Byron was worse in less gifted men, and the nineteenth century provides too many examples of poets who cared less for the revelation of truth through the imagination than for cutting an interesting figure in the public eye. That is why the minor figures of the Romantic age are so dull; for in the end nothing is less attractive than pose.

The evil could go deeper than this, and some of its more sinister manifestations account for the bad name which the Romantic spirit has in some quarters today. Dreams are one thing, and pose is another, but worse than either is the state of illusion or self-deception to which the imagination may drag a man if it is not handled with self-knowledge and self-criticism. In such a state he believes what he wishes and does not ask if it is really true or not. He may delude himself about facts and substitute his private version of them for the reality, or he may delude himself about values and persuade himself that his own wayward or corrupt tastes are a real criterion of worth. Because the Romantic outlook sets so high a value on the individual self, it runs the risk of allowing men to live in their private universes without paying sufficient attention to what happens outside them. In this condition they make their own laws and try to apply them to the common world. This may not prevent them from producing accomplished works of art, but these will be none the less perverted. There are moments, and indeed more than moments, when Victor Hugo allows himself this self-indulgence, with the result that we do not know how seriously to take him. It was this tendency, too, which spoiled much work of the nineties. The Aesthetic gospel, as Wilde propounded it, not only denied that truth is desirable in itself, but attempted to glorify certain things which mankind has condemned. What is wrong, for instance, with *Salomé* is not merely that its rhetoric rings false, but that some of the assumptions on which it is built are abhorrent. The Romantic spirit may be a dangerous poison when it is allowed to work too freely, and it is not surprising that "Romantic" is used as a term of condemnation for actions and thoughts in which an accepted scheme of values is perverted or replaced by others ultimately repellent. Of course, this criticism has little relevance to the great Romantic poets of England, but the danger is real and must not be overlooked.

A second danger lies in the exacting demands which the Romantic outlook makes of its votaries. It insists that a man must exploit to the utmost what is characterisically his own, and especially his individual vision and special inspiration. It places little trust in the forms and techniques which other poets have fashioned for common use, and tradition means little to it. This put the Romantic poets at a disadvantage in comparison with such men as Virgil and Milton, who were sustained in composition by a commonly accepted theory of what poetry ought to be, and approved by general consent in using means fashioned by other men for this end. Of course, their success and their fame came from their masterly use of such means, but we cannot doubt that Virgil was able, despite many misgivings, to write the *Aeneid*, or Milton, after long years spent in public service, to compose *Paradise Lost*, just because they had behind them a tradition which gave them confidence and enabled them to attempt what would otherwise have been insuperable tasks. The Romantics had no such support. They relied mainly on inspiration, and inspiration, left to itself, is notoriously untrustworthy. Those who set all their hopes on it and shape their lives by it may find themselves suddenly robbed of its strength and unable to regain it. This happened to Coleridge in one way and to Wordsworth in another. If Coleridge's collapse was more pathetic, Wordsworth's was more dismal. Neither their art nor their outlooks were of use to them when the crisis came, and their efforts to continue as before show how frail the roots of their inspiration were. If they had belonged to a well-established tradition, things might have been different; for tradition enables a poet to conserve his powers, to recruit his strength from other quarters when he is not able to do everything from his own resources. It even helps him to exert himself in fields for which he is not ideally suited, but in which none the less he may be able to win noteworthy successes. The Romantics relied on what was most unlike others in themselves, on their own peculiarly individual gifts. The result was that, by too much concentration on them, they exhausted these gifts and had nothing to put in their place.

A third danger which threatened the Romantics lay in their conception of the Beyond, of that other world which they found in vision by using the imagination. In dealing with this they were always vague, and such vagueness has its own perils. It might be argued that the poets could not but be indefinite about a matter which was beyond the reach of descriptive words, that they were too honest to claim for it a clarity which it did not possess for them. This is true; but the Romantic vagueness is such that its exponents may convey so little to us that they fail in their main task. The problem hardly arose so long as the poets used or invented myths adequate to their needs. Though the issues presented in "Kubla Khan" or *Prometheus Unbound* or *Hyperion* are indeed vast, they are intelligible and stirring because they are given in concrete forms which have a vivid appeal. But the danger is more apparent when no myth is used, and the poet tries to say all that he can in direct, descriptive statement. Despite their revolt against the eighteenth century, the Romantics had not completely abandoned its habit of abstract expression. It is true that they do not fall into such inept pomposities as Victor Hugo when they talk about "eternity" and "infinity," nor need we doubt that to them these words meant more than they did to him. But there are times when at least Wordsworth and Shelley try to present vast conceptions through direct statement, although they are beyond its reach and can be adequately expressed only in symbols. The result is that in some moments which clearly meant a great deal to these poets, their ideas are wrapped in obscurity and their sense of mystery is ineffective because they lack the art to convey its full significance. We see that something of utmost import is afoot and that the poet is transported outside his usual self, but we hardly know what has happened to him. The skies open, and he soars on the wings of inspiration to explore the infinite, but an impenetrable obscurity hides his goal from our eyes.

Both Coleridge and Poe insist that vagueness is necessary to poetry, and both display its perils. In their desire to secure it, both at times rely more on sound than on visual impressions or intelligible meaning. Poe's repetitions and invented words show his trust that sound will do what is usually done by images. Sound is of course as necessary to poetry as sight or meaning, but it is dangerous to give it too emphatic a place. This Coleridge too seems at times to have done. There are places in his poetry where we feel that though there is a perfectly intelligible meaning, it is there somehow by accident, and that Coleridge did not quite intend it to be what it is. Take, for instance, the end of "Kubla Khan":

> For he on honey-dew hath fed
> And drunk the milk of Paradise.

If we insist that a poem should be understood, we ask what is meant by honey-dew, and are disappointed to find that it is not a very attractive substance. So we suspect that Coleridge has used it because of its sound or because of the vague associations which the combination of honey and dew starts in our minds. Again, a little earlier, he says:

> A damsel with a dulcimer
> In a vision once I saw.

A dulcimer is not a very melodious or a very elegant instrument, and the visual impression is not seductive. But did Coleridge really intend to produce one? Did he not use the word "dulcimer" for its sound, and especially for its consonants which correspond prettily with those of "damsel"? When Romantic poetry aspires too ardently to become music, it tends to leave some of its sense behind. The result is often delightful, but, when we look more closely at it, it reveals a frailty which we do not expect in great poetry.

A more serious danger in this vagueness is that it may come very near to nonsense, as it sometimes does with Poe. In his case we can almost see what happens. His discontent with the actual world was so great that in his desire for escape he half visualized an order of things which is beyond understanding. In it the laws of existence are annihilated, and even the bondage of words is broken by making them serve a new purpose of hints and echoes. What Poe did shyly and solemnly, Edward Lear did with inspired confidence. Like Poe, he was a prey to melancholy and a haunting sense of failure, and, like Poe, he transmuted his misery into melodies in which the music of words is much more important than their sense. He is a master of glowing rhythms. His nonsense poems bewitch the ear, and compared with him even Lewis Carroll has no more than a logical or mathematical elegance. Nor are Lear's subjects entirely alien to a Romantic taste. He too has a predilection for remote places and unusual happenings, even something like Wordsworth's interest in a primitive simplicity of life. Are not most elements of Romantic poetry to be found in the strange situation of the Yonghy-Bonghy-Bò?

> On the coast of Coromandel
> Where the early pumpkins blow,
> In the middle of the woods
> Lived the Yonghy-Bonghy-Bò.
> Two old chairs and half a candle, —
> One old jug without a handle, —
> These were all the worldly goods,
> In the middle of the woods,
> These were all the worldly goods
> Of the Yonghy-Bonghy-Bò,
> Of the Yonghy-Bonghy-Bò.

The accomplishment here is perhaps greater than anything in Poe, but the methods are the same as Poe's, from the ingeniously interrelated rhymes to the emphatic repetitions, and their origin in Lear's personal history bears some resemblance to the sources of Poe's inspiration. Again, the Romantics affected a poetry of melancholy and often wrote songs of a melting sweetness, in which images of grief are wedded to a haunting melody. This Lear often does, as for instance:

> Calico Pie,
> The little birds fly
> Down to the calico tree,
> Their wings were blue,
> And they sang "Tilly-loo!"
> Till away they flew, —
> And they never came back to me!
> They never came back!
> They never came back!
> They never came back to me!

In his emotions and his methods, Lear bears a startling resemblance to some of the Romantic poets, and his unprecedented art raises awkward questions about their achievement.

Lear's nonsense poetry is literally a *reductio ad absurdum* of Romantic methods, and especially of the belief in vagueness. He differs from his grave models not in his means but in his end. He wished to write nonsense, and with the insight of genius saw that the Romantic technique was perfectly suited to it. With him the Romantic indefiniteness passes beautifully into absurdity, and his own inchoate sorrows vanish in the divine light of nonsense. He has indeed his own kind of imagination which is accompanied by a special insight. By transforming his state into that of the Yonghy-Bonghy-Bò or the Quangle Wangle Quee or the Dong with the Luminous Nose, he both invents enchanting figures of fancy and is able to have a clearer insight into his own troubles by placing them in an unexpected perspective. Lear showed how close the Romantic vagueness was to nonsense, and exploited it for his own purposes. The result is outside all literary canons, but none the less miraculous and magical. Lear chose his means deliberately in a full knowledge of their worth. It is a different matter with poets who use not dissimilar means in all seriousness, without seeing their menace to a sublime or a solemn mood. There are moments when Wordsworth and Coleridge and Shelley come near to absurdity, because they try to say more than words will carry. This danger implicit in the Romantic outlook was not always faced openly or surmounted with success.

These dangers which threatened the Romantics must not be confused with the limitations within which they worked, and which gave to their poetry its distinctive character. Those who do not like this poetry may complain of the bounds which enclose it, but it remains true that without these bounds it would not be what it is. Every successful achievement in the arts comes from some limitation on the artist's work. In order to do one thing he must eschew another. Just as the Roman poets of the Augustan age formed their grave and majestic harmonies by abandoning the conversational ease of Catullus, or as the French Symbolists perfected their subtle and musical art by avoiding anything that savoured of realism or Parnassian objectivity, so the Romantics won their triumphs by confining their art to certain fields of experience and excluding much else which has often belonged to poetry but did not really concern them. Such a process seems inevitable to the progress of poetry. The poet must do something new, but he cannot do it without casting aside what he thinks outworn. More than this, he must find the right means to say what concerns him most deeply, and, since he is after all a limited human being, he rightly works in a field where he is at home and able to act freely. This is true of the Romantics, who began as revolutionaries in poetry and were determined not to write like their predecessors of the eighteenth century. The result was that their art, despite its range and variety, is confined within certain limits, and a glance at some of these may help to illustrate the nature of their achievement.

In the first place, as the example of Christina Rossetti shows, the Romantic outlook denied any real place to orthodox religion. It was too individualistic and in the widest sense too Protestant to allow the kind of conformity which she needed. Each poet was indeed concerned with a transcendental order, but it was in some sense his own and shared with no one else. Though all speak of "eternity," they do not mean the same thing by it, and they interpret its manifestations differently. Nor, as we have seen, were they able to give precise accounts of it. It is essentially vague. This is not what the orthodox believer demands of the other world. Christina Rossetti had no doubts that the heaven of her prayers would be as the Bible describes it, and this clarity was an essential element in its appeal to her. What is true of her is true of other religious poets. The celestial landscape of the City of God, as Abélard or Dante or Vaughan sees it, is solid and luminous, and nothing is more alien to their desires than that it should be wrapped in obscurity. Nor is this less true of religions other than Christianity. Homer sees Olympus as a perfect exemplar of the most beautiful places on earth, bathed in a dazzling light and untroubled by snow or rain or cloud. Pindar's vision of the Olympian gods is singularly definite. Their existence is gay with music, a flawless counterpart to the intermittent and transitory joy which men know in their fullest hours on earth. These brilliant and satisfying visions of a celestial world are possible only because they are based on a common belief which men accept as true. In their advance into the unknown, the Romantics had no such faith as this. They had broken too violently with tradition to accept literally its account of another world, and their own ideas of such a world were not at all like those of orthodox faith. Their other world was not something which awaits the delivered soul, but a mystery lurking behind visible things, and a mystery it must remain if it was to keep its hold on the poets. When Wordsworth in later life enjoyed his "evening of extraordinary splendour" and tried to interpret it in terms of Christianity, he had forsaken his most characteristic beliefs, and the result is an inferior version of the "Ode on Intimations of Immortality." There was something in the Romantic outlook which prevented it from being inspired to its best poetry by the visions which had long obsessed other men.

Something also hampered the Romantics from transforming their transcendental longings even into unorthodox religion. It is of course possible for a poet, who is haunted by thoughts of another world but unable to accommodate them to conventional beliefs, to create his own visible shape for it. Virgil, for instance, resembled the Romantics in his sense of the insoluble mystery which encompasses human life. He felt that this world is not everything and is in many ways unreal or like a dream. This mystery he hardly dared to probe, but acquiesced in the impossibility of finding any solid answers to his questions. None the less, he succeeds in producing a religious effect, in making us believe that men are moved by spiritual forces and are the agents of a supernatural destiny. To some degree the English Romantics tried to do the same thing. They cast their thoughts on transcendental matters into myths, like "The Ancient Mariner" and *Prometheus Unbound*. But the results, however rich in inspired insight and impressive vision, are not somehow religious. They may have their own kind of faith and their own sense of the holy, but the emotions which they arouse are not what we associate with religious devotion, however unusual. They are too explicit, too emphatic, too tied to the limitations of their mythological setting, to convey even anything similar to Virgil's sense of man labouring towards some dimly descried and faintly apprehended goal. The fact is that the Romantics are concerned with a mystery which belongs not to faith but to the imagination. It is not something outside themselves which they try to realize, but something which they create largely by their own efforts. Even when they feel themselves in the presence of "eternity," it is not entirely external but has many connections with their own selves. Their approach to the Beyond and to the invisible powers which enclose the visible is determined by their conviction that in the last resort the only reality is mind, and that even the universal mind is manifested in individual human minds. Religion seems to demand a sharper dichotomy between the human soul and the divine, and for this reason the Romantics were unable in the last analysis to create a purely religious poetry.

Secondly, the Romantics, who wished to extend the sphere of poetry and succeeded in covering a much wider range than the Augustans, were limited in their scope by their conception of the beautiful. The ideal of the beautiful, which was followed in different ways by Shelley and Keats and Rossetti, inexorably exalts one kind of experience at the expense of another. The Romantics' test of the beautiful was the effect which it made on them. They recognized it when it mastered their senses and exalted them to some vision beyond. In so complex a matter they are not in any way to be blamed for this view. It is certainly more objective than modern views, based partly on Poe, that beauty is haphazard and subjective, an event which happens for no clear reason in ourselves. The danger of this is that the poet's world may become solipsistic and his work defeat the understanding of other men. Nor did the Romantics fall into the error, as some of their successors did, of thinking that the beautiful is confined to certain classes of experience, known and acknowledged and respected. Such a view not only inhibits free creation but makes nonsense of much older poetry which was written from a very different outlook. The Romantics thought that beauty is a final quality of reality revealed through visible things. It was for them to seek it, and they believed that they knew it by the enchantment which it laid upon them. In practice they might find, as Rossetti did, that it is confined to some single sphere like love, but that did not make them think that it is necessarily and always so confined, and they were ready to recognize it wherever it might appear. With their theory we need have no quarrel, but their practice shows that their conception of beauty was limited by their outlook.

Indeed, we can hardly deny that the Romantics confined poetry to a somewhat limited corner of existence. Of course, in this they discovered many unknown tracts. The rural scene which appealed to Wordsworth, Coleridge's moonlit mystery between sleep and waking, Shelley's ecstatic contemplation of ideas, and Keats' attempt to find the bliss of pure creation were subjects which few, if any, poets had attempted before. The same might almost be said of Rossetti's search for beauty through love and of Swinburne's feeling for the essential, indefinable poetry of things. But this very concentration on what stirred their imaginations meant that the Romantics rejected or neglected many subjects in which other men might find a wonderful magic, and it is significant that Byron, who did not share their beliefs, was able to compose a more varied poetry. In the realistic passages of *Don Juan*, he wrote about contemporary life without subservience to conventional ideas of beauty, and found much to which others were blind. Byron deserves credit for having seen that in the crowded panorama of contemporary life even the most prosaic activities may provoke real poetry. The great Five, and Rossetti and Swinburne after them, were inspired only by the more exciting and more mysterious aspects of man and nature. Even Wordsworth's simpler poems, which were at first so ridiculed for what looked like a too artless simplicity, deal with an isolated life in special conditions which exclude the complexities of urban sophistication. The modern revolt against the Romantics has been partly due to a conviction that they, with their cult of solitude and strangeness, did not write a realistic poetry of the world which they knew. Nor indeed could they have done so. They revived poetry by looking into themselves and isolating unusual experiences in their inner biographies. This turning inward was their answer to the previous age, with its insistence on the externality of things and its lack of belief in the self. From the intensity of their concentration on the self, the Romantics gained some of their greatest successes, but the price paid was a neglect of much which stared ordinary men in the eyes.

None the less, we cannot complain that by their devotion to the mysteries of life the Romantics failed to appreciate life itself. It is of course true that they do not belong to the company of universal poets, like Homer and Shakespeare, in whom everything human touches some chord and passes into music. But they are closer to common life than Pope or Dryden, even than Milton or Spenser. It would be hard to think of another man who combined, as Blake did, an extraordinary power of vision with the tenderest compassion for the outcast and the oppressed, or who, like Shelley, used his Platonic musings to unfold an enormous scheme for the regeneration of the world. Even the staid Wordsworth found a new source of profound poetry in the humble creatures of fell and waterside, in leach-gatherers and old huntsmen, small girls and idiot boys. Even so devoted a lover of physical nature as Keats came to see that the poet must not detach himself from mankind, but live in compassionate understanding of it. And this understanding was in many ways new. It has a new tenderness which is far removed from the aristocratic dignity of the Augustans or the princely splendours of the Elizabethans. In their attempts to understand man in the depths of his being, the Romantics were moved by convictions which give a special humanity to their poetry.

A third limitation on Romantic poetry was set by their conception of what a poet's outlook ought to be. The whole movement has been called the rebirth of wonder, and there is justice in the title. To be sure, all poetry lives by wonder, by the delight of discovery and the exaltation which it brings. But the Romantics certainly stressed the virtues of wonder and gave to it a special prominence in their work. Most of them believed that the spirit must be quickened by releasing it from the bonds of habit, from the conventional frame which stifles a man's capacity, and that this can be done by awaking a delighted amazement even at familiar things. It meant that a poet must regain a special simplicity, which Wordsworth and Coleridge compared to that of a child. What Wordsworth says so eloquently in the "immortal Ode," Coleridge announced in a lecture:

> The poet is one who carries the simplicity of childhood into the powers of manhood; who, with a soul unsubdued by habit, un-shackled by custom, contemplates all things with the freshness and the wonder of a child.[1]

Shelley does not use the comparison with childhood, but in his *Defence of Poetry* says what is in effect very much the same thing:

> It purges from our inward sight the film of familiarity, which ob-scures from us the wonder of our being. It compels us to feel that which we perceive, and to imagine that which we know. It creates anew the universe after it has been annihilated in our minds by the recurrence of impressions blunted by reiteration.

This view was developed by Wordsworth until he formed his theory of the need for wonder and of the part which it ought to play in our lives. For him it is the same as "admiration," and when he speaks of "admiration," he means a lively wakefulness which liberates us from the deadening routine of custom and stirs in us that awe which is the gateway to vision. It is this which he praises in his own *Michael*:

> In his thoughts there were obscurities,
> Wonder, and admiration, things that wrought
> Not less than a religion in his heart.

Through wonder Wordsworth found that excited awe which gave meaning to his worship of nature.

This belief in wonder, which all the great Five held in some degree, affected their poetry. In their reaction against the idea of a common world as the eighteenth century had believed in it, they found their objects of wonder mainly in what is strange and unusual. This is true not merely of Coleridge and Keats but of

Wordsworth and Shelley. Wordsworth rejected the life of cities that he might live close to nature, but in his time nature was strange enough to most people, and Wordsworth sought in it its least familiar and less admired aspects. In his desire for a regenerated world, Shelley lived among strange ideas which were at war with many accepted standards in his time and were thought by most of his contemporaries to be mad or wicked or both. Time has accustomed us to these notions and dulled their paradox. But when the Romantics formed them, much of their attraction lay in their strangeness. And this, more than anything else, determined the course of the Romantic spirit in the nineteenth century. The love of the intrinsically strange because it awakes wonder and creates a peculiar enchantment came to be regarded as the primary task of poetry. That is why Kipling, speaking of Coleridge's "demon lover" and Keats' "perilous seas," says:

Remember that in all the millions permitted there are no more than five — five little lines — of which one can say: "These are the pure Magic. These are the clear Vision. The rest is only poetry." [2]

Today it is hard to see how anyone could give quite that praise to Coleridge and Keats. The lines are indeed wonderful, but they are not the only pure magic or the only clear vision in all poetry. Yet for nearly a hundred years such a judgement would have commanded wide assent, and this shows how the Romantics imposed their love of strangeness on the world.

The element of wonder which meant so much to the Romantics affected their work in a special way. In their desire to restore a lively vision of existence, they rejected the mechanistic philosophy of Locke and went far in the opposite direction, finding their metaphysics in an idealism in which the mind creates reality. But though they were much concerned with ultimate issues, and though at least Coleridge and Shelley studied philosophy, the result for most of them was a belief in a spiritual activity in

which the strict reason plays only a subordinate part. Though
Shelley enjoyed ideas, as few men do, for their own sake, in the
end what counted with him was less reason than the emotions.
Though Coleridge played the philosopher all through his life,
his finest poetry owes little to his philosophical views and exists
almost in defiance of them. But the greatest rebels against the old
concept of reason were Blake and Keats. For Blake philosophy is
the enemy because it destroys our delight and wonder at existence. He fights it with all his weapons and condemns its exponents to Ulro, the lowest of his four states of being, where everything is reduced to rule and line and the creative spirit is dead.
For him intuition and vision are infinitely more important than
reason, and in "Auguries of Innocence" he proclaims that the
simplest things provide arguments which no philosopher can
refute:

> A Riddle or the Cricket's Cry
> Is to Doubt a fit Reply.
> The Emmet's Inch and Eagle's Mile
> Make Lame Philosophy to smile.
> He who Doubts from what he sees
> Will ne'er Believe, do what you Please.
> If the Sun and Moon should doubt,
> They'd immediately Go out.

Blake wanted vivid, visionary experience, not the hesitations and
uncertainties of abstract thought. In his own way Keats agreed
with him. Though in a famous passage of *Lamia* he seems to
exalt sensations at the expense of intelligence, what he really does
is to insist that the imagination is more important than the analytical reason:

> Do not all charms fly
> At the mere touch of cold philosophy?
> There was an awful rainbow once in heaven:
> We knew her woof and texture; she is given
> In the dull catalogue of common things.

The Romantics were far from thinking that intelligence is unimportant or that thought is not necessary to poetry, but they insisted that this thought must be imaginative and not abstract, and that it must look at all the qualities of things and not at their general natures.

This is a reasonable point of view, but it limits a poet's performance. In rejecting philosophy and natural science, the Romantics accentuated the isolation of poetry from the current thought of their time. It was not in this spirit that Aeschylus created his magnificent myths about the great issues which faced Athens, or that Dante put into the *Divine Comedy* all the philosophy and political thought of the Middle Ages, or that Milton justified the ways of God to man by presenting a vast scheme of man's history and place in the universe. There is no eternal or necessary quarrel between abstractions and imaginative vision. But in their distrust of reason, as the eighteenth century understood it, the Romantics found themselves almost forced to concentrate on something which is not indeed irrational but might become so in less powerful hands. The result is that their poetry lacks that element of strict, prolonged thought which gives an additional strength not merely to the great Greeks but to such writers as Racine and Goethe, whose strictly poetical power owes a great deal to the hard thought which has preceded composition and is indeed transcended in the poetry, but none the less is invisibly present and powerful. The Romantics have their moments of inspiring thought and wonderful insight, but they lack this special strength which comes from uniting sustained mental effort to poetry, and their work is therefore limited in this respect.

Within these limitations the Romantics worked, and we should not wish that they had done otherwise; for by this they were able to secure their own territory and make the most of it. They brought to poetry not merely surprise and wonder and vision, which after all may be found in much great poetry, but something else which was more characteristically their own and may perhaps be regarded as the central quality of their art. In

their vivid perception of sensible things, they were able almost
in the same moment to have a vision of another world, and this
illuminates and gives significance to sensible things in such a
way that we can hardly distinguish them from the mysteries
which they have opened and with which they are inextricably
connected. The result is that they shed a celestial light on the
objects of sense and make them examples of something else much
more wonderful. The most haphazard event may so strike them
that in a single moment they see both the individual object and
its eternal significance. Just as a Greek poet like Pindar believed
that there are moments in life when a divine glory illuminates
earthly things and makes men partake of the timeless felicity of
the gods, so the Romantics believed that what matters most is this
interpenetration of the familiar scene by some everlasting presence which illuminates and explains it. It is this which makes
Romantic poetry what it is, and this above all is due to the Romantic trust in the imagination, which works through the senses
to something beyond and above. Blake understood this when he
said in the poem "Eternity":

> He who binds to himself a joy
> Does the winged life destroy;
> But he who kisses the joy as it flies
> Lives in eternity's sun rise.

The essence of Romantic poetry is that in catching the fleeting
moment of joy it opens the doors to an eternal world.

This characteristic differentiates the Romantic poets from
those of classical antiquity and all who have followed their example. The kind of difference may be illustrated in the treatment
of an age-old theme, the song of the nightingale. Virgil is quite
straightforward when he uses it as a comparison for Orpheus'
lamentation for Eurydice:

> Qualis populea maerens philomela sub umbra
> amissos queritur fetus, quos durus arator

observans nido implumis detraxit, at illa
flet noctem, ramoque sedens miserabile carmen
integrat, et maestis late loca questibus implet.[3]

As the nightingale, sorrowing under a poplar's shade, laments the young she has lost, whom a heartless ploughman has seen and dragged unfledged from the nest. All night long she weeps, and perched on the bough renews her piteous song, and fills all the country round with her sad laments.

This is a fair record of the nightingale's song as a classical poet would interpret it. Of course, Virgil introduces his humanizing touches to make the situation more pathetic, but he is concerned with an actual event and with nothing else. He sees no mysteries and is not concerned with any transcendental issues. This is not the way in which Keats listens to the nightingale. For him its song is much more than a mere song; it is also an event in a timeless order of things:

Thou wast not born for death, immortal Bird!
No hungry generations tread thee down;
The voice I hear this passing night was heard
In ancient days by emperor and clown.

Keats does two things at once. He addresses the individual, living nightingale which has inspired his poem, but he passes beyond it to an ideal bird which is a symbol of unrestricted, timeless song. This method and the outlook which it presupposes are glorified by the associations with an unseen world, and the unseen world is more vividly present because it is displayed in a single actual case.

This dual purpose gives a special character to Romantic poetry. By associating single sensible experiences with some undefined superior order of things, the Romantics have enriched our appreciation of the familiar world and awakened a new awe and wonder at it. Such a poetry is, of course, only one kind among many, and it rises from an outlook not shared by all men. If a society has ever existed which is completely content with what it has and asks for nothing else, it would not need such comfort as the Romantics have to offer. But to all who are dissatisfied with a current order or a conventional scheme of things, this spirit brings not an anodyne but an inspiration. From discontent it moves to a vision of a sublime state in which the temporal, without losing its individuality, is related to the timeless, and the many defects of the given world are seen to be irrelevant and insignificant in comparison with the mysteries which enclose it. The Romantic poet appeals to us because he does something which we cannot but respect. He believes that in exercising his imagination he creates life and adds to the sum of living experience. He wishes to be not a passive observer but an active agent in a world which exists by a perpetual process of creation. He takes his part in this process by making men aware of the reality which sustains the changing visible scene and is the cause and explanation of everything that matters in it. We may not accept all his assumptions and conclusions, but we must admire the spirit in which he approaches his task, and admit that the problems which he seeks to solve must not be shirked by anyone who wishes to understand the universe in which we live.

NOTES

NOTES

CHAPTER I

1. John Locke, *The Reasonableness of Christianity*, in *Works* (12th ed.), VI, 135.

2. John Locke, *An Essay Concerning Human Understanding*, in *Works*, II, 11, 3.

3. *A Vision of the Last Judgment*, in *Poetry and Prose of William Blake*, ed. by Geoffrey Keynes (1 vol., 4th ed.; London: The Nonesuch Press, 1939), p. 639.

4. Samuel Taylor Coleridge, *Biographia Literaria*, ed. by J. Shawcross (2 vols.; Oxford, 1907), I, 202. Cf. Coleridge's review of poems of Drake and Halleck in the *Southern Literary Messenger*, April 1836: "Imagination is possibly in man a lesser degree of the creative power of God."

5. Novalis [Friedrich von Hardenberg], letter of February 27th, 1799, in *Gesämmelte Werke*, ed. by Carl Seelig (Zürich, 1945), V, 274.

6. William Shakespeare, *A Midsummer Night's Dream*, Act V, scene 1, 12–17.

7. *Ibid.*, Act V, scene 1, 23–27.

8. W. H. Woodward, *Vittorino da Feltre* (Firenze, 1923), p. 175.

9. Coleridge, *Biographia Literaria*, I, 59.

10. Blake, *A Vision of the Last Judgment*, in *Poetry and Prose*, p. 651.

11. *Letters of Samuel Taylor Coleridge*, ed. by Ernest Hartley Coleridge (2 vols.; London, 1895), I, 352.

12. Blake, Fragment, in *Poetry and Prose*, p. 107.

13. Blake, Marginalia to Sir Joshua Reynolds's *Discourses*, in *Poetry and Prose*, p. 777.

14. *Ibid.*, p. 788.

15. Blake, "Auguries of Innocence," in *Poetry and Prose*, p. 118.

16. Blake, Fragment, in *Poetry and Prose*, p. 128.

17. Blake, Annotations to Wordsworth's Poems, in *Poetry and Prose*, p. 821.

18. John Keats, *Endymion*, I, 795–800.

19. Coleridge, *Biographia Literaria*, II, 5.

20. *Letters of Samuel Taylor Coleridge*, II, 450.

21. William Wordsworth, *The Prelude, or Growth of a Poet's Mind*, II, 255–260, ed. by Ernest de Selincourt (Oxford, 1928).

22. *Ibid.*, XIV, 190–192.

23. *Ibid.*, II, 362–369.

24. Wordsworth, *The Recluse*, ll. 71–72.

25. Blake, Annotations to *The Excursion*, in *Poetry and Prose*, p. 823.

26. *Defence of Poetry*, in *Prose Works of Percy Bysshe Shelley*, ed. by Harry Buxton Forman (4 vols.; London, 1880), III, 104.

27. *Hellas*, ll. 776–785, in *Poetical Works of Percy Bysshe Shelley*, ed. by Harry Buxton Forman (4 vols.; London, 1882), III, 80.

28. Blake, *Jerusalem*, in *Poetry and Prose*, p. 442.

CHAPTER II

1. Blake, *Jerusalem*, in *Poetry and Prose*, p. 434.

2. Blake, *Milton*, in *Poetry and Prose*, p. 375.

3. A. E. Housman, *The Name and Nature of Poetry* (Cambridge, England: Cambridge University Press, 1933), p. 43.

4. Blake, *The Marriage of Heaven and Hell*, in *Poetry and Prose*, p. 181.

5. Blake, letter of July 6th, 1803, in *Poetry and Prose*, p. 869.

6. Blake, *A Vision of the Last Judgment*, in *Poetry and Prose*, p. 638.

7. Blake, Annotations to Berkeley's *Siris*, in *Poetry and Prose*, pp. 820, 818.

8. Blake, *The Laocoon Group*, in *Poetry and Prose*, p. 580.

9. Blake, *Vala, or The Four Zoas*, "Night and First," in *Poetry and Prose*, p. 254.

10. *Ibid.*, "Night the Second," p. 278.

11. *Ibid.*, "Night the Fifth," p. 294.

12. Blake, "Europe," in *Poetry and Prose*, p. 214.

13. Blake, "The Human Abstract," in *Poetry and Prose*, p. 76.

14. Blake, letter of July 6th, 1803, in *Poetry and Prose*, p. 869.

15. Cf. *Poetry and Prose*, p. 371.

16. See *Poetry and Prose*, p. 372.

17. Blake, *Proverbs of Hell*, in *Poetry and Prose*, pp. 183–84.

18. Blake, *Vala, or The Four Zoas*, "Night the Fifth," in *Poetry and Prose*, p. 299.

19. Blake, *A Vision of the Last Judgment*, in *Poetry and Prose*, p. 652.

CHAPTER III

1. Coleridge, *Biographia Literaria*, I, 202.

2. See Forman's note (I, 272) to page 202 of the *Biographia Literaria*.

3. *Prose Works of William Wordsworth*, ed. by A. B. Grosart (3 vols.; London, 1876), III, 442.

4. Coleridge, *Biographia Literaria*, II, 5.

5. Dorothy Wordsworth, in Christopher Wordsworth, *Memoirs of William Wordsworth*, ed. by Henry Reed (2 vols.; Boston, 1851), I, 106: "We have been on another tour: we set out last Monday evening at half-past four. The evening was dark and cloudy; we went eight miles, William and Coleridge employing themselves in laying the plan of a ballad, to be published with some pieces of William's."

6. *Memoirs of William Wordsworth*, I, 107–08.

7. William Hazlitt, *Lectures on the English Poets* (1818), in *Collected Works*, ed. by A. R. Waller (13 vols.; London, 1902–1906), V, 166.

8. *Letters of Charles and Mary Lamb*, ed. by E. V. Lucas (3 vols.; London, Dent and Methuen, 1935), I, 240.

9. Coleridge, *Biographia Literaria*, II, 6.

10. Coleridge, *Miscellanies, Aesthetic and Literary*, ed. by T. Ashe (London, 1885), p. 164.

11. Coleridge, *Biographia Literaria*, II, 6.

12. Coleridge, *Table Talk*, May 31, 1830 (2 vols.; London, 1835), I, 155.

13. *Coleridge's Shakespearean Criticism*, ed. by Thomas Middleton Raysor (2 vols.; Cambridge, Mass.: Harvard University Press, 1930), II, 45.

14. For example, "To R. B. Sheridan" and "Lines on a Friend."

15. Coleridge, *Biographia Literaria*, I, 64.

16. Coleridge, *The Statesman's Manual* (London, 1816), p. 437.

17. Hazlitt, *Lectures on the English Poets* (1818), V, 167.

CHAPTER IV

1. *Journals of Dorothy Wordsworth*, ed. by Ernest de Selincourt (2 vols.; New York: The Macmillan Company, 1941), I, 129 (March 27th, 1802), and 159 (June 17th, 1802).

2. On the question of the actual date of completion, cf. E. de Selincourt's edition of Wordsworth's *Poetical Works* (4 vols.; Oxford: Clarendon Press, 1940–1947), IV, 465.

3. William Hazlitt, *The Spirit of the Age* (London: World's Classics edition, 1904), p. 119.

4. Hazlitt, *My First Acquaintance with the Poets*, in *Works*, XII, 270.

5. Coleridge, *Biographia Literaria*, II, 109.

6. The text of the first version is most easily accessible in E. de Selincourt, *Wordsworthian and Other Studies* (Oxford: Clarendon Press, 1947), pp. 66–76.

7. *Journals of Dorothy Wordsworth*, November 24th, 1801, I, 83.

8. *Unpublished Letters of Samuel Taylor Coleridge*, ed. by E. L. Griggs (2 vols.; London: Constable and Company, 1932), I, 292.

9. Note dictated to Isabella Fenwick in 1843, in *Poetical Works*, III, 464.

10. *The Letters of William and Dorothy Wordsworth: The Middle Years*, ed. by E. de Selincourt (2 vols.; Oxford: Clarendon Press, 1937), II, 619.

11. William Butler Yeats, *Essays* (London, 1924), p. 506.

CHAPTER V

1. The translation is inaccurate. It should be: "Having come by many ways . . ."

2. *Poetical Works of Percy Bysshe Shelley*, I, lxviii.

3. *Ibid.*, I, lxv.

4. *Defence of Poetry*, in *Prose Works*, III, 108, 100.

CHAPTER VI

1. *The Letters of John Keats*, ed. by M. Buxton Forman (Oxford: Oxford University Press, 1935), p. 300.

2. *Ibid.*, pp. 339–40.

3. *Ibid.*, p. 507.

4. *Ibid.*, p. 208.

5. *Ibid.*, p. 324.

6. H. W. Garrod, *Keats* (Oxford, 1926), pp. 119ff.

7. *Collected Essays, Papers, Etc. of Robert Bridges* (4 vols.; Oxford: Oxford University Press, 1933), IV, 131–32, "A Critical Introduction to Keats." I have standardized Bridges' phonetic spelling.

8. *Letters of John Keats*, p. 112.

9. *Ibid.*, p. 315.

CHAPTER VII

1. *Letters of William and Dorothy Wordsworth: The Later Years*, ed. by E. de Selincourt (3 vols.; Oxford: Oxford University Press, 1939), II, 640.

2. Coleridge, *Biographia Epistolaria*, ed. by A. Turnbull (London, 1911), p. 169.

3. *Letters of John Keats*, p. 405.

4. H. E. Rollins, *The Keats Circle* (2 vols.; Cambridge, Mass.: Harvard University Press, 1948), II, 134.

5. *The Works of Lord Byron: Poetry*, ed. by Ernest Hartley Coleridge (6 vols.; London, 1903), IV, 171. See also pp. 272, 484.

6. Byron, *Don Juan*, XI, LX, 7–8.

7. *Letters of John Keats*, p. 413.

8. Blake, *The Ghost of Abel*, in *Poetry and Prose*, p. 584.

9. *The Works of Lord Byron: Letters and Journals*, ed. by Rowland E. Prothero (6 vols.; London, 1901), vol. V, appendix 3, p. 554.

10. Letter of May 25, 1820, quoted by N. I. White, *Shelley* (2 vols.; London: Secker and Warburg, 1947), II, 186.

11. *Works of Lord Byron: Letters and Journals*, letter of February 1st, 1819, IV, 279.

12. Quoted by Ernest de Selincourt, *Wordsworthian and Other Studies*, p. 122.

CHAPTER VIII

1. Poe died at Baltimore on October 7th, 1849.

2. Charles Baudelaire, Preface to *Nouvelles Histoires extraordinaires* (Paris, 1896; vol. VI of *Oeuvres complètes de Charles Baudelaire*).

3. "To Helen":

> *Only thine eyes remained.*
>
> .   .   .   .   .
>
> They are my ministers — yet I their slave.
> Their office is to illumine and enkindle —
> My duty *to be saved* by their bright light.

Le Flambeau vivant:

> Ils marchent devant moi, ces Yeux pleins de lumières, —
> Me sauvent de tout piège, et de tout péché grave,
> Ils conduisent mes pas dans la route du Beau,
> Ils sont mes serviteurs, et je suis leur esclave.

4. "The Haunted Palace":

> And laugh — but smile no more.

Héautontimorumenos:

> Un de ces grands abandonnés
> Au rire éternel condamnés,
> Et qui ne peuvent plus sourire.

Cf. Baudelaire, *Oeuvres posthumes*, pp. 16, 18.

5. Mallarmé, *Les Poèmes d'Edgar Poe* (Brussels, 1897), p. 159: "Sous une de ces facettes, éclatante de feux spéciaux, ce qui toujours fut pour Poe, ou fulgurant, ou translucide, pur comme le diamant, la poésie."

6. The final episode of *La Vida* is based on "Ulalume."

7. The noble *Día de Difuntos* owes much to "The Bells."

8. *Isla de los Muertos* derives its main idea from "The City in the Sea."

9. Semen Kirsanov, *Chetyre Tetradi* (Moscow, 1940), p. 63.

10. *The Poetic Principle*, in *Works of Edgar Allan Poe*, ed. by R. H. Stoddard (6 vols.; New York, 1884), I, 234: "In enforcing a truth we need severity rather than efflorescence of language. We must be simple, precise, terse. We must be cool, calm, unimpassioned."

11. *Ibid.*, I, 235–36.

12. *Ibid.*, I, 235.

13. *Ibid.*, I, 254. Cf. *The Philosophy of Composition*, in *Works*, V, 162: "When, indeed, men speak of Beauty, they mean, precisely, not a quality, as is supposed, but an effect — they refer, in short, just to that intense and pure elevation of *soul — not* of intellect, or of heart — upon which I have commented, and which is experienced in consequence of contemplating 'the beautiful.'"

14. Baudelaire, letter to Armand Frasse, 1858 (*Lettres de Baudelaire* in *Mercure de France*, 1907, p. 176): "En 1846 ou 1847 j'eus connaissance de quelques fragments d'Edgar Poe; j'éprouvai une commotion singulière . . . je trouvai . . . des poèmes et des nouvelles dont j'avais eu la pensée, mais vague, confuse, mal ordonnée, et que Poe avait su combiner et mener à perfection."

15. Poe, *The Poetic Principle*, in *Works*, I, 236.

16. Baudelaire, *La Beauté*.

17. Mallarmé, *L'Azur*.

18. Coleridge, "Limbo," written in 1817.

19. Poe, *The Poetic Principle*, in *Works*, I, 254.

20. Poe, *The Philosophy of Composition*, in *Works*, V, 166.

21. Poe, *Marginalia*, in *Works*, V, 336–37.

22. Did he connect "immemorial" with "in memoria"?

23. Poe, *The Philosophy of Composition*, in *Works*, V, 160. But according to his friend, Mrs. Susan Achard, Poe did not intend this to be taken seriously.

CHAPTER IX

1. *The Collected Works of Dante Gabriel Rossetti*, ed. by William M. Rossetti (1 vol., rev. ed.; London, 1911), p. 671.

2. *Dante Gabriel Rossetti, His Family-Letters*, with a Memoir by William M. Rossetti (2 vols.; Boston, 1895), II, 328. Letter of D. G. Rossetti to his mother: "There is also a splendid anecdote of Keats' proposing as a toast at a gathering – 'Confusion to the memory of Newton!' and, on Wordsworth's wishing to know *why* he drank it, the reply was 'Because he destroyed the poetry of the rainbow by reducing it to a prism.' That is magnificent." The story comes from Haydon's *Autobiography*.

3. *Ibid.*, I, 420.

4. A. C. Benson, *Rossetti* (London, 1904), p. 74.

5. *Collected Works of Dante Gabriel Rossetti*, p. 15.

6. Hall Caine, *Recollections of Dante Gabriel Rossetti* (London, 1882, 1928), p. 248.

7. William Sharp, *Dante Gabriel Rossetti* (London, 1882), p. 413.

CHAPTER X

1. Edmund Gosse, *The Life of Algernon Charles Swinburne* (New York, 1917), p. 212.

2. Swinburne, *Letters* (Bonchurch edition, London, 1927), p. 28 (letter of March 15th, 1865).

CHAPTER XII

1. Collier's report on Coleridge's eighth lecture on Shakespeare, 1811–1812, in *Coleridge's Shakespearean Criticism*, II, 148.

2. Rudyard Kipling, "Wireless," in *Traffics and Discoveries* (New York, 1904), pp. 263–64.

3. *Georgics*, IV, 511–515.

INDEX

INDEX